HEALTHY GRIEF

HEALTHY GRIEF

Normalizing and Navigating Loss in a Culture of Toxic Positivity

Dr. Karen Kramer

ISBN: 978-1-958150-29-0
Healthy Grief: Normalizing and Navigating Loss in a Culture of Toxic Positivity

Hardcover edition November 2023

Subjects
FAMILY & RELATIONSHIPS / Death, Grief, Bereavement
PSYCHOLOGY / Grief & Loss
SELF-HELP / Death, Grief, Bereavement

Published by Inner Peace Press
Eau Claire, Wisconsin, USA
www.innerpeacepress.com

To my son Tyler: May you continue to thrive.

To Michelle G. and Kimberly M.: Your legacies live on.

To Donna M.: This, too, shall pass.

Reader Reviews

"In the tumultuous times and seasons that we live in, Healthy Grief is an answer to the universal travails of humanity. Dr. Karen's words capture the weight of the different types of grief yet she offers her audience opportunities of compassionate, revelatory insights that fosters multidimensional healing. As a mental health counselor, Healthy Grief is a powerful and necessary tool in the prevention, intervention, and post-vention complex trauma recovery process. It reminds her readers the power of choice and to extend grace to themselves as they embrace ownership towards their own healing journey. However, Healthy Grief offers a priceless existential experience that is unique to the author herself... that in your healing journey, you are not alone..."

Jennifer Joy Mojica - M.S., Author of *Dear Voice, Speak*, Mental Health Counselor, Member of the Suicide Prevention Council, and NLP Master Practitioner

"Dr. Karen's 'Healthy Grief' is a profoundly moving and insightful book that guides light through the turbulent and often overwhelming grief journey. As I embarked on this emotionally charged expedition, Dr. Karen's words felt like a reassuring hand to hold, providing solace and wisdom throughout. 'Healthy Grief' is not just a book but a compassionate companion on the journey through grief. It is a testament to her life's work, a gift to those who are hurting, and a beacon of hope for anyone navigating the tumultuous waters of grief. Dr. Karen's wisdom and heartfelt guidance will undoubtedly be a source of comfort and healing for countless individuals for years to come. This book is a must-read for anyone seeking solace and understanding in the face of loss."

Minister **Georganna W. Lewis**, Certified Advanced Grief Recovery Specialist; Amazon Best Selling Contributing Author of *Reach Your Greatness* with James Malinchak (ABC *Secret Millionaire*) and Nick and Megan Unsworth; Author of *Grief is No Longer the Boss of Me, A Personal Story and Simple Action Steps for Surviving Grief and Thriving in Life.*

"Loss is inevitable in life, and as a best-selling author on stress relief, I know grief's long-term impact when left unresolved. During the recent devastating loss of our beloved mutual friend, Dr. Karen and her techniques from Healthy Grief *helped guide us through the shock and heartbreak. Her guidance, marked by kindness and empathy, is a valuable resource for navigating the complexities of grief with her five stages to healing and destigmatizing this challenging journey. I wholeheartedly endorse* Healthy Grief *for anyone seeking solace and understanding during times of loss. It's a remarkable contribution to healing and growth."*

Sara Nakamura - NCBTMB, Owner of StressXpert.com, International Speaker and Best-Selling Author of *Stressed Out And Don't Know What To Do?*

"Here's the great thing I love about Dr. Karen. Not only can she help you with almost any situation in your life, whether it's grief, whether it's figuring out what the new transition is for you at this stage of your life, or whether it's just creating a life that you truly are passionate about. She has blueprints. She has recipes. She has an amazing resume, background, life experiences, and qualifications to help get you from where you are to where you want to be. But the best thing about Dr. Karen is that she comes from the heart. She's a true giver. She's a true survivor, and she's on a mission to make real positive change in this world. She will help to change your life."

James Malinchak - Featured on ABC's Hit TV Show *Secret Millionaire*, Founder of www.BigMoneySpeaker.com, and Author of the Top-Selling Book *Millionaire Success Secrets*

Table of Contents

Part III ~ Stories of Resilience

Part IV ~ Resources

Foreword

*D*r. Karen Kramer is a specialist in grief recovery. The *Healthy Grief* book has a model for how you can do just that so you don't somatize it into your body, which a lot of people do.

I love what Dr. Karen is doing, and I love her passion for it. She has so much life experience of her own and with her clients, and she is constantly adding on and becoming more aware.

She also is someone who can help you get from where you are to where you want to be. She works a lot with women who are going through transitions, whether it's an empty nester, leaving a company, having a divorce, or dealing with the death of a spouse. These are different forms of grief.

If you're someone who's dealing with grief, you've lost your job, you've lost your identity, or if you're someone who is just not happy with your life, or you're suffering, this book is for you. I have friends who recently lost their child, which I think is one of the worst things you have to confront in life.

I love the Healthy GRIEF Framework – very, very powerful. Most people don't know how to deal with that. It's a taboo subject in our world.

I think the idea of somatizing is important. If you've got something going on in your body that's unhealthy, you can go and deal with the symptoms. But what you really want to look at is what's causing it. Therefore, if you can remove the cause, the symptoms disappear, as they did with Dr. Karen's son and also with the clients she's worked with.

I saw a quote recently that said, "You either can spend money on wellness now or spend money on illness later." It's much better to do it now as prevention.

All of these life transitions remind me that you wouldn't go to Africa without a guide. And, yet we tend to go through some of these jungles and swampy areas of life without some navigational support. Dr. Karen is a person who's been down the river, knows where the rhinoceroses live, and knows how to get you that experience that we all want when we go on a safari.

So think of the transitions and griefs of life as this adventure. But you need someone to help you go through the places where you don't have the education, the training, the skill sets, nor the mindset to do it in a way that leads you to feeling happy, fulfilled, and joyful.

There's no reason to be struggling. There's no reason to be unhappy. You've got someone here, Dr. Karen, who can help you do that.

So I encourage you to read this book and take advantage of the skills she has. And if you do, you'll be thanking me. I promise you!

Jack Canfield
Known as "America's #1 Success Coach," co-author of the *Chicken Soup for the Soul* book series, author of *The Success Principles*, and featured teacher in the movie *The Secret*.

Preface

*A*nd then, he was gone.

"I'm fine," I would reply when asked.

I kept busy, diving headfirst into tasks.

"Grieving?" I'd scoff, "Who's got time for that?!"

Then it happened...

I had one of those days.

Emotions overwhelmed me like a tidal wave.

I lost control.

I yelled at my family, cursed at loved ones.

This wasn't my usual self, not by a long shot.

What leads to a cancer diagnosis? What leaves one heart-broken following the loss of an elder? What leaves three young children devastated after the passing of their two estranged parents? Illness, misery, and early death – the one thing these three have in common is unresolved grief.

In the two months leading up to the publication of this book, I experienced the profound loss of four individuals in the previously-described manner. These heart-wrenching situations serve as a reminder of the pressing need for the book you have in your hands. By going through your own healthy journey through loss, you not only heal yourself but also create a healthier and safer environment for your loved ones. Tragedies stemming from unresolved grief need not claim lives nor leave emotional terroil in its wake, and this book seeks to prevent such devastating losses and unintended impact.

When grief strikes, it can bring us to the brink of despair. In these vulnerable moments, we may question our sanity, wonder if we're isolated in our struggles, or even fear that we're somehow flawed. You are not alone. These moments connect us as humans, and I'm here to start a conversation around them.

In a world that often encourages us to "tough it out" and discourages crying, we frequently deny ourselves the time and space to process our emotions fully. But what if we could change that?

Shaken by the aftermath of my meltdown while drowning in my own grief – my family tiptoeing around me – I knew I needed help.

I decided to seek therapy, hoping for support. After a 40-minute session, the newly licensed therapist diagnosed me with "situational anxiety" – a label that offered little assistance. I was then directed to an Anxiety Support Group. To be honest, I barely recall it.

Still in search of answers, I consulted my doctor, suspecting perimenopause might be contributing to my heightened emotions. After merely two minutes of explaining my self-diagnosed grief over my loss and my tumultuous day, the doctor promptly prescribed me drugs. As someone who rarely took over-the-counter medication, I was hesitant to flood my body with chemicals!

Desperate for solutions, my husband suggested I visit a seven-day destination spa I had dreamt of for years. There, I focused on healthy eating, exercise, indulged in spa treatments, and enjoyed days of relaxation far from daily life's pressures. Yet, within two hours of returning home, I found myself bickering with my loving husband.

What was the common thread? My therapy diagnosis, the prescribed drugs, and the spa week away all addressed the symptoms but failed to identify the root cause of my grief.

Six years later, when the love of my life walked out on me, I was determined not to return to institutions that labeled and medicated me.

At first, as a leadership development and corporate coaching professional, I believed I could DIY (do-it-yourself) my way through my divorce. I was wrong. We often hinder our own healing when we're trapped in our grief. "You cannot solve a problem with the same mind that created it," as Albert Einstein famously said.

Then, my path took an unexpected turn when I discovered the field of Neuro-Linguistic Programming (NLP). This transformative body of work not only helped me find harmony and healing in my life again, but did so without the burden of therapeutic labels or medications, offering long-lasting results.

My healing journey not only led to my personal recovery but also to a new perspective on the mind. It equipped me with the tools to facilitate profound mindset shifts, not just within myself but also with my coaching clients. This understanding set me on a course to guide more individuals through the intricate terrain of grief and loss, all while preserving the cherished memories of the past, restoring the equilibrium of the mind and body, and illuminating a path toward living life to its fullest once more.

This is where you come in.

Welcome to a journey where we'll explore grief, coping with life's setbacks, and the incredible resilience within each of us. Let's challenge the status quo and find the right support for our unique paths to recovery.

Let's normalize conversations about grief. No longer must we isolate ourselves in the shadows, feeling alone, doubting if others can understand us, or fearing we are broken and solitary on this path of grief. No longer should we be rushed to "get over it" or "fixed."

We all encounter loss. I've personally observed the profound impact of unaddressed grief on the body – within myself, my family, and my clients. However, I've also witnessed the transformative power of releasing grief from the body. My primary objective for this book is to guide you toward a healthier way of processing loss. Together, let's destigmatize conversations about loss, navigate the journey of grief with empathy and support, and provide our bodies with the tools to be resilient in the face of the inevitable losses.

This book is for you whether you've been labeled, medicated, or instructed to suppress your emotions. Through the 30 candid stories, research, and trusted techniques, we'll unveil the five-stage **Healthy GRIEF Framework**, proving that healing goes beyond treating symptoms. May the pages in this book be your guides and your beacons of encouragement. Know that you, too, will move through this.

As you will see in the stories shared throughout these pages, therapists, psychiatrists, doctors, and other well-meaning, educated professionals play vital roles in our culture. This isn't about pitting options against each other; it's about finding the right support for YOUR path to recovery. You have options!

I don't possess all the answers. Some of the concepts shared may not resonate with you. Take what aligns with your truth, and leave the rest. I'm doing my best to provide information for those who genuinely need this book and the help it can offer.

This book is about living a rich life that transforms the way we make decisions, create, parent, lead, love, grieve, and die. In doing so, it helps us understand ourselves, our relationships, and the legacy we leave on this world.

You deserve a life filled with compassion, understanding, and the tools to cope with whatever comes your way. From my heart to yours, I offer unwavering support in this book to help you grieve healthfully and embrace the beauty of your unique path to finding your new normal. And may you continue to have the courage to love and live life to the fullest.

Let's embark on this empowering journey together!

Introduction

Splash!
It happened.

The world spins.

What once was, is no longer.

And there you are ... still existing.

You are trained to shove everything down deep.

Which is exhausting!

So you release ...

You let go ...

You let go of the weight of the sorrow you've carried for so long ...

bubble to the surface.

Be free!

And there you lay...

floating above the water's edge...

easily...

effortlessly...

Feeling the warmth of the sun penetrate, nurture, and ...

hold your precious heart.

In the vast ocean of human experience, grief is an unrelenting wave that crashes into our lives when we least expect it. It startles us like a sudden splash, leaving us soaked in sorrow, disoriented, and struggling to find our footing in the turbulent waters of loss.

Grief is an intrinsic part of the human condition, a universal emotion that transcends the boundaries of time, culture, and circumstance. It doesn't discriminate; it visits us in moments of profound personal loss, such as the death of a loved one, the end of a cherished relationship, or the shattering of our dreams. Grief is also the silent companion of broader societal and global losses, manifesting in times of collective trauma, upheaval, or change.

However, I'm going to let you in on a little secret.

The key to healthy grief isn't just one thing.

It's not about following a specific process or timeline.

It's not about burying your feelings or trying to "fix" your emotions.

It's about embracing "all the things."

It's the waves of emotions, each unique and raw, crashing against the shores of your heart.

It's the quiet moments of reflection, like the stillness of a forest after a gentle rain.

It's the support and connection you find in unexpected places, just like discovering a treasure chest nestled deep within the layers of your experience.

There's no one-size-fits-all solution to grief.

Just like in gardening, where the perfect plant won't magically transform your landscape, the perfect solution won't instantly heal your pain.

It's a journey of gradual growth and transformation, where you work on different areas of your emotional landscape to create something uniquely beautiful.

The wonderful thing is there are many different ways to process grief. The challenge is there are many different ways to process grief. What, then, is the "right" way?

This book is not here to give you the "right" answer on processing grief, because it's different for every single person. You are unique, and so is your grief.

But this isn't merely a book about loss and sadness. We dive into the heart-wrenching stories of individuals who have confronted loss head-on and emerged transformed. It is a testament to the resilience of the human spirit, a roadmap to navigate the uncharted waters of grief, and a guiding light for those who feel lost and alone in their mourning.

Whether you've picked up this book while navigating a loss, assisting someone through their grieving process, or simply seeking to understand the concept of "toxic positivity," it's crucial to recognize that each of us will encounter various forms of grief in our lifetime. This book is your guide to help you find your special path through loss.

Our society offers abundant resources and encouragement for success, acquisition, winning, and the pursuit of happiness. Educational systems, books, seminars, podcasts, and YouTube channels are overflowing with "How-to" guides for dating, career development, personal finance, and optimal health and beauty.

Yet, there's a noticeable void when it comes to preparing and guiding us through the inevitable experiences of loss, letting go, and grieving. There's a scarcity of resources on how to cope with a breakup or divorce, release long-standing friendships, manage job loss or financial setbacks, face foreclosure or bankruptcy, accept and move through aging and health issues, let go of lost or failed expectations, handle the necessity to downsize or relocate, or healthfully grieve the loss of a loved one.

This book is intended to help you develop better resilience when faced with life's adversities and losses, focusing on those most common throughout our lives. As you journey through these pages, may they provide guidance on how to:

> ✿ **Engage in, rather than avoid, meaningful conversations about grief and loss.**
>
> ✿ **Avoid the biggest mistakes grievers make that can lead to life-threatening diseases.**
>
> ✿ **Discover the negative impact of TOXIC positivity on healthy grieving (and what you can do instead).**
>
> ✿ **Learn the five stages to unlocking your unique path to healing even if you have been grieving for decades.**
>
> ✿ **Find hope through inspiring and powerful stories.**

In the context of this book, we define **grief** as "a deep emotional sorrow experienced after a significant loss when what once was is no longer." While grief is often associated with death and dying, our definition encompasses a category of grief known as disenfranchised grief and encompasses a wide range of emotions and situations.

Disenfranchised grief is characterized by a lack of acknowledgment and public support because the nature of the loss is not recognized or valued by others. Such forms of this type of grief are usually invisible to others. Examples include seemingly minor disappointments like not being selected for a school play to more significant heartaches like your first romantic breakup; from the disappointment of not gaining admission to your preferred college to the loss of a job; from the emotional turmoil of relocating away from home to coping with accidents or health challenges; from navigating the complexities of divorce to adjusting to an empty nest; from transitioning into retirement to moving into a retirement home; from dealing with infertility or loss of memory due to dementia; and loss of hopes, dreams, and expectations.

For most, feelings of grief gradually wane with time. However, for a small group, the intensity of grief persists and interferes with daily life. **Prolonged grief disorder** (also referred to as **complicated grief**) describes the intense and persistent grief that disrupts daily life by dominating one's thoughts and feelings, making it challenging to find relief.[1]

Prolonged grief disorder was added to the Diagnostic and Statistical Manual of Mental Disorders (DSM) in March 2022. It is not surprising that this disorder was added during the notorious COVID-19 pandemic, and, according to the American Psychological Association, "After studies over several decades suggested that many people were experiencing persistent difficulties associated with bereavement that exceeded expected social, cultural, or religious expectations."[2] While this recognition serves to raise awareness about the prevalence of grief and the need for support, it may undermine the fact that grief and its recovery time can vary greatly among individuals. It's essential to acknowledge that not every form of prolonged grief needs to be labeled as a "disorder." On the other hand, this recognition helps provide more support for those struggling with persistent grief.

In addition, **compound** (or **cumulative**) **grief** arises when a series of losses occur in a relatively short time frame. The COVID-19 pandemic that began in Spring 2020 serves as a prime example of compounded grief. It encompassed losses of normalcy, routine, safety, predictability, job and financial security, social life, and loved ones.[3]

Traditional losses often bring a complex web of disenfranchised and compounded grief. Take divorce, for instance, where the loss extends far beyond the marriage itself. It can entail the loss of identity, financial stability, routines, friendships, family support, assets, homes, security, safety, normalcy, and even cherished hopes and dreams. The impact of divorce grief ripples through multiple lives, including children, extended family members, friends, and coworkers.

This book does not address severe afflictions or trauma, yet does explore some. The American Psychological Association defines trauma as "an emotional response to a terrible event like an accident, rape, or natural disaster."[4] Although there is some common ground with grief, **traumatic grief**, which emerges in response to sudden and unforeseen losses, activates post-traumatic survival mechanisms in addition to the usual process of mourning.

We will explore various forms of grief, both major and minor. Also, what one person may perceive as a minor loss, such as the death of a beloved pet, can be significant for another. It's not so much about the event itself as it is about your emotional reaction to it, both initially and over time.

Addressing more extreme forms of grief, as previously described, often requires the expertise of mental health professionals with specialized training in complicated grief work. This book serves as a source of support yet should not replace professional assistance, when needed. Knowing when it's time to seek professional help is crucial to moving forward healthfully.

Whether you're looking for scientific understanding, practical strategies, inspirational stories, or quick assistance, you can find it within these pages. Journey through the chapters of Part I to explore the cultural, psychological, and physical factors that influence your perceptions of loss and grieving. Move to Part II to navigate the five-stage **Healthy GRIEF Framework** which serves as a guide to find your unique path. In Part III, encounter 30 powerful stories that offer comfort in the recognition that none of us walk this path of grief alone. Follow along with their stories using the QR code at the beginning of Part III. There is hope! Part IV unveils various resources including quick tools, processional support, and crisis hotlines. Make sure to check out all the free downloads!

Although the parts of this book are laid out in intentional order to build on each other, jump around as needed. If you need some **quick resources**, flip to Part IV. If you need a **framework of support** to help yourself or someone else through grief, skip to Part II. If you want to nerd out on the **science that influences grief**, start with Part I. If you are seeking some **hope and inspiration** to know there are opportunities on the other side of loss, dive into Part III.

Whether you are currently grappling with grief, standing on the precipice of loss, or seeking to support a loved one on their journey, this book is for you. It is a lifeline, a companion for the turbulent seas you encounter, and a reminder that, even in the midst of the storm, there is a way to navigate the currents of grief and emerge stronger on the other side.

Together, let us dive into the depths of sorrow, ride the waves of emotion, and discover the profound truths that lie beneath the surface of our grief-stricken hearts. There is hope, and there is healing.

Let's begin!

Part I

Nurturing Resilience:

The Role of Culture, Mind, and Body in Grief

Introduction

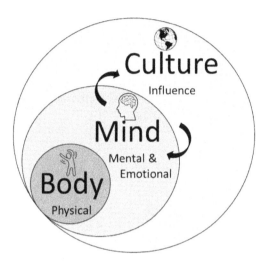

*L*ife often flows smoothly, carrying us along its currents, where we experience a sense of balance and control. However, there are moments when this tranquil journey is disrupted by the abrupt arrival of grief – an unanticipated intruder that enters unannounced, reshaping the very landscape of our existence.

We are a product of the systems in which we live, and the systems that live within us. To understand loss, let's immerse ourselves in the profound influences on the intricate systems of grief.

In Part I, the powerful influences of culture, the intricate workings of the mind, and the mysterious interplay of the body take center stage. Much like the ever-shifting tides and currents of the sea, they determine whether we remain adrift in its turbulent waters or embark on a path toward a healthier recovery.

To heal, we must navigate these complexities, gaining an understanding, and find harmony amidst the tumultuous waves of sorrow.

Culture
Exploring the Influence of our Outer World

"The fact that millions of people share the same vices does not make these vices virtues, the fact that they share so many errors does not make the errors to be truths, and the fact that millions of people share the same forms of mental pathology does not make these people sane."

~ Erich Fromm, *The Sane Society*

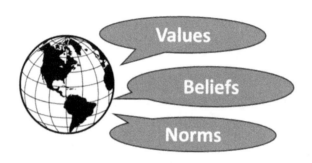

Susan was just 15 when her 42-year-old father was diagnosed with colon cancer. Everyone told her to "Just stay positive" and "Everything will be okay." In the months that followed her father's death, Susan walked smiling through the world as she knew everyone wanted her to. Susan was upbeat. Susan was strong. On the outside, she was continuously cheerful. No one asked how she was really, and Susan didn't tell them. She didn't even tell herself. This is the story of psychologist and author, Susan David, as depicted by Susan Cain in her book *Bittersweet.*[5]

Susan's story illuminates a reality that many face in their grief journeys. The cultural and societal expectations to "stay positive" weighed heavily on her shoulders, painting a vision of strength over her true emotions. The contrast between her external demeanor and internal turmoil underscores the intricate interplay of cultural norms, toxic positivity, and emotional expression.

Cultural systems profoundly influence the molding of individuals, communities, and entire societies. Their impact extends to the realm of grief recovery, offering invaluable insights into what either supports or obstructs our journey toward healthy grieving.

At the core of culture are its values, norms, and beliefs. **Values** serve as *guiding principles that steer decisions, influence priorities, and shape actions*. Cultural values embody a society's beliefs, morals, and ethical foundations, essentially defining what is considered "good" or "right." For example, some cultures prioritize community and strong family bonds, while others emphasize personal autonomy and independence.

Norms, on the other hand, are the u*nunwritten rules and expectations governing our conduct within a society*. They dictate what is deemed acceptable or unacceptable behavior. Cultural norms manifest in various ways, affecting how people interact, communicate, and conduct themselves in social settings. For instance, making eye contact with strangers may be viewed as rude in some cultures, while in others, it signifies respect.[6] The differentiation between values and norms is that values represent broad, overarching ideals, whereas norms consist of specific directives that prescribe particular actions or exclusions.

Beliefs are our *perceptions of the world and shape our interpretation of events and decision-making*. Karma, for example, rooted in Hinduism and Buddhism but widely adopted in various cultures, is the belief that one's actions in this life will determine their fate or circumstances in future lives.[7] It emphasizes moral responsibility and cause-and-effect. This cultural belief plays a significant role in shaping behaviors, traditions, and customs within their respective societies.

Cultural influence, channeled through values, beliefs, and norms, permeates various aspects of our lives. However, this cultural immersion can be so profound that it often goes unnoticed, akin to a fish unaware of the water it resides in until removed from its natural habitat. To gain a deeper understanding of our own cultural influences, it is helpful to explore some of the categories of systems (or "fish bowls") that shape our cultural norms and values:

1. **History, traditions, and customs** allow societies to preserve and pass down their heritage, ensuring that vital knowledge and practices endure across generations.

2. Diverse **languages, dialects, and communication styles** affect how ideas and emotions are conveyed.

3. **Education systems** impact curriculum, teaching methods, and student-teacher relationships, shaping attitudes toward education and academic success.

4. **Rituals and traditions** provide a framework for ceremonies, celebrations, and significant life events.

5. **Religious beliefs and spiritual practices** set standards for behavior, profession, marriage, gender roles, dress, rituals, dietary preferences, and perspectives on life and death.

6. **Gender roles, norms, and expectations** influence the division of labor, family roles, and perceptions of masculinity and femininity, including the display of certain emotions during times of grief.

7. **Family norms** shape the structures and concept of family, impacting expectations for marriage, parenting, caregiving, and intergenerational relationships.

8. Traditional **healing methods and mental health approaches** related to well-being are integrated into the physical and emotional grief recovery process.

Cultural systems wield a profound and positive influence on the values, beliefs, and norms surrounding grief. Consider these three examples:

1. The **cultural expressions of grief** encompasses various outlets like mourning attire, artwork, music, and storytelling, offering individuals a means to share their loss.

2. **Community and social support** helps alleviate the burden of grief by providing both emotional and practical assistance to those in mourning.

3. **Sharing stories** of the deceased and their impact on the community can be therapeutic, helping individuals remember and honor their loved ones.

When an individual's personality aligns with their cultural systems, it often leads to enhanced emotional well-being, smoothing the grieving process. However, cultural influences can become toxic when they hinder or negatively impact an individual's ability to healthfully recover. When personal beliefs and values conflict with that of the cultural system, inner turmoil can ensue.

Here are situations where cultural influences can be detrimental to one's grieving process:

1. Certain cultures **expect individuals to remain stoic** and not openly display their grief, leading to suppressed emotions which hinder healthy emotional expression and grief processing.

2. Some cultures encourage a swift return to normalcy and social activities after a loss, **pressuring to "move on" quickly** and potentially impeding the grieving process.

3. Cultures that **stigmatize discussions around mental health** or seeking therapy can discourage individuals from asking for professional help when dealing with complicated grief, depression, or anxiety, exacerbating their ability to heal.

4. While cultural rituals can be comforting, overly **rigid or restrictive rituals and expectations** may pressure individuals to conform, stifling the authenticity of their grieving process.

5. Cultural norms may **dictate specific roles and responsibilities** for grieving family members, creating overwhelming expectations that hinder their healing.

6. Cultural disparities may lead to **isolation or a lack of understanding** from the broader community, intensifying feelings of loneliness and sadness.

7. Cultural influences may **pressure individuals to conform** to a specific way of grieving, even if it contradicts their emotional needs and coping mechanisms, resulting in feelings of inadequacy and guilt.

8. Cultural influences that **emphasize guilt or shame** around death or grief can be particularly toxic, hampering the ability to process grief effectively.

9. In some cultures, the **expression of nontraditional grief responses**, such

as anger or guilt, is emphasized to retain approval, leading to unresolved grief.

10. The **expression of toxic positivity**, an excessive focus on maintaining a relentlessly positive outlook while denying or suppressing negative emotions, can hinder the natural grieving process by invalidating complex emotional experiences.

This book offers a framework, stories, and resources to help you navigate your grief journey. Culture, with its values, beliefs, and norms, profoundly shapes how individuals cope with loss and heal. Identifying the systems that hinder or help our ability to grieve supports individuals like Susan Davis. This understanding is crucial for providing effective support and care to how we mourn, remember, and heal.

Your Journey:
Reflection and Action

In regards to your grief:

*What **values** guide your decisions, priorities, and actions?*

*What **beliefs** influence your interpretations of events and decision-making?*

*What **norms** govern the way you interact in society?*

Mind

Exploring the Psychology of Our Inner World

"Thought is not reality; yet it is through Thought that our realities are created. It is what we as humans put into our thoughts that dictates what we think of life."

~ Sydney Banks

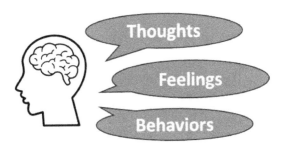

On a bustling morning, blaring sirens disrupted my routine. A three-truck fire brigade on our quiet rural street, battling flames engulfing my aunt's house, evoked vivid memories. It transported me back to a devastating house fire my parents endured almost 20 years earlier.

Recollections of my father's struggle with insurance agents, the despair in his eyes surveying our scorched home, and the backstory of his resilience in a tumultuous childhood as a caregiver for his siblings and alcoholic father at age 12 flooded my mind. Memories conjoined with present reality as my father, 84 at the time, stood amid the ruins of his lifetime achievements.

These vivid images painted a poignant picture, connecting the dots between my aunt's burning house, the simple coffee cup my father held, and the intricate threads of human connection that bind our experiences, thoughts, and emotions.

Welcome to the systems of the mind.

The mind encompasses our thoughts, feelings, and behaviors, shaped by cultural values, beliefs, and norms. Researcher and author Brené Brown aptly stated, "When we don't understand how our thoughts and feelings relate to each other, we become disembodied from our own experiences and disconnected from each other."[8]

To discuss this further, let's define some key terms related to the mind. At the core of the mind's system, we will explore thoughts and thinking, feelings and emotions, and actions and behaviors.

In everyday language, "thought" and "thinking" typically refer to conscious cognitive processes that occur independently of sensory input.[9] **Thinking** is *the act of using your mental faculties to consider, analyze, and reason about information or ideas*. It involves mental activities like problem-solving, decision-making, reflection, and contemplation allowing you to plan, strategize, and make judgments. **Thoughts** are *the products or results of thinking*. They are the mental representations or ideas that arise during the thinking process. Thoughts can encompass a wide range of content, including beliefs, memories, emotions, ideas, and mental imagery. In summary, "thinking" is the active, dynamic cognitive process, while "thoughts" are the mental content or ideas that emerge as a result of thinking. When you think, you engage in a mental activity or process, and the results of that process are the thoughts that fill your mind.

Although often used interchangeably, feelings and emotions are distinct concepts.[10] **Emotions** are *immediate bodily sensations*, while **feelings** are *influenced by emotions but shaped by mental thoughts*. For example, restlessness at a party can be labeled as feeling awkward or exciting based on one's mental interpretation. Feelings, however, are shaped by an individual's unique cognitive processes, beliefs, and past experiences, and can persist over a longer duration compared to the relatively fleeting nature of emotions.

Actions are *specific, intentional, and goal-oriented movements or efforts that individuals choose to take*, while **behavior** is *a broader concept that includes a wide range of actions, both intentional and unintentional, as well as consistent patterns of conduct exhibited by an individual*. Behavior can encompass not only actions driven by conscious intentions but also involuntary or habitual responses. Taking action requires awareness and conscious decision-making with intention behind the behavior. Behavior, on the other hand, includes a broader range of actions and reactions which include not only purposeful actions but also automatic or unconscious responses.

Moving forward, we'll more commonly refer to thoughts, feelings, and behaviors as we dive into the psychology of the mind. However, these are intertwined with thinking, emotions, and actions as well.

In the previous chapter, we talked about how beliefs are shaped by our culture. But beliefs aren't just influenced by culture; our own life experiences play a big role too. Let's explore how they are created.

During childhood, especially in the formative years before the age of 10, our self-perception and worldviews begin to develop. Impressions formed during this period leave a lasting impact. For instance, if we happen to overhear our parents arguing about financial matters or undergo a family divorce at a young age, our subconscious mind retains these initial imprints on money and relationships. These early experiences shape our beliefs about ourselves, others, and the world affecting our decisions, priorities, and behaviors.

By definition, all beliefs are limiting. By believing one thing (such as a certain religious or political view) you are limiting yourself to not believing in another. The question is whether a belief helps or hinders achieving the positive result you want. For purposes of this book, we will refer to **limiting beliefs** as *views about yourself, others, and the world that can negatively impact your ability to process grief in a healthy way.* They may include thoughts like "I'm not worthy" or "I'm not enough." These beliefs can lead to codependent behaviors, narcissism, people-pleasing, declining confidence, guilt, and more.

Imagine this scenario: You come from a family with strong traditional or religious beliefs against divorce, but you go through a divorce yourself. This clash between your family's values and your personal experience can lead to a lot of inner turmoil and self-doubt.

Our minds have this incredible ability to soak up influences, even when we're not aware of them. These influences can quietly chip away at our happiness, damage our relationships, and even harm our health. Given the example of divorce, this underlying influence might lead you to feel unworthy or inadequate. These feelings, rooted in beliefs formed during your early years, shape how you think about yourself and how you interact with the world.

Our lives derive meaning from our interpretations, and it is our thoughts that give events significance. A conversation with a friend about my previous year's challenges brought forth a profound realization. During that year, I confronted the loss of my oldest brother, my mother, and witnessed another sibling's declining health. Yet, amid these challenges, I also encountered moments of triumph including launching a new business venture. How I responded to these events hinged upon my interpretations of them. It is not the events themselves but rather our thoughts about them that influence our reactions.

This interconnected web of thoughts, feelings, and behaviors of the mind become particularly evident during times of crisis, like grieving. Our reactions to life's challenges are deeply rooted in unhealed wounds and their impact on our emotional experiences.

Have you ever found yourself overreacting to a situation, like a minor argument that suddenly escalates into a major blowout? These intense reactions stem from deep-seated triggers within us. The key lies in pinpointing these triggers – those specific words, gestures, or tones that ignite powerful emotions. In some cases, these triggers have roots that stretch far back, beyond our conscious recollection. Therapy techniques can develop an awareness of these triggers, along with the context and the emotions they provoke, which can pave the way toward emotional freedom.

Unhealed wounds often lead us to project our emotions onto external events. These unresolved emotional wounds color our perceptions and amplify our reactions to global and personal events. Through personal experiences, we can uncover how these projections manifest in our lives.

A previous client, Julie (name changed), serves as an example of how certain past wounds can give rise to fear and lead to the suppression of emotions. During group work, Julie would feel uneasy when anyone expressed sadness around her. She would quickly encourage them to see the positive side of things and try to "fix" their issues. However, this often frustrated the person experiencing the emotion, especially within the context of our supportive and nonjudgmental coaching retreat.

After a private coaching conversation with Julie, I discovered that a fear of negativity was at the root of her behaviors. Julie's inclination towards maintaining a positive outlook came from a fear that originated in a near-death experience. Any encounter with negative emotions, whether from others or within herself, triggered memories of that accident and her subsequent depression.

Understanding the systems of the mind, its beliefs, and their effects on thoughts, feelings, and behaviors is essential for healing, growth, and emotional liberation during grief. It is the intricate flow of how a house fire and a coffee cup are immersed in a string of memories, thoughts, and emotions. As we delve deeper into this journey of self-discovery and healing, remember that the key to unlocking the doors of emotional liberation lies within our understanding of the mind's intricate systems and the profound interplay of memories, thoughts, and emotions that guide us through the maze of grief.

Your Journey:
Reflection and Action

In regards to your grief:

*What **limiting beliefs** about yourself, others, and/or the world influence your thoughts?*

*What unhealed emotional wounds of the past are affecting your **feelings** now?*

*What **behaviors** have hindered or helped your healing process?*

Body
Exploring Hidden Response to Grief

"But strange that I was not told that the brain can hold in a tiny ivory cell God's heaven or hell."

- Oscar Wilde

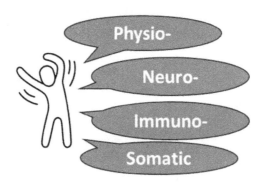

As posted by client, Stephanie, on her Facebook page:

Today marks five years since I lost my soulmate...

Usually by April, I start to spiral ...

This year is different. Cancer changed things in a big way. During one of my conversations with one of my doctors he told me my tumor has been growing for about five years. ... The grief and sorrow that I chose to hold on to, broke my body down in ways I could not imagine.

When I lost [my husband] Ronald I became so depressed and sick, hospitalized, diagnosed with broken heart syndrome and little did I know a tumor started developing in my colon, pretty much at the bottom of my stomach. This is where I usually say I could feel the sorrow in the pit of my stomach. My body listened to my pain. The body truly is amazing. My body followed what my mind was feeling. I can only speak for myself and my own cancer diagnosis, but I know this is my truth.

Five years later, my body is telling me enough, this is your wake up call.

I have taken some drastic steps to heal my body, mind and soul. I never wanted to let the grief go, it was my way of honoring my husband. My cross to carry for the rest of my life for not saving him that day, I've carried the guilt this entire time and have never been able to forgive myself. I was willing to go to the grave with that.

But, then in comes cancer. … Let's just say, message received loud and clear. I need to heal my heart and mind first. I have to live for my kids; for Ronald and for the first time, I realized I need to live for me too. I believe for me… stress was my silent killer.

So today, for the first time on this day, the sadness is not so devastatingly deep. I can breathe… never again will I give this day power over me or my children. Never. … God is showing me it's time to forgive myself.

… I think Ronald is telling me it's okay to let go of this pain.

So, now my next journey is healing and learning to love myself again.

"I never get angry," says a character in one of Woody Allen's movies. "I grow a tumor instead." While this phrase might be from a fictional character, many cases mentioned in this book, especially those of cancer patients (like Stephanie), have confirmed the truth of this remark. (Read Stephanie's full story in the chapter "Childhood Trauma, Death, and Diagnosis.")

Grief, left unprocessed, can have profound implications on our bodies. To comprehend why, we must explore the intricate relationship between our values, beliefs, feelings, thoughts, behaviors, and physical well-being.

Welcome to the systems of the body.

If you read no other chapter, read this one. The core of this book is to help you understand the impact that chronic, ongoing grief can have on the body. We cannot discuss the body without exploring what affects it.

Fortunately, fields of research have become more interdisciplinary and comprehensive, allowing us to test and further understand the interplay. Here are some of the fields of study that relate to and encompass the mind and body, which we will integrate into this book (though is certainly not an exhaustive list). The basic terms representing the individual fields of study include **bio** (life), **psycho** (thoughts and behaviors), **social** (cultural factors), **physio** (physical), **neuro** (nervous system), **immuno** (immune system), and **somatic** (body), among others.

Since grief is not commonly researched across disciplines, I will use stress as an example to help identify the following fields of study:

- **Psychology** is the scientific study of the human mind and its functions, especially those affecting behavior in a given context. For example, psychological responses to stress could include irritability, anger outbursts, frequent arguments, inability to rest or relax, changes in eating habits, and sleep pattern alterations.

- **Physiology** is the science of the functions of organisms, including the chemical and physical processes involved.[11] Physiological responses are the body's automatic reactions to stimuli. For example, physiological responses to stress could involve a faster heartbeat and increased breathing.

- **Psychophysiology** is the study of physiological signals recorded from the body or brain and their relationships with psychological processes. An example is a migraine caused by stress.

- **Somatic psychology** focuses on the body as distinguished from the mind or spirit. For example, stress can cause some people to develop headaches, chest pain, back pain, nausea, or fatigue.

- **Psychosomatic** refers to physical illnesses or conditions caused or aggravated by mental factors such as stress. It explores the relationships among social, psychological, and behavioral factors on bodily processes and quality of life.

- **Immunology** is concerned with immunity, and stress has been linked to various aspects of the human immune system. Acute stress, for example, can lead to the mobilization of specific types of cells in the bloodstream in a "fight or flight" response.

✿ **Neuroscience** deals with the structure and function of the nervous system and brain. Short-term stress responses, as an example, involve the amygdala and the hypothalamic-pituitary-adrenocortical (HPA) axis, which regulates hormones like cortisol.[12]

✿ **Psychoneuroimmunology** explores the interactions among behavioral, neural, endocrine, and immune processes. Stress, for example, activates neural circuits that involve immune responses.

✿ **Developmental psychopathology** studies the impact of adverse experiences on mind and brain development. For example, an article by the APA Journals Articles Spotlight on developmental psychology addresses a wide variety of disorders, from those long known to involve heightened stress sensitivity and sensitization, such as major depressive disorder, bipolar disorder, anxiety disorders, and psychosis, to disorders for which an emphasis on stress mechanisms is more unique, such as tobacco addiction.[13]

✿ **Interpersonal neurobiology** looks at how behavior influences emotions, biology, and mindsets in others. The *Neurobiology of Stress* journal, as an example, serves as a platform for disseminating research and review articles spanning basic, translational, and clinical investigations into stress and its associated disorders.[14] Their primary emphasis is on the effects of stress on the brain, spanning from cellular mechanisms to behavioral functions. It also explores stress-related neuropsychiatric conditions including depression, trauma, and anxiety.

✿ The **biopsychosocial model**, introduced by George Engel in 1977, emphasizes the need to consider not only biological factors but also psychological, social, and cultural factors when understanding a person's medical condition.[15] In the 1980s and 1990s, this model significantly influenced clinical research, leading to increased federal funding and a substantial body of research exploring the links between stress, depression, immune function, neuroendocrine function, cardiovascular and cancer risks, and disease occurrence.[16]

We are biopsychosocial creatures, and our health or illness reflects our relationship with the world we inhabit. However, despite the advances in the studies above, various fields of psychology and medicine still rely on outdated disease models that no longer meet the scientific and social demands of the field. For example, mainstream medical practice often disregards the role emotions play in physiological functioning. Yet, ample scientific evidence shows that a person's lifetime emotional experiences profoundly influence health and illness. Disease in an individual can tell us about the origin and broader culture in which that person's life unfolds.

Prominent figures such as physician Dr. Gabor Maté and psychiatrist Dr. Bessel van der Kolk have explored how life's tribulations and grief can become embodied, leading to a variety of physical and emotional manifestations. This phenomenon underscores the powerful connection between mind and body, shedding light on why the body's response to emotional distress is so impactful.

The Body Keeps the Score, by Bessel van der Kolk, summarizes several decades of research into the nature of trauma.[17] Drawing on Van der Kolk's work and that of many others, it reveals the discoveries of a new generation of disciplines, including neuroscience, developmental psychopathology, interpersonal neurobiology, and more. These fields have shown that trauma causes actual physiological changes in the brain, including a recalibration of the brain's alarm system, increased stress hormone activity, and alterations in the filtering of relevant mental functioning.

The Myth of Normal, authored by Hungarian-Canadian physician Gabor Maté and his son, Daniel, encompasses psychology, medicine, and social critique.[18] Maté dives into the perplexing rise of health problems, such as diabetes and autoimmune diseases, in Western nations, despite substantial investments in healthcare systems. He attributes this phenomenon to Western culture's deeply rooted materialistic and individualistic values which have generated excessive stress and trauma, ultimately contributing to the surge in illness.

Maté's exploration extends to the realm of modern medicine, which often disregards these psychosocial factors by treating the body in isolation. He argues for a new paradigm that recognizes the intricate connections systems between health, the mind, and the socio-political context. According to Maté, disease should not be perceived as external to the self and body but rather as an expression of internal tensions. The neglect of these needs can lead to conditions like cancer and autoimmune diseases. *I whole-heartedly agree!* (See more about Maté's research, autoimmune disease, and loss of identity in the chapter "Identity.") Ultimately, Maté contends that the prevalence of sickness should be expected as a consequence of the medical profession's failure to recognize the intricate connections between physical and mental health. It is this thinking that led my doctor to prescribe drugs to numb my emotional symptom of grief.

My client Stephanie's experience serves as a powerful example of this intricate connection of the disciplines. Her journey through grief and her later cancer diagnosis underscores the importance of addressing the emotional underpinnings of our physical health. The trauma of losing her husband, coupled with unprocessed emotions, led to a somatic response – a tumor. Stephanie's path towards healing also demonstrates the potential for recovery when we acknowledge the connection between our emotions and our well-being, and release what's standing in the way of the healing process.

Both the work of Maté and van der Kolk challenge the prevailing paradigm in the psychiatry and medical industries, and call for a more holistic approach to well-being. This is not the fault of the practitioners in these fields; it is how they are trained. It is ingrained in our culture that doctors and therapists know best. It is ingrained in the medical field that cancers are things that need to be radiated, chemically attacked, and/or surgically removed.

However, the finger can't be wagged at the institutions that trained our well-intended medical and therapeutic professionals either. We live in a world that wants immediate results and "quick fixes." We don't want to know that unresolved grief over the death of a parent, an unforgiving grudge over a boss who fired you, the unrelenting hurt from that high school break-up, or a deep-seated belief of "I'm not good enough" stemming from a childhood trauma has anything to do with our current pain, ailment, or diagnosis. It is so much easier to just be physically or mentally diagnosed or labeled for your symptoms: prescribed drugs to numb or temporarily "fix" those symptoms; and scheduled for a medical procedure to radiate, remove, or temporarily "mend" the symptoms. It is the prevailing Western societal popular thought that it is so much easier to manage the "dis-ease" of the body than what created it in the first place. I debunk this idea in our future chapters.

Fortunately, more research is becoming mainstream to help medical professionals and patients alike know about alternative treatments. Books such as *Profound Healing* by Cheryl Canfield[19] and *CURED: The New Science of Spontaneous Healing* by Dr. Jeffery Rediger,[20] just to name a few, are challenging the status quo.

According to the Center for Disease Control and Prevention (CDC), the three leading causes of death in the United States in 2022 were heart disease, cancer, and unintentional injury (as indicated in the following figure from National Vital Statistics System).[21]

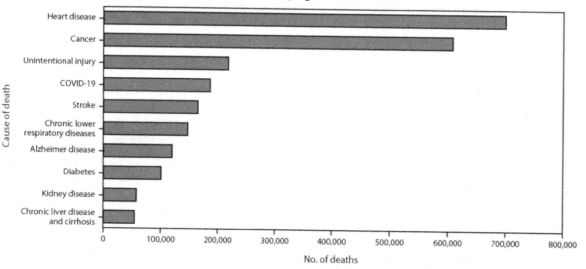

Leading Underlying Causes of Death

As a practitioner who works with subconscious programming, I have witnessed in many clients the profound ways in which the body can heal once traumas, triggers, and limiting beliefs are released. *Not all the time and not in all cases, yet it is possible.* My all-time, go-to book to quickly assess and reassess the healing of the mind and body is Wendi Jensen's *The Healing Questions Guide.*[22]

Jensen's book and body-related questions assists me in helping my client identify where and how the body is reacting to and storing grief. Using "heart problems" as an example, let's explore the psychosomatic and psychoneuroimmunological responses to the lead cause of death. (Cancer questions are explored in the chapter "Childhood Trauma, Death, and Diagnosis.")

Heart Problems:
1. What will it take for me to become aware of and understand the laws of love I have not yet understood?
2. What feelings of compassion am I resisting to feel?
3. What would my life look like if I no longer needed the approval of those who are incapable of giving it to me?
4. What is going on in my family that needs healing? What will it take for me to contribute to that healing?
5. Who do I need to forgive?
6. What will it take for me to completely forgive myself?
7. What responsibility am I trying to get rid of?
8. What do I need to do to heal the relationship that hurts so badly?
9. Who am I hoping will rescue me but they never show up? What will it take to relieve them of this expectation and rescue myself?

Congestive Heart Failure:
1. What will it take to convince me I am worth loving?
2. What value is there in predicting that I will probably be rejected? What would be a healthier outlook about my possibilities?
3. Who have I allowed to dictate whether or not I am worth loving? What will it take to remove my need for their approval from my life?

Heart Attack:
1. What will it take for me to open myself up so I can let more love in?
2. What value is there in seeking money, power or position over love? What would be a healthier and happier endeavor?
3. What will it take for me to have the courage to express love to others?
4. What will it take to accept myself as lovable?
5. What will it take to heal all the regrets, sorrows, and remorse I feel for rejecting and resisting love in the past?

Heart Valve Problems:

1. What will it take to open up and let more love in?
2. What love am I resisting to feel?
3. What would it feel like to be even more loved than I already am?

When we truly pay attention to and listen to our body, it will tell us all we need to know to truly heal. You will experience the power of Jensen's book throughout the inspiring stories in Part III, as well as how I use questions like those above in my client mindset breakthrough coaching practices.

Throughout the rest of this book, we will use "**body**" as the code word for all the complex scientific terms describing the interactions between *culture* (which encompass values, beliefs, norms) and the *mind* (which include thoughts, feelings, and behaviors) on the intricate system of one's physical well-being.

Our bodies bear the weight of grief, and when left unresolved, it can manifest as additional health issues. The purpose of highlighting this is to encourage you to recognize and release it before it inflicts irreversible harm on your well-being. This book, along with the subsequent **Healthy GRIEF Framework**, is crafted to bolster these concepts and, more importantly, to support YOU in discovering your unique path to healing.

Healthy grief isn't merely a matter of kindness to your body; it is vital for living!

Your Journey:
Reflection and Action

*Where in your **body** do you feel grief?*

*When you think about your grief event, where in your **body** do you feel the pain or sensation?*

In Conclusion

*I*n conclusion, we covered the intricacies of grief, diving into the systems of how culture, the mind, and the body shape our capacity to heal amidst sorrow.

Culture exerts its influence by shaping our values, beliefs, and norms, which in turn impact our behaviors and emotional responses in times of loss. While cultural influences champion positivity and happiness, they can become toxic when they clash with personal beliefs, cultivating expectations of quick recovery, mental health stigma, isolation, and feelings of guilt or shame.

Our minds hold the key to understanding our emotional responses and behaviors, driven by early childhood experiences and beliefs influenced by culture and personal history. Unhealed emotional wounds further underscore the importance of comprehending the effects of our beliefs on our thoughts, feelings, and behaviors.

The chapter on the body sheds light on how unprocessed grief takes a toll on our physical well-being. Across various fields of study spanning psychology and medicine, we uncover the intricate interplay between biological, psychological, social, and cultural factors in health and illness. A fundamental pillar of this book is the recognition of the significance of identifying and releasing unresolved grief to prevent irreversible damage to our bodies.

Good news! As we embark on the journey ahead, think of us as explorers venturing into the vast emotional ocean. Our guide will be the five-stage **Healthy GRIEF Framework**, designed to help us process loss healthfully. This journey is enriched by our understanding of how culture, the mind, and the body interact within the intricate landscape of grief.

Let's venture on!

Part II

Exploring the Healthy GRIEF Framework:

A Roadmap to Healing

Introduction

"Grief does not obey your plans, or your wishes. Grief will do whatever it wants to you, whenever it wants to. In that regard, Grief has a lot in common with Love."

\- Elizabeth Gilbert

*P*art II is your companion if you're grieving, experiencing that deep emotional sorrow, or coping with the aftermath of an event that disrupted your life as you once knew it.

Various models have been developed to assist in the grief process. Traditionally, grief was thought to follow a linear path – popularized by the five stages of grief from the psychiatrist, Dr. Elisabeth Kübler-Ross in her 1969 book *On Death and Dying*.[23] However, as David Kessler (an expert of grief) aptly puts it, "Each person's grief is as unique as their fingerprint" (from the *Unlocking Us* podcast with Brené Brown).[24] It is not linear, and it can be messy. Grief is a natural, intrinsic response to profound loss. It's not something to be avoided, fixed, or numbed.

This section provides a framework for you and those you support, offering a normalized conversation to facilitate healthy processing and guide you along your unique journey towards a "new normal." The **Healthy GRIEF Framework** is a graceful approach to supporting the process and emotions as it focuses on communication and sharing experiences. It helps soften the experience, bring comfort to those involved, and gives grace to the highs and lows of the grief journey. It adapts to flow with the organic experience you may have during times of change.

The goal of the **Healthy GRIEF Framework** is to more easily transition from acute grief to integrated grief as quickly and healthily as possible without succumbing to the prolonged grief disorder. **Acute grief** occurs in the initial period after a loss, almost always including strong negative feelings, and can dominate a person's life.[25] **Integrated grief** is a result of adaptation to the loss. Although grief is not "over," it finds a way in their life versus dominating it. The goal of this book is to healthfully integrate your grief experience.

In each of the upcoming chapters, you'll find not only a detailed exploration of each stage but also practical insights into how it manifests in your life. We'll dive into why each stage is significant, what it entails, actionable steps you can take, and, for those in a supporting role, how you can extend a helping hand to someone navigating the treacherous waters of grief.

It's essential to remember that your journey through grief is profoundly personal and unique. Our aim here is to equip you with the tools to recognize your current position on this path using the framework as your guiding map. Each stage will be tailored to your specific needs, aiding you in navigating your way towards a healthier grieving process.

Let's jump in!

Foundation
Transition Time and Dancing with SARAH

"If it weren't for the rocks in its bed, the stream would have no song."

~ Carl Perkins

he **Healthy GRIEF Framework** stands as a testament to the synergy of leadership and psychology, grounded in rigorous research and enriched by the depth of my client experiences. At its core, the **Healthy GRIEF Framework** comprises five stages. Together, they provide a holistic approach to explore the deep complexities of grief and guide you toward healing.

Before we explore each stage, let us first lay a foundation for our framework. We begin by examining the crucial **transition times** and the **psychological phases** that weave throughout the intricate grief journey.

Transition Time

Clinical psychiatrist Dr. Ted Rynearson said, "There are really only two stages of grief – who you were before and who you are after."[26] When "life happens" and what once was is no longer, you have just entered Dr. Rynearson's second stage. To help demystify the path through the grief experience, let's lay the foundations for "who you are after."

Throughout my work at the Center for Creative Leadership since 1993, I have guided individuals ranging from new managers to C-suite executives through various organizational changes including merges and layoffs. One leadership model referred to often is the Bridges Transition Model, developed by William Bridges and introduced in his 1991 book *Managing Transitions: Making the Most of Change.*[27] This model provides valuable insights for individuals and organizations, helping them navigate the personal and human aspects of change. While its focus is specifically on "organizational change," it is a foundation of the **Healthy GRIEF Framework**.

Bridges differentiates between two terms - change and transition. **Change** is *an external event that happens to you*, and **transition** is *an internal process that develops as a result of the change event*. In regards to grief, "change" represents the grief event that initiated the "transition" which encompasses the psychological journey of thoughts, feelings, and behaviors as you internalize and adapt to the new circumstances brought about by the change (or grief event).

Therefore, **transition time** is the term used to discuss the journey one takes from the beginning of the grief event to the point they feel they have "moved forward" in life. Recognize that (depending on the type of grief) the journey truly never ends or is "over."

Modified from Bridge's model, the transition time for the **Healthy GRIEF Framework** is ordered as **End**, **Middle**, and **New**, and further described below:

End: Transition begins with the change (grief) event – when what once was is no longer – or the "end of a chapter" in life before transitioning to another.

Middle: This transition is at any point between the "End" and "New" marked with psychological readjustments and uncertainty. During this time, motivation, productivity, and the focus on daily tasks may decrease. At the same time, negative thoughts (like "I can't do this alone") and emotions (like sadness, fear, or anxiety) may increase.

New: This is a gradual ease into a "new chapter" in your life. It involves cultivating new insights, values, and attitudes in transitioning to and creating the "new normal." "It acknowledges the impact of loss, celebrates the positives, and guides you toward a new way of life."

While the "New" transition time gives something to work towards, grief is not something to "get over," just "move on" from, or a specific destination to meet. It is something to strive for and to be in flux.

Now, let's explore the emotional phases of grief.

Dancing with SARAH

Clinging to the life we once had can give rise to various thoughts and emotions.

Donna O'Toole is quoted as saying, "To find a safe journey through grief to growth does not mean one should forget the past. It means that on the journey, we will need safe pathways so that remembrance, which may be painful, is possible." At the very least, when you feel overwhelmed by grief, the SARAH model offers comfort by helping you pinpoint your current location on "the map" towards the "new normal." This simple act of identifying your place provides clarity about your emotional state and position in the grieving process.

"Dancing with SARAH" (or simply SARAH) is a light-hearted nod to "being in the flow" of the thoughts and emotions that come up, "dancing" versus "fighting" with your psychological experiences. I often utilize this well-known model with corporate clients as a practical framework for navigating unsettling news and guiding individuals through corporate transitions. However, I have also used it coaching teenagers navigating this thing called "life" as well as coaching clients going through divorce. The SARAH model has been a key takeaway to understanding the psychological cocktail mix of emotions one feels when life doesn't go as planned, including grief.

SARAH is loosely based on Dr. Elisabeth Kübler-Ross' model of grief. Having done her research on terminally ill patients, Kübler-Ross' Five Stages of Grief was not intended to be used linearly nor was it to apply to any type of grief. Almost all recent research has refuted the idea that grief progresses in predictable, sequential stages. Therefore, SARAH is just a guide.

What makes SARAH so helpful? It's easy to understand and remember.

Let's begin by exploring your reflections on the psychological experiences one may have during the grief process.

First, what emotion might one feel in the initial stages of grief starting with the letter "S" (the first letter of SARAH)? For example, when my parents' house caught on fire, I recall the mental toll it took on my father. He couldn't answer simple questions to the insurance agent such as the year the house was built and who else lived in the house. That look in his eyes when he turned to me for help said everything. My dad was in shock!

If you answered "**Shock**" without looking ahead, you are like most with whom I've presented SARAH. Other word associations are *sadness, surprise, stress,* and *shame*. The goal is not to "get it right;" the goal is to have a general idea on what people may feel when they first experience a grief event.

From there, you might expand on words related to these emotions yet don't start with "S" such as *numbness, confusion, disappointment, despair, loneliness, heartbreak, hurt, overwhelm, embarrassment,* and *guilt*.

As the emotions start to flow, what letters might come next starting with the letter "A"? "**Anger**" is the most common answer, yet other associated words are anxiety and anguish. Additional words related to the previous, yet don't start with "A" include *frustrated, hate, worry, fear, hopelessness, contempt,* and *disgust*.

How are you doing so far? I'm sure you are getting the hang of it. Again, this is supposed to be *easy* to remember.

Next, let's imagine someone is in the pit of heightened emotions during grief. What might "R" stand for? If you guessed "**Resistance**," you are correct! And, if you are like most people when I present this model, you likely came up with other words like *reject, rage, rebel, react, regret, resentment,* or my favorite – "*rock bottom*." Additional related words that don't start with "R" include *avoidance* and *denial*.

Now, let's imagine someone is starting to emerge from the emotional depth of their grief. Starting with the letter "A," what might one be feeling? "**Acceptance**"! Other words associated with this second "A" are *action, assistance, appreciation, assimilation,* and *accommodation*. Additional words related to the previous, yet don't start with "A" include *gratitude* and *thankful*.

Before we move on, let me emphasize again: This is not intended to be linear; it is only to understand a basic flow of emotions. Additionally, you will likely cycle back and forth through the various emotions before reaching "Acceptance." And even if you accept the grief event, you have every right to cycle back and forth to and through various emotional states. Grief can be a messy cocktail of emotions. It doesn't mean you are crazy; it means you are normal.

And, the last last letter of SARAH is "H." What might that stand for as someone is far enough through their journey of grief? Yes, "**Healing**"! Bonus points if you just yelled out "Healthy Grief"! This is our ultimate goal - to *healthfully* transition through the experience of grieving. Other associated words are *hope*, *help*, and *happiness*. Additional related words that don't start with "H" include *joy, contentment, calm, peace, relief, tranquility,* and *peace*.

Bottom line: The goal is to mark your "You are here" X on the map of emotions using SARAH as your guide. You do not have to remember all the associated words. Just find five representing each of the letters that resonate with you, and let your imagination do the rest. Easy-peasy!

Here's the basic flow of SARAH – **Shock**, **Anger**, **Resistance**, **Acceptance**, and **Healing** – mapped along the transition time (as mentioned previously).

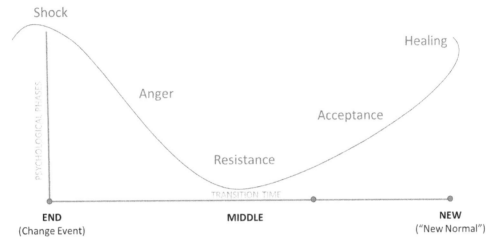

Before continuing, it is worth emphasizing again that YOUR experience through grief is going to be unique. No matter the words you use to describe what you are feeling, it's important to know that whatever you are feeling is a normal and natural part of the process. Let your process be your process. Your map to healing might just look something like this...

Stages of Grief

When it comes to prolonged grief and trauma, these will require a trained mental health practitioner to help you navigate the process. This book should only be a supplement to your healing journey.

We have explored the **transition time** of grief (End, Middle, and New) and understood the psychological phases of **SARAH** (Shock, Anger, Resistance, Acceptance, and Healing). With that foundation, let's jump into the **Healthy GRIEF Framework** of Gather, Relate, Involve, Ease, and Focus.

Your Journey:
Reflection and Action

*What's your biggest **takeaway** from this chapter?*

*Where are you in the transition time of your grief journey - **End**, **Middle** or **New**?*

*Reflecting on **SARAH**, what key emotions have you felt today?*

Gather
Mind the Facts

*"Don't sacrifice the beauties of tomorrow by focusing
on the sorrows of yesterdays."*

~ Dr. Karen Kramer

You are here if you have ever:
- Felt the "world stand still" when you got that call from a friend or family member?
- Lost touch with what day it is?
- Gone to bed with the gnawing feeling in your stomach because you frankly "forgot" to eat?

Welcome to the first letter in the **Healthy GRIEF Framework**. *G* stands for Gather *the facts associated with the event*. This is the intellectual or logical mind aspect of the GRIEF process.

This is the start of the **transitioning time** (or the "**End**") when the grief begins or when what once was is no longer. However, Gather can also happen at any point during the transition time when there is a need to collect more information to fully process the loss.

Gather involves reflecting on the losses, yet may not be able to fully process information about the grief event itself. During this initial time, it may be difficult to focus on simple tasks. The most notable emotion experienced during this initial phase of the grief process is likely shock representing the first emotion in **SARAH**.

The **goal** in this stage is to *gather enough information to process the major shift that just occurred which includes anytime information is needed to help move your forward.*

Signs of progress through the initial Gather Stage include the shock and numbness wearing off and starting to feel more alive, recognizing life is still going on around you and trying to catch up, and taking care of some of the basic necessities of life such as food (or at least acknowledge them). This may include more awareness of yourself, life around you, and the grief event itself.

Let's explore another type of grief. Anticipatory grief is a type which refers to the feeling which takes place before an impending loss.[28] An example may be mourning over the eventual passing of an ill loved one. Non-death-related examples include anxiety associated with military deployment, apprehension upon a tornado or flood warning, anticipation of corporate downsizing, fear over a scheduled mastectomy procedure, or distress surrounding an impending divorce. For the purpose of this book, we incorporate all types of grief and define it as *the deep emotional sorrow experienced after a significant loss when what once was is no longer.*

> Grief is the deep emotional sorrow experienced after a significant loss when what once was is no longer.
>
> ~ Dr. Karen Kramer

Any grief event that initiates the "end" of what once was can activate a new cycle of grief including when the anticipatory grief begins. Following are lists of some events that may activate the "End" of what once was leading to the Gather Stage of receiving or requiring more information to full process.

Health-related events might include:
- ◊   Health / mental diagnosis (ADHD, cancer)
- ◊   Incident / accident (car, etc.)
- ◊   Health decine (dementia, old age)
- ◊   Hospitalization (heart attack, car accident, risky surgery)

◊ Major health decision (chemotherapy, hospice/palliative care)

◊ Death of a loved one, suicide

◊ Loss of physical / mental abilities

◊ Loss of (mastectomy, arm, leg) or ability to use (paralysis) a body part

◊ Perinatal loss (miscarriage, stillbirth, neonatal death)

◊ Elective abortions

Relationship-related events might include:

◊ Event / awareness of stability/safety (infidelity)

◊ Decision (commitment to reconcile, divorce, separation, break-up)

◊ End (divorce, break-up, or partner moves out)

◊ Blocking (not attending an event, blocking communication, unfriending on social media)

◊ Loss of child custody (full or part-time)

Events related to career, job, or finances might include:

◊ Laid-off

◊ Retired

◊ Becoming an entrepreneur

◊ Becoming a "stay-at-home" parent

◊ Loss of title / position

Identity-related events might include:

◊ Committing to unpopular opinion/decision (no COVID-19 vaccines, no chemo for cancer, political vote, an act contrary to one's religious beliefs)

◊ Declaring (and making) a big shift in your life

◊ Stigma by a family member or self (incarceration)

◊ Significant birthday milestone ("30 is old," "AARP knocks on my door at 55")

◊ Loss of independence / freedom

Whether you are the Griever or Responder, let's discuss effective and not-so effective ways other's my receive or respond to the change event.

What to Say

It's one thing for you to begin the grief process – death, job loss, divorce – it can also be shocking to others when you share the news.

During this phase, communication is important. Share relevant facts and tailor the information to the person, especially for children, so they can fully understand yet avoid overwhelm.

At the onset of the grief event, the first thought is when, where, and how do I communicate (or ask about) the grief event?

Let's imagine I said "My mother died." To that statement, how might you respond? Would you say "I'm sorry," or "My condolences." It is likely you would as many of us in a Western society are conditioned to respond in that manner.

Then what? What might you do next? Would it get awkward? Might you change the subject out of awkwardness? Many do as, in western society, we are not formally conditioned on how to respond to other people's grief.

Here are some responses shared with me by those who wrote stories for this book.

To a divorce:

To a death:

In general:

As a Griever, how might you feel?

As a **Supporter**, have you ever used any of these lines? *I have!* If so, reflect on the purpose for your statements. Is it because you felt uncomfortable and were trying to make *yourself* feel better? Or were you honestly just trying to find a way to make *them* feel better yet didn't know what to say?

Toxic positivity during times of grief can take a wide variety of forms. Some examples include the ways in which Supporters initially respond to the Griever's grief. Keep the previous comments in mind, here is a view on similar statements and why they would be considered toxic:[29]

◊ *"Just be strong"* - While meant to be sympathetic, this prevents the Griever from sharing their experience.

◊ *"You'll find someone else."* - While an attempt to comfort, it also doesn't acknowledge the Griever's pain.

◊ *"Happiness is a choice"* - This implies that it is the Griever's own fault for not "choosing" to be happy.

How, then, *do* you best respond to one's loss?

As a Supporter, increasing your awareness equips you to provide and receive more authentic support during challenging times. Start by actively identifying toxic expressions and strive to foster an atmosphere where both you and others can openly share your emotions, be they positive or negative, without facing judgment.

Simply put, you can just say "I'm with you," or "I'm thinking of you." Avoid "I know how you feel" or "I understand," because everyone's experience of grief is different. See page 61 for some suggestions.

Each grief experience is unique. Responding to a Grievers should be unique to, sensitively based on the personal needs of the Griever, and thoughtfully considered depending upon the situation. Be authentic, be kind, and be you.

Ultimately, it is less about finding the right things to say; it's more about maintaining a supportive presence and giving support to someone free of any judgment, hidden agenda, need to "fix," or to get to a specific outcome. (See chapter "Ease" for more tips to support.)

The more we normalize conversations around grief, the better we become at engaging with others and finding our own style of support. Let's get better at our response to grief.

Your Journey:
Reflection and Action

*What's your biggest **takeaway** from this chapter?*

*In the Gather Stage, what **information** do you need today to help move you forward on your grief journey?*

What should I say to someone grieving?

Of their list of 64 phrases pertaining to grieving the death of a loved one, *here are a few of my favorites for general use from What's Your Grief.*[30]

- ◌ "There are no words."
- ◌ "You can talk to me about [it/them] whenever you want - in 5, 10, 30 years."
- ◌ "You aren't going crazy."
- ◌ "Your grief reactions are normal / appropriate."
- ◌ "Tell me about [it/him/her]."
- ◌ "Grief is not an expiration date."
- ◌ "You don't have to talk. I will just sit beside you."
- ◌ "I'm sorry for your loss."
- ◌ "It sucks!"
- ◌ "I don't know what to say, but I will listen."
- ◌ "You will never get 'over it,' yet you will get through it."
- ◌ "There is no right or wrong way to grieve. Your life has been changed forever."
- ◌ "You're allowed to feel and be exactly as you are because this is your experience and no one else's."
- ◌ "I remember ..." (and share a positive memory)
- ◌ "It's okay not to be okay."
- ◌ "We'll get through this together."
- ◌ "You are not moving on, you are moving forward."

Relate
Emotions of the Heart

"Give sorrow words; the grief that does not speak knits up the o-er wrought heart and bids it break."
~ William Shakespeare

*U*ou are here if you have ever:
- ☀ Felt lost?
- ☀ Unable to put words to your grief?
- ☀ Think you are doing "just fine" because it's been three weeks and you are back to "the usual" as if nothing major happened?

Welcome to the second letter in the **Healthy GRIEF Framework**. *R* represents **Relate** to the emotions (associated with the grief event) by acknowledging your own thoughts and feelings while also actively listening to others'. This aspect forms the emotional core of the GRIEF process.

Transitioning time is all along the continuum from "End" to "New," and encompassing any of the emotions in **SARAH**.

The **goal** in this stage is to *acknowledge the emotions of the grief process.*

Signs of progress in the Relate Stage include an ability to connect with (verses avoid) what you are feeling, able to more accurately articulate your thoughts and feelings. In doing so, you have more agency and control over your emotional ups and downs as you understand their purpose in your grief journey. This may include being able to engage in more effective conversations with others about your feelings, wants, and needs.

In this chapter, we'll explore emotions related to SARAH as an ability to understand, label, and heal. We end the chapter with some tips on how best to support Grievers.

Naming Your Feelings

As Shakespeare said, "There is nothing either good or bad, but thinking makes it so." Turns out, he was right. Becoming more conscious of our thoughts allows us to have more choice over our emotions.

If you struggled to come up with the SARAH descriptive emotions in the chapter "Foundation," you are not alone. Interestingly, according to a research study by Brené Brown, "Most people can only name three emotions: happy, sad, and angry. Increasing our emotional vocabulary can be life-changing because without language, we don't have the words needed to describe our experience, so we remain trapped in darkness not knowing ourselves and our behavior."[31] And... who wants to be trapped in grief with no way out? I don't!

Being able to identify, describe, and put names to your feelings is closely tied to your ability to heal. Harvard psychologist Susan David references our emotions as beacons adding "They help you to identify what you care about most, and motivate you to make positive changes."[32] Similarly, Brené Brown states, "People who can distinguish between a range of emotions are much better able to manage the ups and downs of daily life."[33] If our goal is to healthfully process through grief, we need the emotional language to do so.

In her recent book *Atlas of the Heart*, Brené Brown outlines 87 human emotions and experiences based on her research and extensive literature review. To help keep it simple for our use in this book associated with grief, SARAH (at its core) only focused on five emotions. Below is SARAH and related emotions and psychological experiences associated with those in the model. The goal is to help name the various emotions one may feel throughout the grief process. When we name them, we are better able to identify where we are in the process, therefore, feeling less lost. Note: Not all are emotions. Some are thoughts and a few are actions. Either way, it gives a framework on which to process.

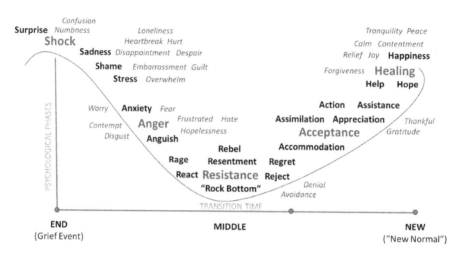

We'll enhance our understanding of grief-related emotions by using the SARAH clusters of words. Of the 54 emotions listed in the previous model, we will define 35 of them based on Brené Brown's research and two based on psychologist Jean Piaget's cognitive development therapy.[34] Since some of the definitions of the remaining 19 emotions overlap, and (frankly) not to overwhelm you, let's become more familiar with just the 37 emotions listed below.

Shock Cluster

Confusion - "Has the potential to motivate, lead to deep learning, and trigger problem solving."

Surprise - "An interruption caused by information that doesn't fit with our current understanding or expectations. It causes us to reevaluate."

Sadness Cluster

Sadness - It is "...vital for developing compassion and empathy. It comes from loss or defeat – real or imagined. It is not depression and not grief. Sadness moves us..."

Disappointment - "Disappointment is unmet expectations. the more significant the expectations, the more significant the disappointment. ...

When we develop expectations, we paint a picture in our head of how things are going to be and how they're going to look."

Despair - "Despair is a sense of hopelessness about a person's entire life and future. When extreme hopelessness seeps into all the corners of our lives and combines with extreme sadness, we feel despair."

Heartbreak - "Heartbreak is always connected to love and belonging. ... Heartbreak is what happens when love is lost."

Hurt - According to a research team by Anita Vangelisti "Individuals who are hurt experience a combination of sadness at having been emotionally wounded and fear of being vulnerable to harm. When people feel hurt, they have appraised something that someone said or did as causing them emotional pain."

Loneliness - "At the heart of loneliness is the absence of meaningful social interaction - an intimate relationship, friendships, family gatherings, or even community or work group connections."

Shame Cluster

Shame - "Shame is the intensely painful feeling or experience of believing that we are flawed and therefore unworthy of love, belonging, and connection." We keep shame hidden because we believe we are not enough and deserve to feel ashamed of who we are. Examples include raging at your kids, bankruptcy, DUIs, and incarceration.

Embarrassment - "Embarrassment is a fleeting feeling of self-conscious discomfort in response to a minor incident that was witnessed by others."

Guilt - "Like shame, guilt is an emotion that we experience when we fall short of our expectations or standards. However, with guilt, our focus is on having done something wrong and on doing something to set things right, like apologizing or changing a behavior." It is a feeling that "I behaved badly."

Stress Cluster

Stressed - "We feel stressed when we evaluate environmental demand as beyond our ability to cope successfully. This includes elements of unpredictability, uncontrollability, and feeling overloaded." It's a reflection of our mind, not our body.

Overwhelmed - "Overwhelm means an extreme level of stress, and emotional and/or cognitive intensity to the point of feeling unable to function."

Anxiety Cluster

Anxiety - "The American Psychological Association defines anxiety as 'an emotion characterized by feelings of tension, worried thoughts and physical changes like increased blood pressure.'" Generalized anxiety disorder involves excessive worry about everyday concerns, with all forms of anxiety stemming from an intolerance for uncertainty.

Worry - "Worry is described as a chain of negative thoughts about bad things that might happen in the future."

Fear - "Fear is a negative, short lasting, high alert emotion and response to a perceived threat." Anxiety is future-based, while fear is now.

Anger Cluster

According to Brené Brown, although researchers indicate that anger is a primary emotion, her research indicates that it is a secondary emotion believing there are a lot of other emotions underneath anger. Here are the anger clusters associated with SARAH.

Anger - "Anger is an emotion that we feel when something gets in the way of a desired outcome or when we believe there's a violation of the way things should be."

Contempt - "Contempt, simply put, says 'I'm better than you. and you are lesser than me.'" According to John and Julie Gottman, in the *Love and Respect Workbook*, "Contempt is perhaps the most corrosive force in marriage."[35]

Disgust - "According to emotions research pioneer Paul Ekman, disgust 'arises as a feeling of aversion towards something offensive.'"

Disgust - is trying to avoid being "poisoned" by something or someone.

Frustrated - When things don't go as planned. "Frustration sometimes overlaps with anger. Both anger and frustration can result when a desired outcome is blocked. The main difference is that with frustration, we don't think we can fix the situation, while with anger, we feel there is something we can do."

Hate - "According to researcher Robert Sternberg, hate is a combination of various negative emotions including repulsion, discuss, anger, fear, and contempt.'"

Anguish Cluster

Anguish - "Anguish is an almost unbearable and traumatic swirl of shock, incredibility, grief, and powerlessness."

Hopelessness - "Hopelessness arises out of a combination of negative life events and negative thought patterns, particularly self-blame and the perceived inability to change our circumstances." Hopelessness is strongly related to suicidal ideations.

Resistance Cluster

Avoidance - "Avoidance, the second coping strategy for anxiety, is not showing up and often spending a lot of energy zigzagging around and away from that thing that already feels like it's consuming us."

Regret - "Both disappointment and regret arise when an outcome was not what we wanted, counted on, or thought would happen. ...With regret, we believe the outcome was caused by our decision or actions."

Resentment - "Resentment is the feeling of frustration, judgment, anger, 'better than,' and/or hidden envy related to perceived unfairness or injustice. It's an emotion that we often experience when we fail to set boundaries or ask for what we need, or when expectations let us down because they were based on things we can't control, like what other people think, what they feel, or how they're going to react."

Acceptance Cluster

Accommodation - a term developed by psychologist Jean Piaget's in his theory of cognitive development.[36] It describes what occurs when new information or experiences cause you to modify your existing understanding of the way things "should be." It is the process we use to adjust and change our understanding of something to incorporate new information and experiences.

Assimilation - to take in (information, ideas, or culture) and understand fully, and is also part of Jean Piaget's theory of cognitive development.

Gratitude - "Gratitude is an emotion that reflects our deepest appreciation for what we value, what brings meaning to our lives, and what makes us feel connected to ourselves and others." Gratitude is correlated with better sleep, creativity, and decision-making skills, and decreased entitlement, hostility, and aggression. Being thankful is a close synonym.

Healing Cluster

Calm - "Creating perspective and mindfulness while managing emotional reactivity."

Contentment - "The feeling of completeness, appreciation, and 'enoughness' that we experience when our needs are satisfied." Contentment is associated with greater well-being and life satisfaction.

Happiness - "Feeling pleasure often related to the immediate environment or current circumstances." Happiness is a stable, longer-lasting feeling of being in control that is more internal than external.

Hope - Hope is a function of three things - setting realistic goals, having a means for achievement, and having a sense of agency. It is a thought, not an emotion. Hope helps us get through adversity and discomfort.

Joy - "An intense feeling of deep spiritual connection, pleasure, and appreciation." Joy and gratitude are strongly related.

Relief - Researchers Ira Roseman and Andreas Evdokas describe relief as "feelings of tension leaving the body and being able to breathe more easily, thoughts of the worst being over and being safe for the moment, resting, and wanting to get on to something else."

Tranquility - "'Tranquility is associated with the absence of demand' and 'no pressure to do anything.'"

Language holds tremendous power and serves as a conduit for meaning. However, it's crucial to note that feeling your emotions doesn't always necessitate immediate action. There are instances where it's vital to allow yourself the time and space to sit with these emotions, process the situation, and accept your feelings before taking any action. Also, make sure to not suppress them.

In a widely renowned TED Talk titled "A Gift of Power and Emotional Courage," Harvard psychologist Susan David cautions us about the consequences of suppressing negative emotions.[37] She highlights that if we avoid experiencing these feelings, they will persistently undermine us. Research on emotional suppression corroborates this, revealing that when emotions are brushed aside or ignored, they tend to intensify or amplify. While it may seem like we're asserting control over unwanted emotions through will-power or avoidance, in reality, these emotions end up exerting control over us. (Refer back to my opening Preface as a perfect example.)

How to Support?

Engage in conversations about feelings and the implications of the change. Observe (without judgment) the Griever's thoughts, emotions, actions, and reactions to understand the impact of the change. Introduce the concept of SARAH (see chapter "Foundation") as a framework for discussing and recognizing their own and others' emotional stages without judgment.

Be present, listen attentively, and empathize without judgment. Listen and take the time to truly hear and empathize with the Griever. Honor emotions and ask open-ended questions. Create a safe space for expression.

Resist the urge to fight anger with more anger. Show empathy and allow others to express their anger. Communicate your points only after validating the Griever's emotions. Encourage healthy outlets like exercise, safe venting, or therapy.

Expressing and validating emotions is crucial to navigate the grieving process and embrace change. Regularly revisit and monitor the Griever's journey through the grief phases, respecting their unique path and timing.

The most healing thing you can do for a Griever is to be a witness to their pain – to allow them to be seen, heard, and understood. The best thing you can do as a Griever is be a witness to your own pain by understanding and flowing with and through your emotions. Dance with SARAH!

Your Journey:
Reflection and Action

*What's your biggest **takeaway** from this chapter?*

*In the Relate Stage, what range of **emotions** have you felt today?*

Involve
Steps into Action

"The man who moves a mountain
begins by carrying away small stones."

~ Confucius

You are here if you have ever:
- ✹ Slept for days to the point people are starting to ask questions?
- ✹ Had logistics to attend to and not a clue as to where to start?
- ✹ Felt overwhelmed?

Welcome to the third letter in the **Healthy GRIEF Framework**. *I* stands for **Involve** *yourself in forward movement*. Think of this step as the *action-oriented* aspect of the GRIEF process. It is an opportunity to reorient your mind, body, and emotions back to life while doing so on your own timeline.

Although there may not be a lot of movement in the initial "End" (when the grief event occurred), taking action in the Involve Stage can happen throughout the **transition time**. Shifts towards finding a new way of life beyond what once was requires taking action. Various emotions may bubble up throughout **SARAH**, yet taking healthy action will help to move towards the acceptance and healing phases.

The **goal** in this stage is *to take action*.

Signs of progress in the Involve Stage include more engagement in life activities and more traction. This may include increased energy, more motivation, and more clarity.

In this chapter, we'll explore how to take action and what you can do as a Supporter.

What to do?

The *Involve* stage of the **Healthy GRIEF Framework** is a critical point to help Grievers to shift out of "the pit" of the SARAH Model, and move from the acute grief to integrated grief. Where **acute grief** occurs in the initial period after a loss when grief dominates the person's life, **integrated grief** is the result of adaptation to the loss.[38]

The key here is to take action!

However, in general, there tends to be two types of action-oreinters. First are the "action takers" who quickly jump into busyness related to the grief change event OR doing anything else as an avoidance tactic for going through the grief process (specifically emotions). The second type are the "non-action takers" who disconnect from life for months and years as they slowly slip into deeply emoting through the grief process, otherwise known as a form of **prolonged grief disorder**. Finding a middle ground is helpful and healthy for the grief process.

The goal for taking action depends on the type of grief and how you are psychologically reacting to it. There are a couple different ways to approach it. And here are some tactics that emerged both from my research and client experience.

Disassociate

Disassociating, or deliberating detaching or distancing yourself from particular thoughts, emotions, and behaviors, has its benefits and challenges. One benefit is that it gives your mental, emotional, and physical body a break from engaging in the emotion of grief. One example is pretending a lost or estranged loved one is just gone temporarily. Another is taking a vacation and pretending that everything is normal "back home." It is a form of denial. Ongoing dissociating (or denial) may be an avoidance tactic of the inevitable and can create bigger problems if experienced for a long period of time, yet can create some temporary release in small doses.

Distract

Another form of "action taking" is distraction. This can help a Griever who is overwhelmed and flooded. Although there are pros and cons to being distracted, a pro is that it gives a Griever a way to physically, mentally, and emotionally engage in an activity not related to the grief. It can create forward movement in their life.

This is all about doing something to keep oneself busy. For example, while going through my first divorce, I threw myself into my doctoral work. After my father died. I jumped into managing the estate. Although it was related to the logistics of the grief process, I was using it to distract me from the grief. On the flipside, as I describe in more detail with my full story later in "A Father's Passing," distracting oneself long-term to avoid going through the emotions of the grief can have devastating results. Use this in small doses.

Also identify the purpose for the distraction. For my divorce, I had a sense of control over my doctoral work when I could not control my divorce. This was a positive distraction for a short period of time until I could reengage back into the divorce process. After my dad died, I had a limiting belief (referred to later as "Little Miss Karen") that prevented me from engaging in the emotions of the grief process. This, to quote Susan David, is when emotions can come back with a vengeance.

So anything that is keeping you busy, that is good for only a period of time. However, if you choose to stay there, thinking, "Great, I'm doing great for the grief process, because I'm not feeling all the feelings," then decide the time limit you will place on reengaging into the grief change and transition process. You may be purposely avoiding what is inevitable because of the emotions that are underneath. Recognize the pros and cons of distraction.

Distractions may look like going back to work, engaging in education or a hobby, or engaging in a vacation or hanging out with friends to have fun.

Give Yourself Grace

After the shock wears off, productivity will likely decrease (unless you are engaged in denial or distraction, as previously indicated). This means your "energy battery" may wear out sooner than "normal." Your ability to focus on and pay attention to even simple tasks may wane. Some refer to this as "brain fog" or "grief brain."

This may look like sleeping all day or taking naps, avoiding running into people or not returning messages, reading all day or binge watching Netflix. The goal is to give yourself time, space, and permission to just... be.

Don't expect it to take a certain time. If you take time off of work and still feel you need more time after that passes, request it. Bereavement and grief are not time bound to a week off of work or a year to recover.

The best advice my financial and trust attorney told me after my mother died is that the process could take years (not months), and that I didn't have to jump into the paperwork immediately.

If you have children, family, a partner, work, or others who depend on you, seek support so you can focus on what you need. See the next chapter for more tips on how to ask for support.

As with any activity taken in this phase, pay attention to your mood, your energy levels, and life around you. Although there is no time designated for this, life may place pressure or expectations on you such as work and family demands, both logistically as well as well-intended and caring concern for your well-being. Therefore, give yourself a time frame and communicate that to others. Also note when professional help is needed to support shifting you into other action-oriented tasks to help you healthfully process grief.

It's okay to feel the feelings; it's not okay to stay there.

> It's okay to
> feel the feelings;
> it's not okay
> to stay there.
>
> ~ Dr. Karen Kramer

Take Time

When thinking about jumping into action, it's okay to do it slowly. Establish one, two, or three tasks to do. Start with the basics that are going to help fuel your body to keep it moving forward and then slowly start integrating other things.

This could be as simple as getting out of bed before noon, taking a shower, brushing your hair, and putting on fresh clothes. It could be going to work for a few hours, taking the children to school one day, or making one meal. Slowly integrating yourself back into life. Find a pace that works for you, and not one that other people are going to force on you.

Examples:

- ◊ Focus only on the current day
- ◊ Focus on highest priorities like health, work, and family

Focus on Immediate Needs

This is where you start taking concerted efforts towards the immediate needs of the grief event. Examples may include:

- ◊ Make a critical decision on your health - chemo, surgery, testing, or hospice
- ◊ Have honest communication with kids, family, loved ones
- ◊ Be vigilant with medical directives and needs
- ◊ Manage the estate / finances
- ◊ Plan the funeral / celebration of life, or deal with paperwork
- ◊ Find a caretaker, lawyer, doctor, or therapist
- ◊ Contact insurance, social security, or financial institutions
- ◊ Box up items for a move / clean up

Nurture Your Body

Food, sleep, and exercise are key ingredients for a healthy mind and body. This also supports your emotional expression. In times of grief, it is not uncommon to be off a "normal" movement and nutrient regime. Based on your abilities, find ways to care for your body.

Examples:

- ◊ Eat regular and healthy meals
- ◊ Exercise - gym, homework, treadmill
- ◊ Get out in nature - walk, hike, swim, boat, ski, fish
- ◊ Engage in hobbies - read, garden, art, travel, cooking, music
- ◊ Do things you love - catching sunset at the beach, dancing, singing
- ◊ Explore new places - road trips, new restaurants
- ◊ Do some self-care - hair cut, mani-pedi
- ◊ Engage in holistic healing modalities - Massage, Reiki, meditation, sound bowls

◊　Write, Journal

◊　Religion - pray, read the bible, confession

◊　Read, listen to podcasts, education

Honor Yourself and Others

We are social creatures. If you find yourself isolating yourself out of embarrassment, feeling a burden to others, overwhelmed and just don't know what to say, don't want to have to explain the change, etc. find ways to ease back into connecting with other humans.

Connecting with others during times of grief can fill the soul. We will discuss more in the next chapter. Here are some examples of actions you can take to just connect with others while also honoring yourself.

Examples:

◊　Say YES to offers of help and support

◊　Set healthy boundaries and ask for what you need

◊　Minimize time with unhealthy relationship interactions

◊　Consciously choose with whom, when, and how to inform others of your grief journey

◊　Spend quality time connecting with loved ones

◊　Remember to celebrate yourself in the process - birthdays, holidays, quiet time

◊　Volunteer to build a social network and purpose

◊　Laugh and joke with others

Note: If interacting with others involves minimizing time with unhealthy or toxic relationships, see Part IV Website Resources for more information on setting healthy boundaries.

Establish a Routine

The next step is engaging in actions that can move you forward towards your "new normal." This may take days, weeks, months, or years. It's less about the time, and more about the action steps to keep one foot in front of the other.

Examples:

- ◊ Create a routine with an ideal schedule
- ◊ Maintain healthy boundaries and continue to ask for what you need
- ◊ Be intentional with your time
- ◊ Rediscover your purpose and what you want

How to Support?

Engage the Griever in practical tasks, respecting their needs and preferences. Encourage open communication, support, and collaborative decision-making to foster unity and forward momentum. Embrace the idea that this may take more time than you might process; everyone's grief journey is different.

During this stage, Grievers may still *resist* change. They may reject any change created by the grief event, and may deflect by focusing on other issues. They may use logic and reasoning as a defense mechanism.

Practice patience and attentive listening are crucial (see the chapter "Ease" for tips). Set appropriate boundaries and recognize these behaviors as protective shields against discomfort and loss. Keep in mind that Grievers may be reacting out of their loss, and not to take things personally, and… set appropriate boundaries regarding any physical, mental, or emotional harm to them, yourself, and others. (See Part IV Resources for support.)

If applicable and appropriate, provide action plans with clear time frames and success indicators. This will depend on the type of grief and not to be used to rush something through the process of grieving. Encourage small, achievable steps that appear manageable and realistic for the Griever. Support goals, celebrate wins, and tackle easily attainable tasks first. And … your timeline may not be the same for the Griever.

By involving Grievers in action steps, it assists their progress through the SARAH phases from any range of emotions associated with *shock*, *anger*, and *resistance* and gently guides them towards *acceptance* and *healing*. In that phase, they can more easily embrace their loss and find hope for the new chapter of their life.

You do not have to do it all. You do not have to do it all at once. And you do not have to do it alone. Your process is unique and will take whatever time you need.

You certainly should not process your grief by yourself which is a reason why the next chapter is all about finding by whom and what support you need to move forward in your healthy grief journey.

> You do not have to do it all. You do not have to do it all at once. And you do not have to do it alone.
>
> ~ Dr. Karen Kramer

Your Journey:
Reflection and Action

*What's your biggest **takeaway** from this chapter?*

*In the Involve Stage, what **one action step** can you take today that will help you move forward on your grief journey?*

Ease
Hands of Support

*"All the water in the world cannot drown you
unless it gets inside of you."*

~ Eleanor Roosevelt

*Y*ou are here if** you have ever:

✺ Run out of toilet paper because you just haven't felt like going to the grocery store?

✺ Desperately needed help, yet didn't want to burden anyone?

✺ Thought that no one is going to understand the pain you are in?

Welcome to the fourth letter in the **Healthy GRIEF Framework**. *E* represents **Ease** *through the transition with the support of professional and/or informal help*. Think of this stage as the *supportive hands* that guide you through grief.

Seeking support is best to begin at the start of the **transaction time** although the type of support needed will change throughout your grief journey. Various **SARAH** emotions may be expressed.

The objective of the Ease Stage is to support you to and through the *acceptance* phase (of SARAH). It is certainly a milestone in the healthy grief process. By this stage, you have let go of the grip on "what once was," or at least the expectation for things to go back to the way they were before or how they "should be." Depending on the grief event, this may include acknowledging that your loved one will not return, relationships change, children grow up and move out, careers change, friendships wane, health shifts with age, and things in life come and go.

Acceptance doesn't mean being okay with the loss, but rather adjusting to a changed life. Acceptance also doesn't end grief; it's a series of smaller moments over time.

Even if you've accepted the grief change, there may still be various emotions including confusion, uncertainty, and impatience. Expressing your feelings is crucial. You won't have all the answers as you journey ahead.

The **goal** for this phase is to *ask for and accept support*.

Signs of progress include, for example, seeking support to plan and attend change-related events (such as a funeral) or professional support to sign important papers (such as in a divorce, trust, or medical agreement). This may accompany increased energy, motivation, engagement, and utilizing support.

In this chapter, we'll discuss ways Grievers can seek support including some reason why they may shy away from it. Supporters, your tips to helping others through grief is also shared.

How to Ask for Support

When is the best time to ask for support? As soon as possible. When you think you need help, that's the time to ask for it. Not at the point where you actually need it.

Reach out even if it is to say, "Hey, this is what's going on in my life. I'm not quite sure when I'm going to need help." Or "Hey, my mom just passed away. I could really use some help going through her closet because I know that's going to be emotional. I don't know when, but are you available to help me when I do?" Asking doesn't mean you need help immediately.

Asking for help before hitting "rock bottom" will save you time, money, and energy. This is your opportunity to advocate for your own needs, and remember that healing involves acceptance, integration, and moving forward.

> When you think you need help, that's the time to ask for it. Not at the point where you actually need it.
>
> ~ Dr. Karen Kramer

First, let's acknowledge some reasons that may prevent you from seeking support.

Embarrassment

When my husband walked out, I hid behind my fake smile for months before I finally told more than just a few of my close friends. Unfortunately, I was also missing out on opportunities for help. When I started sharing, I was surrounded by coworkers, friends, and family who provided an ear to listen, shared their related stories of encouragement, and provided resources (like a therapist referral) to help me move forward.

If embarrassment is something holding you back, start small by telling at least one person.

Burden

Do you feel like a burden? I did when I was going through my grief journey, many of them! In reality, others may be grateful to share your grief load and help support you. One gentleman told me, after his son died, "I just needed toilet paper, someone to clean my bathroom, and to mow my lawn." He found that his neighbors and friends were happy to help him with those tasks because he gave them the *gift* of letting them know what he truly needed.

What may feel like a burden (to ask) can be a present to others. You are giving them a gift of letting them know how to best support you in a time of need.

Others Are Not Helpful

There will be people who, with all good intentions, are just not helpful. This could include those who may attempt to "fix" your grief by offering suggestions or telling you what to do. If this is the case and you are finding yourself becoming frustrated for not feeling seen, heard, or understood, politely excuse yourself. Honor that the Supporter is doing the best they can with all-good intentions. The information coming next will help them support you.

There will also be those who, for various reasons, will not be fully emotionally available to process with you. That's not something I felt I could do with my husband after my father passed. Instead, there were many times I snuck off to cry in the bathroom or silently wept at night. This, by the way, is not an experience I hope you find yourself in which is why I'm providing various suggestions. (Note: I'm also the one who thought I could D.I.Y. my way through my own divorce. Not a good strategy!)

I hid my sadness from my husband because I didn't feel seen, heard, or understood at the time; instead, my grief to him was something to "fix," and he was frustrated for not being "able to fix" me. This is not a fault of either of ours; we just didn't have the tools available for me to fully express what I needed and for him to understand how best to support. If you can relate, keep reading.

In addition, do you have those friends that are great to have fun with yet may not be the ones you turn to when you need emotional support? Likely so, and let that be okay. Not everyone in your life is going to be available to support you during your grief. It's more about them and less about you. Don't take it personally. The goal is to find those people who can support you.

It's Not Just You

Also, grief is not just all about you. Depending on the type of grief, there may be others who need you to get support - for you and for them.

For example, if your parent passed away and you have young children who depend on you, not only are your children going through their own grief over losing a grandparent, they are losing their own parent to grief. This is a version of **compound grief**. This can also occur during a divorce. Let me repeat that. While you are going through the grieving process, seek help at least for those who depend on you. *Members in your household may also be going through grief. If you are not ready to seek help for yourself, at least seek help for them.*

> Members in your household may also be going through grief. If you are not ready to seek help for yourself, at least seek help for them.
>
> ~ Dr. Karen Kramer

"Okay, Okay! How do I ask for help?"

I'm glad you asked! Here are various ways to seek (and receive) formal and informal support to help you healthfully *ease* through the grief process.

Raise awareness through education and experiences such as:

◊   Books (like this one), Podcasts

◊   Courses, Programs, Seminars

◊   Education and Certification Programs

◊   Religion - Reading the Bible

Process grief through experiences that work with your beliefs and opportunities such as:

◊   Therapy, counseling, coaching

◊   Support groups

◊   Religious services

◊   Mediums, psychics, spirit guides

Seek support groups (**formal or informal**) who serve different functions (such as emotional support, encouragement) which can be formed around:

◊   Religious Groups

◊   Coaching/Therapy

◊   Business/Network

◊   Health

◊   Hobbies

◊   Military

Seek individuals (or collective) informal support who serve different functions (such as emotional support, encouragement, childcare, groceries) through:

◊   Friends - current, past, and new

◊   Coworkers, colleagues

◊   Family, partner, husband/wife

◊   Neighbors

◊   Classmates

Engage in professional/formal services such as:
- ◊ Legal - divorce, family, probate, trust, personal injury
- ◊ Medical - doctors, specialists, social worker, dietitians, caregivers
- ◊ Psychological - therapist, counselor, psychiatrist, NLP practitioners
- ◊ School - counselor, vice principal, principal, teachers
- ◊ Religion - church (or place of religious services)
- ◊ Military

It's important to recognize that fully comprehending the depth of the pain and disbelief over a life-altering event, and processing the experience cannot be rushed. **It's okay to feel the feelings. It's not okay to stay there.** In cases of prolonged grief, seek professional help. Seeking appropriate support becomes crucial in such cases. Profound traumas require professional support to heal effectively. Additional resources can be found in Part IV.

The support you need right now may be different tomorrow or a week from now. Start with where you are now. If you are feeling alone or are geographically alone (due to no partners, distant family, or no local friends), there are many ways to seek support. See Part IV for ideas. The goal is to *reach out*.

How to Support?

When someone is going through the grief process, in general, they may be 1) in a fog and unable to give you an answer on what they need, and/or 2) don't want to "burden" you or are embarrassed by asking for what they really need.

If you are not sure how to reach out, start with words or phrases used in the letter on the next page. Use it as an email, a phrase or two for a quick text, or (best yet) pick up the phone and give them a call.

From logistics to emotional support, following are some recommendations.

Note: However you choose to support the Griever, be authentic and honest with what you will and will not provide. It can do more damage to say you will "always be there" for them, yet not return their phone calls or texts. This can be more hurtful to the Griever who has taken the effort to reach out.

Letter of Support

Dear Friend,

I hope this message finds you as well as can be expected during this time. I just wanted to let you know that you're in my thoughts.

Grief is an incredibly personal and unique experience. I won't pretend to know exactly what you're going through, yet I'm here to listen and support you in any way you need. No judgments, no advice, just a willing ear and a shoulder to lean on whenever you're ready to talk.

Your feelings are entirely valid, and you don't need to compare your pain to anyone else's. There's no need to put on a brave face or hide your grief under a facade of busyness. Your journey through this is your own, and it deserves the time and space it requires.

I know that sometimes talking to those closest to us can be challenging because they want to make our pain go away. While their intentions are good, it's not always easy for them to just listen and be present. That's where I come in. I'm here to listen without judgment or an agenda.

Please remember that it's okay to prioritize yourself during this time. Self-care is essential, and you should never feel guilty for taking care of your needs. You matter immensely, and your well-being is a priority.

Feel free to reach out to me anytime, in any way that suits you. Whether it's a call, a text, or a message, I'm here and ready to offer my support, whenever you're ready to talk.

Sending you warm hugs and all the strength you need. Take care, my friend.

With love and understanding,
Me

Logistical Support

Offering specific support is the best. They can always say "no." For example, when I was going through my divorce, people offered help yet I was not good at asking for help or even accepting it. It was only when a dear friend said "I'm at the grocery store. I'm going to get you what I think you need unless you tell me otherwise." That was what I needed at the time. You can always say, "[This] is what I am doing for you. If there is something more (or different) I can do for you, please let me know. I care about you, and I want to be there to support you." You know the Griever the best. Offer them something that you know they may need and will not protest. Sometimes just offering to come over with a cup of coffee and sit on the couch to just listen can be just the support one needs, and for others, that may be too much.

When someone is grieving, the basic necessities tend to be needed first such as groceries, cooking, cleaning, taking care of the kids, etc. After my mother died, a dear friend texted me a link from her GrubHub account and told me to order dinner for me and my son. Although a part of me wanted to graciously decline, I realized I was in no condition to make dinner and gladly accepted.

The goal is to help make the Griever's life as easy and simple while their life is consumed by grief. Here are some suggested ways to offer help:

- *Childcare* - babysitting, school/sport transportation, tutoring
- *Food* - "easy to make" groceries, pre-prepared meals, delivery meals (DoorDash, Uber Eats, GrubHub) or create a meal train (mealtrain.com)
- *Cleaning* - mowing lawn, cleaning bathroom, washing dishes, offering a maid service, laundry
- *Transportation* - to grocery store, for kid's school/sports, medical, legal
- *Resources* - recommendations for a doctor, lawyer, mortuary, childcare provider, real estate agent, financial planner, caregiver

Bottom line: Tell the Griever what you plan to do. Give him/her the opportunity to graciously accept, decline, or modify your offer. And, if this suits you, let him/her know you are there for emotional support.

"Holding Space"

Sometimes the best support is a willing ear to just listen. It's about witnessing someone's grief and giving it permission to be spoken. For grief to be seen, heard, and witnessed by another can be the most powerful tool for healing.

First, as a Supporter, be aware if **your grief triggers** and emotional wounds are being activated by the other's grief. For example, if you have recently been divorced and are still bitter, will you be able to put your thoughts, feelings, and beliefs aside to be completely present for the divorcing Griever? If not, it may not be the best support for either of you, and may end in a toxic cocktail of emotions further reinforcing the grief.

One tendency is to "fix" someone by giving them advice. *I know I've done it!* If this is your natural response, take a moment to explore that purpose for you. Are you attempting to ease your *own* discomfort over their grief? Are you impatient for them to "move on" or "understand" something? Do you like to be in control? Being present with a Griever is not about fixing, controlling, or managing their grief for them. It is… wait for it… about listening, witnessing, and understanding their grief.

Unless the Griever explicitly asks for it, trying to "fix" a griever in an emotional state (although done with good intentions) may be met with anger, sadness, or shutting down because they may not feel heard, seen, or understood for what they are going through.

Now that we have explored some things that may get in the way of "holding space" for a Griever, here are some key tips:

1. **Be Present**: Give your full attention. Put away distractions, such as your phone or other electronic devices, and focus on the conversation.
2. **Offer a Safe Space**: Create an environment where the grieving person feels safe to express their feelings, thoughts, and emotions without judgment. This could also be done in conjunction with physical activities like going for a walk or hike; a friend-date for a meal, coffee, or the movies; or going shopping, to the beach, etc.

3. **Use Active Listening**: Show that you're actively engaged in the conversation by nodding, making eye contact, and using verbal cues like "I see," "I hear you," and "Tell me more." I once supported a grieving coaching client during a phone call with little more than using the phrase "Tell me more."

4. **Ask Open-Ended Questions**: Encourage the Griever to share their experiences by asking open-ended questions like "How are you feeling today?" or "Can you tell me more about your memories?" A tip I picked up from my dear friend Alise Cortez's book *Coloring Life* is (if the grief is the passing of a loved one) to ask to share their fondest memory of that person.[39]

5. **Validate Their Feelings**: Let them know it's okay to feel the way they do. Statements like "It's completely normal to feel this way" can be comforting. Use the SARAH model (in the chapter "Foundation"), if appropriate and helpful.

6. **Respect Silence**: Sometimes, Grievers need moments of silence to process their emotions. Don't rush them or feel the need to fill the gaps with words.

7. **Be Patient**: Grief can be a long and unpredictable process. Allow the person to express their feelings at their own pace, and don't rush them through their process.

8. **Respect their Coping Style**: Understand that people cope with grief in different ways. Some may want to talk, while others may need time alone. Respect their coping style and boundaries.

Supporting someone through grief requires patience, empathy, and understanding. Remember that everyone's grief experience is unique, and your role is to be a compassionate listener and a source of comfort. The most precious thing you can do for someone grieving is to give them the gift of being seen, heard, and understood. This is less about what you say or do, and more about your genuine presence and authentic care.

> The most precious thing you can do for someone grieving is to give them the gift of being seen, heard, and understood.
>
> ~ Dr. Karen Kramer

The Secure Relationship

June 10 · 🌐

When your partner is in pain, emotional or physical, their brain can't take in logic and details. What is most comforting to suffering is engaged, but non-anxious presence. It often involves soft touch and it sounds like phrases which are simple and soothing. The more simple the better. This is because pain exists in the part of the brain which is the most primitive...it transcends words and information. It doesn't speak "words," it speaks "feels." It's the same part of the brain shared by distressed babies and horses (among many other animals). How would you soothe a baby in distress? How would you soothe a horse in distress? Nobody tries to talk babies and animals out of hurting because they intuitively know it's not possible. When left to intuition, most people (regardless of gender) will instinctively show up with soft, simple, soothing phrases. Growing up in a culture where logic is encouraged over emotional attunement, independence over interdependence, stifles this essential part of our humanity and for our relationships to thrive we need to learn how to reclaim it. The next time your partner is in distress, try to show up as a soothing presence, not a fixer. You can give advice later if you need to, but don't lead with it. To be a comforting presence the goal can never be to "take the pain away"......but paradoxically comforting presence is the very thing which creates the space for the pain to move through at its own pace.

#thesecurerelationship #thesecurerelationshipmft #secureattachment #securelove #healthycouple #healthycouples #relationships #relationshipadvice #emotionallyunavailable #emotionalsupport #emotionsmatter #emotionallyavailable #emotionalwellbeing #communicationiskey

👍❤️ 16K   528 comments   7.4K shares

Although the depth of the pain over a life-altering event, and processing the experience cannot be rushed, recognize when they may need professional support. Prolonged grief and profound traumas require professional support to heal effectively. Seeking appropriate support becomes crucial in such cases.

Professional Support and Resources

For most, grief symptoms decrease over time. However, for a few, the intense feelings of grief persist, becoming severe enough to prevent them from continuing life in a healthy manner. This can lead to **prolonged grief disorder** Personally, I am not promoting further psychological labeling for a "dis-order" or something that defines the specific time by which someone "should" process grief. However, this "disorder" provides additional awareness and resources for grievers.

Knowing when you need professional help can be the key to healthfully moving forward. Profound traumas require professional support to heal effectively. Refer to the resources found in Part IV for crisis hotlines and other resources.

To fully embrace the Ease Stage, seeking and accepting help is crucial. It not only aids *acceptance* but also paves the way for the *healing* phase ahead.

Your Journey:
Reflection and Action

*What's your biggest **takeaway** from this chapter?*

*In the Ease Stage, what **formal** or **informal** support do you need today to help you move forward?*

Focus
Future Vision

"Suffering ceases to be suffering,
the minute it finds meaning."

~ Viktor Frankl

ou are here if you have ever:

- 💥 Been irritated with people telling you to "move on," yet now curious what that might look like for you?
- 💥 Felt the mix of positive and negative emotions about the future at the same time?
- 💥 Found yourself dreaming of what life *could* be like?

Welcome to the final letter of the **Healthy GRIEF Framework**. *F* stands for **Focus** *on the future or the "next chapter" in life*. Think of this as the stage where you gain clarity of vision within the grief journey. It is about finding your true center of interest and activity through grief.

The objective of this stage is *to move to the **New** (or "**New Normal**") transition* time representing a revitalized identity and a new path in life. This phase marks the unique start of fully stepping into one's own purposeful and value-aligned life which gives form to the opportunities of "What's Next?" Define your "new normal," envision your goals and values, and experiment to find what works best. Find balance in integrating "what once was" into your "now and future" (depending on the type of grief). Celebrate small victories and progress as you create new traditions and purpose.

This is more closely related with the ***healing*** phase of **SARAH**. The healing phase is the ultimate milestone in the healthy grief process. This when grief has been *integrated* into your life (as opposed to *acute grief* when the loss dominates your daily life).

By this stage, depending on the grief event, the Griever fully embraces the concepts of the new reality and recognizes its benefits. Grief has been integrated in their lives - "it" was an event that occurred, life does move forward yet without the grief playing a pivotal part in their everyday life. This doesn't mean that the grief ends; it is a "new chapter" in the journey of grief. As quoted by Donna Matthews (you will read her story in the chapter "A Loss of a Child"), "Grief doesn't shrink; we need to learn to grow our life again around our grief. Our life gets bigger around grief as we interact with others and have new experiences."

The **goal** is to *develop your "new normal" as you move forward in life.*

Signs of progress include newfound energy, sense of purpose and meaning, and increased motivation. This may include a surge of energy towards a revitalized identity and a new path in life, an embrace of new experiences, and a desire to create and sustain healthy habits and routines. We will explore steps that can lead you there.

It's important to recognize that fully comprehending the depth of the pain and disbelief over a life-altering event, and processing the experience cannot be rushed. Grief work is not about reaching a point where all pain disappears but rather developing the ability to remember the change (or life before it) with more positive feelings than painful. Healing occurs as acceptance deepens, allowing individuals to integrate their loss into their lives and move forward.

In this chapter, we'll explore the healing phase and the various emotions associated with it. We'll discuss how Grievers take advantage of this phase as well as how they will know what it looks, feels, and sounds like. We'll end with a quick tip for the Support, as well as what to expect of grief moving forward.

How to Create Your "New Normal"

Your "New Normal" is not necessarily a destination, yet we will approach it as such just to have a target to move towards. Think of this as opening up the "next chapter" of your life, or stepping into the "new season."

Here are a couple of ways to do that.

Find Meaning and Purpose in Life

Hope helps us get through adversity and discomfort (hence the reason why it is a key part of this **Healthy GRIEF Framework** of *Focus* and psychological SARAH phase of *healing*). Identifying one's meaning and purpose in life can give one hope.

As you will read in a future story about Jan's loss of identity due to retirement (in the chapter "Retirement"), being able to give new meaning and purpose in her life prevented her downward spiral into depression. Purpose can be working for racial justice, teaching children to read, making inspiring art, or creating and giving out cards to strangers to make them smile. It's a way to blend one's passion, talents, and care for the world in a way that infuses our lives with meaning. Having a purpose in life is associated with all kinds of benefits. Not only does it feel good to have a sense of purpose, research suggests it is tied to having better health[40] and longevity.[41]

But how do you go about finding your purpose? Sometimes, just having someone talk to you about what matters to you can make you think more intentionally about your life and your purpose.

Kendall Bronk, a researcher who directs the Adolescent Moral Development Lab at Claremont Graduate University says that people can find a sense of purpose organically or through deliberate exercises and self-reflection.[42] She and her colleagues have found that exercises aimed at uncovering your values, interests, and skills, as well as practicing positive emotions like gratitude, can help point you toward your purpose in life.

One way to find meaning and purpose is to identify your *ikigai*. *Ikigai* describes an ancient philosophy that has enveloped the way Japanese people live. Some believe it's even the reason for their happiness and longevity. Western culture has been known to adopt it as their way of discovering a meaningful career. According to *ikigai*, purpose and meaning are found by searching for the intersection between what you love to do, what you're good at, what the world needs, and what you get paid for.

This is further supported by research on *centenarians* – people who live healthily past 100. During the process of researching the roots of biocognitive science for his book *The MindBody Code*, neuropsychologist Mario Martinez interviewed dozens of centenarians.[43] He found that these centenarians had four essential beliefs that they all share. These include beliefs that:

◊   aging is simply the passing of time

◊   you have all the time in the world

◊   you have the agency within you to enhance your life and health

◊   everyone loves you, which is also known as healthy narcissism

Finding our purpose is a great way to connect with life. Brené Brown, in her book *Daring Greatly* emphasizes that, "Connection is why we're here; it is what gives purpose and meaning to our lives."[44] In her "Press on with Purpose" blog post, she further expresses her purpose to "know and experience love."[45] *I echo her sentiments.*

Forgiveness

American author, speaker, and humanitarian Marianne Williamson once wrote, "Unforgiveness is like drinking poison yourself and waiting for the other person to die." It seems simple, yet it is a key ingredient if we are truly going to healthfully heal through grief.

Forgiveness in the context of grief, might be directly towards others, yourself, or God or the Universe. And the list goes on.

If you can relate to this, there is an opportunity for you to embark on a journey of forgiveness. To begin, pinpoint the aspects that require healing and the individuals you wish to forgive. Validate your emotions concerning the harm inflicted upon you, understand their impact on your actions, and endeavor to let them go. Consider reaching out to a qualified professional (such as those listed in Part IV) or joining a support group for additional guidance and support.

One popular forgiveness technique is called *ho'oponopono*. Being part of the Polunesian culture and having experiencing traditional *ho'oponopono* that is much different from many westernized versions, I have to add a personal caution: It is with sadness that such a sacred tradition to the rich Polynesian culture has been watered down to a technique far from its true nature.

Traditional *ho'oponopono* is practiced throughout the South Pacific including Hawaii, Samoa, Tahiti, and New Zealand. At its true core, this technique is conducted by indigenous healers often within the extended family by a family member. According to the *Hawaiian Dictionary*, "Ho'oponopono" is defined as "To put to rights," and "Mental cleansing; family conferences in which relationships were set right (*ho'oponopono*) through prayer, discussion, confession, repentance, and mutual restitution and forgiveness."[46]

There are, however, powerful forgiveness techniques in use today that just happen to also be titled "*Ho'oponopono.*" This includes one I use with my own clients. See Part IV for additional resources.

Celebrate the Transition

"When I die, I don't want a party." I knew what my mother meant. She meant she didn't want us to go out of our way to honor her after she passed. Having already hosted a number of celebrations of life for our departed family members, I reminded her that the "party" was for the living. "Please don't deny us the opportunity to honor YOU with our stories."

On that day, I stood at the top of the steps, clutching a microphone and gazing out at the numerous individuals who had gathered by my backyard pool. We had come together not only to pay tribute to my mother but also to remember my brother; they passed two weeks apart. The stories and memories that people shared on that day, whether about my mother, my brother, or both, illuminated the profound impact they had on the lives of others. My mother and brother had left a permanent mark on the hearts of those who knew them. It was an invaluable gift to us - the living.

What "celebration" might you have to honor this transition in your grief journey? Here are some ideas to get your creative juices flowing:

◊ Celebration of life, memorial, funeral

◊ "Bye-Bye to the Tatas" to celebrate a double mastectomy

◊ Divorce Bashes (like a Bachelor or Bachelorette party)

◊ College send-off party

◊ A military duty send off or welcome home party

◊ Empty Nester Bash

◊ Recovery Milestone for progress overcoming an addiction, eating disorder, or mental health challenge

◊ Pet Remembrance Ceremony

◊ "New Beginnings" Gathering for almost any fresh start

What would you add to the list? Be creative. This is anything that celebrates the closing of one aspect of your life and embraces the new.

How will you know?

How will you know when you are in this phase? What does it look like, sound like, and feel like to know you have successfully and healthfully grieved? This is different for everyone. The question is, how will YOU know?

This doesn't mean you will ever tear up over the loss of something you once had. It means you can remember the good times too, bounce back more easily when emotions bubble up without self-criticism or judgment, and honor the existence of similar situations without being triggered into the past.

Below are some examples. Note those that relate most to you.

In general, you are able to:

◊ Send sympathy and condolences to others without feeling the need to share your own grief (for your OWN sake)

◊ Listen to someone's well-intended suggestions on what you should or shouldn't do with your grief, thank them for their opinion, and do what YOU feel is best for you without guilt or pressure

◊ Patiently "hold space" for, actively listen to, and objectively be present for another's similar grief journey

◊ Congratulate or support someone without "trauma bonding" over the negativity around your own experience

◊ Attend a funeral, wedding, baby shower, birthday or any celebration related to your grief without being triggered

◊ Wish someone a happy marriage, anniversary, birth of child, birthday, or death condolences on social media without being triggered

Based on my research, here are some examples of healing through the grief journey. The goal is to find what YOUR "new normal" is for you.

◊ Be able to openly talk about the grief event without succumbing to deep emotions

◊ Forgive oneself and/or others and move forward with their life

◊ Set and maintain boundaries for healthy relationships

◊ Take time to self-reflect, learn, and grow from the experience

◊ Help, motivate, and inspire others with their grief story

How to Support

Follow the Griever's lead, and celebrate in their journey!

This is Not the "End" of Grief

Grief is an experience. There will be moments when a picture, a smell, a holiday, a name, a social media post, or anything might remind you of your grief. Maybe it's finding the recipe to grandma's famous apple pie hidden in your baking drawer. Maybe it's the cologne of someone passing you by that reminds you of your lost love. Maybe it's the death-versary, their birthday, or the features on your smiling child's face.

During such moments, you'll recognize that you've navigated the grieving process in a healthy manner when these episodes of grief grow less frequent, and your capacity to rebound becomes increasingly effortless. If this is not the case, please find professional help to support you. See Part IV for additional support.

The primary objective of this book is to ensure that grief, along with the adverse emotions it brings, doesn't take residence in your body, compromising your immune system, or fostering minor ailments that could potentially escalate into serious health issues. It's important to clarify that this isn't meant as a pessimistic outlook but rather as a source of motivation to encourage you to liberate yourself from the emotional burden that might otherwise hinder your ability to fully embrace life. Your well-being and vitality deserve the chance to thrive among the living.

This doesn't mean to "move on" as if the event never happened (although you certainly can, if that is your choice). It means that you *do* have a choice. It means that this thing called "grief" and the once gut-wrenching emotions no longer dictate how you are going to live your life.

Albert Einstein once said, "In the middle of difficulty lies opportunity." When you truly open yourself up to this "new chapter" of possibilities, it may just be what you need to get clear on your wants, needs, purpose, hopes, and dreams.

Your Journey:
Reflection and Action

*What's your biggest **takeaway** from this chapter?*

*In the Focus Stage, from today's vantage point, what does the "**new normal**" look, feel, and sound like to you?*

In Conclusion

*"When you come from a place of curiosity, y
ou open yourself up to possibilities."*

~Dr. Karen Kramer

*H*ow was grief modeled for you growing up or at different periods in your adult life? What positive and not-so-positive experiences shaped the way you view and cope with life's challenges? What grief are you experiencing now? What have you learned so far that you can apply to your own life?

Navigating grief can empower us to let go, move forward, and embrace the life we desire. Alternatively, it can trap us in repetitive patterns, leading towards compound grief or prolonged grief disorder. However, there is always hope.

The **Healthy GRIEF Framework** emerged from my research, experience with clients, and my successes and failures in supporting my youngest son through grief. Little did I know, as I laid on my bed with my nine-year-old in shock on that mid-October evening, that our lives would be forever changed. What once was, was no longer (as shared more in the chapter "Death, Divorce, and Illness"). I watched helplessly as my son's once-bright spirit faded away. I was losing my son! It wasn't until he turned 17 that I discovered the techniques to unlock his hidden grief, enabling him to become the thriving young adult he is today, now approaching 21.

In honor of my son's successful recovery and the success of many of my clients, I offer you this framework. I continue to use this framework in everyday life. It opens the doors of communication by gathering information, checking on their emotions, involving them in the process, seeking support, and encouraging a healthy focus on the future.

Your grief is your own experience, and you will move forward with it in your own way and on your own time. May the **Healthy GRIEF Framework** provide guideposts to help you along your journey. Let's breathe life into it through the various stories of loss and recovery in the next section.

Part III

Stories of Resilience:

Applying the Healthy GRIEF Framework for Healing

Introduction

"The unexposed is the unhealed."

~ William Paul Young, *The Shack*

*O*ur lives are composed of a medley of experiences, all of which coalesce into what we call "life." We possess the choice to either lament life's challenges, setbacks, and obstacles or reframe them into learning opportunities.

To normalize conversations about grief, we must confront the "hard" dialogues. Part III serves this purpose. As your guide, we explore how to apply the **Healthy GRIEF Framework** through stories as case studies associated with death, intimate relationships, relationships with others, identity crises, maternity grief, health challenges, and a trilogy of losses.

Incorporating insights from Part I, where applicable, most stories conclude with an examination of:

🌍 **Culture**: How values, beliefs, and norms influence expressing negative and positive emotions in the grieving process

🙂 **Toxic Positivity**: How positivity aids or hinders healthy grief progression

🧠 **Mind**: How personal beliefs, values, and attitudes shape thoughts, feelings, and behaviors during loss

🤸 **Body**: How unaddressed traumas, triggers, and unresolved grief impact the body's healing process

Drawing on Part II, each story is also analyzed using the **Healthy GRIEF Framework**, giving you a roadmap for your own healing journeys. It encompasses:

🧠 **Gather** the facts

♡ **Relate** to the emotions

👣 **Involve** in action steps

🤲 **Ease** with support

👁 **Focus** on the future

Section by section, we navigate grief stories from personal, client, friend, colleague, and acquaintance experiences. Each storyteller was specifically selected for this book. May their words breathe life into your own path toward healthy grieving. Raw and authentic, these narratives resonate with deep anguish, struggles, messages of hope, guidance, tips, and advice. Sprinkled throughout are supportive statistics and research that validate various aspects and types of grief, enriching you with elements to aid their personal journeys.

The first section is centered on the most common form of grief: **death** or the "passing" of a loved one. We explore four moving stories from the loss of a child to the loss of a parent.

Next, the second section explores the second most prevalent grief form: the loss of an **intimate relationship**. These five narratives encompass break-ups, divorces, infidelity, reconciliation, and rediscovering love.

Transitioning from intimate relationships, the third section explores **other relationships** weaving in and out of our lives, encompassing friendships, family ties, coworkers, and acquaintances. Estrangements, ambivalent friends, and divisiveness are the stepping stones through these three stories.

In the fourth section, we dig into the intricate relationship between grief and **identity**, exploring how life transitions can evoke a sense of loss and inspire the quest for a renewed sense of self. Drawing on insights from Dr. Gabor Maté's research in *The Myth of Normal*, we examine the significance of identity formation and its influence on well-being. These six narratives are set against the backdrop of transitions, including the shift from corporate life to entrepreneurship, adapting to a new identity in retirement, overcoming childhood trauma, embracing the challenges of middle age and menopause, and navigating evolving father-daughter dynamics.

In the fifth section, we dive into the realm of **maternity** grief, encompassing experiences like miscarriages, infertility, and more. We start with a focus on two heart-wrenching stories and conclude on a lighter touch.

The sixth section explores the profound impact of **health** on our identity and life journey. Whether shaped by birth, accidents, diagnoses, or end-of-life experiences, these three series of three narratives explore the unique paths of health-related grief.

In the seventh section, the spotlight turns to the intricate interplay of a **trilogy of grief experiences** in an individual's life, including career, identity, death, childhood trauma, diagnosis, divorce, physical disabilities, and illness.

Many tears were shed in the making of this book, mostly in this section. You are blessed with the 30 narratives that graced these pages with their own journey of loss and triumph, or at least the "triumph" they have found on their path through this thing called "grief." Robert A. Neimeyer, a psychology professor at the University of Memphis and a clinician, once wrote, "Grieving is a process of reconstructing a world of meaning that has been challenged by loss." There is hope and healing in those stories - a gift I impart to you.

In our deepest moments of sorrow, we crave the comfort of someone who has felt a comparable ache, even if the causes of our grief may vary. Our longing is for our sadness to be acknowledged and understood, rather than brushed aside or belittled by individuals who cannot bear witness to our emotions due to their own reluctance or incapacity to confront sorrows of their own. Join the storytellers of these 30 stories along their journey by scanning the QR code or going to bit.ly/HG-Resources to listen to them narrate while you read along.

bit.ly/HG-Resources

By sharing these stories, I invite you to open your conversations about grief. Your own journey is important. When we can share the stories of our valiant and most heartbreaking moments with each other, we build connections. Share your own story with me via email to HealthyGrief@DrKarenKramer.com.

Ultimately, these stories are here for you to discover narratives and insights from these journeys, both familiar and distant, to enrich your own paths to healing.

So, let's journey on!

Healthfully grieving when your loved one's life is no longer.

DEATH

" Loss is a byproduct of living. "

~ Kirsti A. Dyer, MD, MS, FT

*T*he most common form of grief we will all experience is death. I commonly refer to it as a "passing," as in a transition from this world to "another."

This chapter is not about getting hung up on terms or even religious or life and death beliefs. It is about how to healthfully process through the inevitable – at some point in your life, you will experience the death of someone close to you.

The first of three stories is my own. It incorporates the passing of my own father along with how I not-so-gracefully went through the grief process (as I alluded to in the Preface), how it was influenced by a limiting belief, and how it inspired the writing of this book.

The second is Donna's story about the loss of her own daughter... while going through divorce, becoming an empty nester, and having her parents move to another state... all in the middle of COVID-19. Her story packs a punch with realism and raw energy. In the review of her story, we explore a need for regular mental health check-ups.

In the third narrative, we navigate Timothy's journey, set against the heart-wrenching news of his mother's diagnosis. This ignites a recurring pattern in Timothy's life, one that he breaks which sets him on a road to love, grace, joy, and inner peace.

We end with Stella's story written within weeks after the passing of her father. She honored the sadness and realism of his life while building upon the healthy coping skills she had gleaned through previous life experiences.

Each tale concludes with a review through the lens of the **Healthy GRIEF Framework**. Find a story or more that resonates with your own journey, or one from the past. Take note and gain insights from their part of their journey to add to your own.

My Father's Passing: Daddy and "Little Miss Karen"

"I thought you died!"

I was five years old when I first began to comprehend that my parents were "different."

"Are those your grandparents?" a classmate inquired.

Grandparents? Certainly not!

However, my young and impressionable five-year-old mind began to weave a new perspective about the world, leading to a cascade of thoughts like this:

Grandparents are old.

Old people die.

My parents are old.

My parents are going to die.

At that time, I didn't quite understand the concept of death beyond the idea that people simply vanished forever. It's fascinating how our developing brains form associations and interpretations.

I entered this world as a latecomer to my parents' lives. My mother was nearly 45 when I was born, and my father was 47. My brothers were 16 and 21 at the time. I experienced a joyful and nurturing childhood within the embrace of a close-knit family. We thrived on nearly 15 acres of interconnected family land. While my developmental years were relatively uneventful in terms of major life occurrences, the untamed imagination of a young child's mind can still roam far and wide.

One Saturday morning, I woke up to the radiant sun filtering through the sheer white curtains of my bedroom window, the time nearing noon. I wriggled out of bed, wiping away the Sand Man's remnants from my drowsy eyes, and embarked on a search around the house for Mommy, Daddy, or my brother Ed. Yet, they were nowhere to be found!

Panicking, I dashed out the back door onto our expansive acres, calling out for Mommy and Daddy in distress. My mom was the first to hear my frantic cries and beckoned me over, her gloved hands soiled from using a post hole digger to set up new grape lines in her garden.

"What happened?!" my mother inquired, visibly concerned about my state of agitation.

Through tearful hysteria, I managed to convey, "I... thought... you died!"

In that moment, it seemed like an innocent misinterpretation of a child. Little did I grasp the extent to which this event would imprint an unconscious yet traumatic memory, fueling a lingering fear of losing my parents.

When I was 20 years old, my father shared (while driving me to the airport for a Las Vegas trip with friends) that he had been diagnosed with prostate cancer and was scheduled for surgery. I recall my dad sharing this news with me in his characteristic gentle manner, but that same five-year-old Karen who once believed her parents had perished on that Saturday morning stirred within me.

I was numb, unsure of how to react. My friends detected something different about me during our short flight from San Diego to Las Vegas, although they remained unaware of the exact reason. I became emotionally withdrawn. Despite external attempts to engage in the enjoyment surrounding me – friendship and the vibrancy of Las Vegas – I remained inwardly dormant. When night fell, after retiring to the hotel room, my mental whirlwind commenced. No longer preoccupied by external stimuli, my mind raced, feelings surged, and emotions cascaded.

As emotions swelled, I silently slipped into the bathroom, curling up beneath the sink. In this private enclave, I wept as I hadn't in years. I felt like I was thrown back into those backyard fields on that day when I was five. This was the true onset of my grieving process.

Hearing me weep, my dear friend Steve found his way into the bathroom, managed to curl up under the sink with me despite his 6 foot, 4 inch frame in a way that could only make me laugh. However, that wasn't the only time Little Miss five-year-old Hysterical Karen came out to "play."

A few months later, my dad went in for surgery. The surgery went well. However, I could not bring myself to visit my dad while in recovery at the hospital. Seeing my very active and strong father in an incapacity state reactivated what I now dubbed "Little Miss Karen." She only went away when my dad was back to his normally active self.

When I was 37, my parents passed the role of Trustee and Executorship of their will and trust from my oldest brother to me. However, I found myself avoiding the conversation about my role with my dad in a way that I would otherwise consider irrational. I had no good, conscious excuse for my avoidant behavior when it came to talking about the details of the will and trust.

In January 2012, my father experienced a fall resulting in a fractured hip. With his close family at his side, he chose to undergo a risky hip surgery. Against all odds, he emerged from the surgery to commemorate his 90th birthday the following day. His unwavering determination fueled a remarkable recovery, gradually restoring his strength to engage in physical therapy and regain mobility. Yet, despite the remarkable comeback, our focus needed to shift beyond the confines of his hip.

During this time, his PSA levels were on the rise, indicating the return of his prostate cancer. The numbers had been under scrutiny for a year or two, although I had unconsciously disconnected myself – both physically and emotionally – from conversations regarding his health.

In April 2012, my father suffered a minor heart attack that led to a decline in his cognitive faculties, particularly concerning financial matters. By the start of July, it was evident that my father was approaching the twilight of his life. Over the next six months, I fully stepped into my role as the trust's executor. Drawing upon my adeptness at taking action, organizing, and managing finances, I carried out this responsibility that had been passed on from my eldest brother. My father's guidance had indeed prepared me well for this task.

Yet, amidst the practical aspects of my father's care and estate, I unintentionally distanced myself from the emotional turmoil of "Little Miss Karen"

– the scared child within me, afraid of losing her father. My days were filled with overseeing my parents' financial matters, coordinating doctor's appointments, managing in-home physical therapy sessions, and arranging for caregivers. I took on the role of the dutiful and responsible daughter, embodying the archetype of a caretaker.

However, within this period, what escaped my realization was the profound importance of genuine connection with my father. An opportunity for father-daughter bonding lay amidst those precious final months, but my focus on managing the logistical aspects of his life inadvertently led to detachment. While moments of connection did occur, in retrospect, I wish I had invested more time in fostering a deep connection rather than approaching the end of his life as a detached business transaction.

The realization came gradually that my father's time was drawing near. He began to describe visions of his departed barbershop chorus friends, beckoning him to join them on the other side. He even started to sing the songs they had once harmonized. The inevitable prelude to his passing arrived as he entered a pre-death coma, similar to the one my 36-year-old niece had experienced four years prior (as told in the chapter "End of Life").

During this critical phase of my life, my best friend provided invaluable support. Together, we navigated the complexities of hospice care and making sense of the array of medications. Drawing from the knowledge I had gained when caring for my niece four years earlier, I confidently administered familiar sponges and drops of morphine.

In one instance, there was a humorous interlude involving a suppository pill. Turning to my best friend, I quipped, "I love my dad, but he's going to leave this world full of sh*t." The lighthearted moment served as a welcomed relief from the somber atmosphere, while also providing a sense of comfort in her unwavering support.

As the night settled in, my mother and I stationed ourselves beside my father's bed. My mother slept on a mat on the floor, while I occupied my zero gravity chair next to my father. My loyal friend took up a spot on the living room couch, offering emotional companionship throughout the night.

In those final hours, I embraced the responsibility of tending to my father's needs. Every hour, I roused from my slumber to monitor his breathing, moisten his lips, administer prescribed drops of morphine, and meticulously document each detail on the notepad beside his bed.

Around 1:30 in the morning, I awoke for the hourly check, prompted by the familiar sound of his labored, uneven breathing. Gently stirring my mother, I prepared for what was inevitably approaching. Within moments, my father took his last breath, marking his peaceful departure from this world.

Ironically, my father's life ended within the confines of my childhood bedroom – the same room where, almost four decades prior, "Little Miss Karen" had awakened with the unsettling belief that her parents' demise was imminent. This time, however, the reality was undeniable. My father had transitioned into the realm beyond.

I was "Daddy's Little Girl." I was the youngest of three, and the only girl. Raised with only brothers, my dad was thrilled to finally get his little girl. We were very close. My "daddy" was now gone.

Anyone who knew me then would know I was the model will and trust executor. I called and took my mom to the trust attorney, paid and managed bills, and coordinated the planning of the celebration of life for my dad (planned a month after his passing). I was doing all the things I thought I needed to do… inadvertently distracting myself from the grieving process.

A month later, I found myself faced with the heart-wrenching decision to put my beloved 18-year-old cat, Smudge, to sleep. Smudge had been a steadfast companion throughout my journey, accompanying me from the inception of my career to various roommate scenarios, the birth of my first child, a divorce, and even the union of my second marriage. He was more than just a pet; he was my "first baby." However, his health had begun to deteriorate, mirroring the situation with my father. I knew the time had come to say goodbye. As I held my ailing cat in my lap in that cold stark veterinary office and made the somber choice to put him to rest, waves of grief engulfed me. The floodgates of emotion burst open, and tears streamed down my cheeks, releasing a flow of emotions I had suppressed during the last seven months of my father's decline.

Upon returning home with my beloved pet's remains, my husband and youngest children began digging a grave for him to rest. It was a somber parallel, as I dialed my mother's number to share the news of my feline's fate.

However, before I could utter a word, my mother informed me of a decision she had made under the sway of my middle brother, Ed. This decision involved disinviting Ed's ex-wife and step-son from Dad's forthcoming celebration of life – a decision that my mother, older brother, and I had collectively made just two weeks earlier. This sudden reversal left me feeling hurt and abandoned by those who had agreed on the initial plan. On a typical day, such a situation might have unsettled me, but I would have engaged in a conversation to find common ground. Yet, this time was different. My hurt transformed into anger and rapidly escalated into a rage I had rarely experienced before.

I vented my fury by screaming at my mother before abruptly hanging up the phone. My frustration drove me to storm down to her house – a mere five-minute walk away – where I confronted her face-to-face. Fueled by my emotions, I seized the phone from her while she was mid-conversation with my older brother and unleashed my anger into the receiver before disconnecting the call. The feelings of abandonment resurfaced, intensified by my conviction that my older brother Gene had also let me down. After this confrontation, I left her home and proceeded to my middle brother Ed's residence on the same property, pounding on his door in my emotional turmoil. (I later learned that my mother had alerted him to my state and advised him not to open the door.) With no response, I returned to my house, seized my phone, and left a series of expletive-laden messages on Ed's voicemail. This outburst, so far from my typical demeanor, emerged in full view of my husband and children, who were attempting to navigate the chaotic situation while continuing their task of preparing Smudge's burial site.

In retrospect, it is clear that I had entered the grief cycle in its full intensity. The emotions that I had pushed aside, dissociated against, and distracted myself from had reached a tipping point. The cumulative weight of suppressed feelings, combined with the loss of my father, and the impending loss of my cherished cat, had ignited an overwhelming emotional release. The storm of emotions that I had unwittingly kept at bay had finally crashed upon me with an unrelenting force.

Beneath the surface, I was still struggling with the weight of grief. My irritability had become a palpable presence, casting a shadow over my interactions with my family. One afternoon, about two months after my father's passing, I vividly remember a moment of overwhelming frustration. I found myself raising my voice and shouting at my nine-year-old son for neglecting to tidy up his toys in the dining room. The intensity of my anger reached a breaking point, and I instructed him to leave for his grandma's house, just a brief five-minute walk away.

In the midst of this emotional turmoil, my husband and his visiting friend remained silent in another room. As my emotions surged and I felt myself crumble, my husband cautiously entered the dining room. There, he found me huddled in a ball, my tears flowing unchecked. It was then, amid the raw emotion, that I recognized the urgent need for help, a recognition that I could not allow my emotional turmoil to wreak further havoc within my family.

In pursuit of guidance, I embarked on a search for a therapist. The professional I connected with was relatively new to her field, and I sensed a certain unease stemming from my extensive credentials – a background including two master's degrees, a PhD, and experience as an executive coach and leadership development facilitator. The irony lay in the fact that, despite my academic achievements, the problem at hand required a fresh perspective. As Albert Einstein wisely said, "We can't solve problems by using the same kind of thinking we used when we created them."

Yet, the therapy session that followed led to a diagnosis of "situation anxiety," an assessment that seemed more like a checkbox completion than a meaningful step toward resolution. Afterwards, I was steered towards an anxiety program, a recommendation that left me uninspired and untouched by acknowledgment of my grief journey. It's important to note that my experience with therapy wasn't universally negative; I had found support through therapy in the past. This particular instance, however, seemed like a missed opportunity. It felt as if I had been labeled, boxed into a category, and handed off to a group training regimen.

Driven by a desire to unearth the root cause of my emotional outbursts, I reached out to my doctor with the thought that I might be undergoing early menopause at the age of 43. A mere two minutes into sharing the story of my father's passing and recounting my episodes of anger, my doctor hastily prescribed a hormonal medication. She even went so far as to suggest that she could administer the patch on my arm that very day. It was important to me to clarify that I have never taken prescription medications nor over-the-counter drugs without a genuine need. Consequently, the idea of embarking on a medication regimen was a step I was unwilling to take.

Propelled by a third burst of anger, my husband proposed a seven-day retreat at a destination health spa I had been considering for some time. The experience offered an appealing combination of strenuous exercise, rejuvenating treatments, nutritious meals, and an escape from the chaos. However, my return home was marred by renewed arguments with my husband over minor matters within just two hours of my return. This time, my irritation had nothing to do with him and everything to do with the internal turmoil I was battling. It was as if a rubber band was wound tightly around my chest, ready to snap at any provocation.

All the avenues I explored – psychological labels, medications, and even the retreat – offered only temporary respite. They failed to address the true underlying issue: the grief stemming from the loss of my father and the restrictive beliefs fostered by "Little Miss Karen." This transformative experience fueled my dedication to open the VillaVision Wellness and Retreat Center and provided the impetus for me to put pen to paper and share my story in this book, as well as the more successful tools and experiences used to finally heal through my journey.

Grief is an inherent, natural aspect of existence. All of us have an expiration date, and I am profoundly grateful that my father lived long enough to be part of my adult life, well into his 90s.

May my experiences inspire a paradigm shift, encourage a normalized dialogue around grief, and offer pathways to resiliently navigate the unique voyage to finding harmony in your life again.

Dr. Karen Kramer
San Diego, CA

The Story in Review

As you find with all stories in this book, each path to find healing is unique. The following is a review to help you connect previous concepts in this book to this story. In this case, we'll start with my own.

Culture: In *The Myth of Normal*, Dr. Gabor Maté emphasizes that mental health issues are not just individual problems, but are often symptoms of a larger systemic problem. This message can be helpful for anyone struggling with feelings of shame or self-blame. However, to the point of the book's subtitle, *Trauma, Illness, and Healing in a Toxic Culture*, it is not about blaming individuals; it's about solutions that lay within the cultural norm that perpetuated the problem. The crux of the matter lies in how traditional medical and healthcare practitioners are trained to swiftly diagnose surface-level symptoms, often overlooking deeper issues suc h as grief and trauma. Unfortunately, they also operate in a society that emphasizes quick fixes and yearns for a "magic pill" solution to both physical and psychological challenges. It's crucial to note that my intention is not to point fingers at healthcare professionals or therapists; rather, this issue is deeply ingrained in our cultural and societal norms that want a "quick fix" (such as a diagnosis, pill, or surgery) rather than to take the time to identify and release the core issue. There are various forms of support to help you through loss. Find those that help you healthfully grieve, including identifying the root cause, not just numb or mask the symptoms of grief. See Part IV Resources for additional suggestions.

 Toxic Positivity: Pretending that everything was "okay" and that I was "coping well" had its price. I was trying to fool myself (*Resistance, Denial*), and it prevented me from getting the help I needed in the beginning (*Ease*).

 Gather: Each grief story may have many *Gather* stages (when "ending" and beginning along the transition time) in the same story line. Mine was no different. The main shifts in this story included when my dad first told me he had prostate cancer, when his health started to decline upon breaking his hip, his near-fatal heart attack, and his final passing.

Relate: "Little Miss Karen" was driving my emotional state based on an irrational belief made at age five (*Psychological influence*). *Dissociating* from my emotions and *distracting* myself with busy work such as the affairs of the estate, helped me only so far. However, as emphasized by the work of psychologist, Susan David, the emotions I had been avoiding came back with a vengeance. Making the choice to put my beloved cat to sleep a month after my dad's passing kicked off the emotional flow through grief in a way that created a negative ripple effect throughout my family.

 Involve: Most of my action steps in this story were associated with *dissociating* and *distracting* myself from my feelings. These included taking care of my father's medical and estate affairs. However, planning the celebration of life and managing the details of the estate on behalf of my mom did engage my talents for finances, details, and event planning which added some fun and break from focusing only on the loss of my father.

 Ease: Seeking therapy and medical support, *in my case,* did not help me. However, I do highly recommend seeking support through grief. Now that *prologue grief disorder* is an identifiable mental health diagnosis, there are more resources to help those going through grief than there were in 2012. See Part IV for additional resources. I am also leery of any label or diagnosis that does not further support someone seeking to identify the core of the issue. The support that did help me was having my family and best friend with me during these critical times to ease the pain of the process. The greatest and longest-lasting support was the deep subconscious work through NLP, Time Line Therapy®, and Hypnotherapy that allowed me to identify, honor, and reconstruct "Little Miss Karen."

 Focus: Since my father's passing in 2012 and releasing the frightened "Little Miss Karen," I was more present during the decline and death of other family members. It is my experience, along with the techniques I use with my clients today, that fueled the development of the VillaVision Wellness and Retreat Center and the creation of this book – to help more people heal through grief. Bottomline, there are various ways to move forward after a loss. May this book provide a plethora of paths for *you* to do so.

The Loss of a Child:
A Perfect Storm

Grief doesn't shrink; we need to learn to grow life again around our grief.

*M*y sorority sister, Karen, posted this Facebook question: "In what ways have you experienced grief?" Oh, the hook for me! I responded, "Good question and a large one when you consider all the types of losses in life that cause grief." Karen knew from my Facebook posts I had a depth of knowledge about grief from my personal experience. I haven't shied away from putting out/sharing pieces of my story to friends. Life is too precious to candy-coat; sometimes pain needs to be seen, expressed, shared, and that realness has been part of my grief process.

Karen and I later had a chat. She shared she was writing a book on grief and asked if I would write about my story to share in her book. Timing of this request was right for me, I wouldn't have been up for the task until now. My thoughts still run around after all the backstories, but I can express my thoughts and my process in hopes it might provide connectedness and comfort to someone else.

Like I responded to Karen's Facebook question, grief is big. My grief is the kind that is the horror story for parents. The one that creeps up in the night. The one that you'll shove down so deep under your bed, just like the boogie man who made you shutter. The fear springs from the thought of its spector that will pull you into a hole you don't know how you'll survive. You know this fear that I'm talking about: the death of your child.

For me that possibility had been standing behind me as I tried not to have it happen. Of my two incredibly precious children, my daughter Maryne, lost her life due to her mental illness. An illness she battled with, I'm sure, longer than I knew, but had appeared when she was 11. She died eight days before her nineteenth birthday. I know society says, "died by suicide," but that phrase sweeps away the illness that led to her death and instead puts the cause on the person for dying. How easy is that to label, to check a box, to eliminate the insidious illness that is the true cause?

I hope you hear my anger. Anger is a part of grief. One of the many feelings that tumble around in no particular order. Grief felt like an emotional lottery, I didn't know which emotion would pop up throughout the day. Places, songs, anything that connected me to my daughter could be a trigger and still can, though thankfully not as frequently. Two emotions caused by grief that continue to be triggered in me are anger and guilt. These two made me not want to exist during difficult struggles with them. The feelings remind me of something I heard about people who are in a fire, on fire. There's a moment where they decide to succumb or decide to live. These victims, in terrible, incomprehensive pain, have to decide to keep surviving each day they are in the burn ward. That is the most similar description I can give. I have to choose to live each day in pain. If you are unaware of this, let me inform you, it is now medically understood that emotional pain triggers in our brain in the same place as physical pain. Let that sink in for a moment. Think of a time when your heart felt like it hurt, it did! Your brain can't tell the difference between the two. I can understand why it's easy to get lost in emotional suffering looking for ways to numb it, looking for that sweet release of pain like a burn victim when they receive morphine. When my pain was intense I had unhelpful patterns of behavior. Typically, I couldn't stand to be home by myself, so, to avoid that, I went out shopping. Eventually, I found healthier activities, like hiking or kayaking, but I still struggle to use this as a numbing distraction. I also began therapy with the person who had been my daughter's therapist. Maybe this sounds odd. However, speaking to someone who knew the family and knew my daughter's struggles helped comfort me and helped me feel understood. Eventually, we have to make the time to be with our grief. Shoving it down and ignoring it will ultimately seep into your body in unwelcome ways. Whether it's running and numbing, having no patience or tolerance, or hypertension in your body, it's there. A saying from Buddha helped me to understand why I suffered and still do: suffering is caused by clinging and grasping for what we can't have. Yes, so true! I cling and grasp for my daughter, therefore, I suffer. I've learned to accept this as my life now. Maybe in time I won't grasp and cling so hard.

Looking at the moment I found my daughter, I remember the details that have come back over time. The brief details I will share are that after performing CPR, talking to the police, and going to the hospital, the decision was made to remove life support and let Maryne's body die. In that moment, all I knew to do was ask the nurse to put down the arm rail. I needed to be right next to my baby. She was brought to life through my body and I needed to be next to her as she died. I wrapped my arm over her and snuggled next to her, like I had over the years when she went to sleep, until she took her last breath. My ex-husband and my younger son Mitch were also there, but I don't remember what was said or what they did, nor could I focus on them. I couldn't even consider the loss my son was experiencing. It was the end to an illness that had been lost, and the beginning for me of learning more than I had any idea or understanding I would. Let me make this clear, this growth or learning I experienced isn't a silver-lining, God's plan, or any other label used to try to put grief into a neat package of "good out of bad." If you simplify anyone's painful experience, it only serves you to make you feel better, not the person experiencing the pain.

Nine days after Maryne died, I went back to work. At the time, it was my survival strategy. Continue to be alive by getting up each day, get Mitch off to school, and pretend everything was okay. I had learned this strategy during the 10 years I worked at a preschool, and during the time my daughter's illness emerged. I used this to immerse myself into the daily task at hand. It helped me block out any of the difficulties in my personal life. This was my initial attempt to cope. I could avoid the heartbreak until I drove home. Then the reality would rise up, resurfacing as tears streamed down my face, sobbing and holding the steering wheel tight until I made it home. Doing my best to "pull it together" before I walked inside.

My son, Mitch – my baby boy, my anchor. I tried to find help for us. I tried talking to him to check-in on how he was holding up. I know that my efforts weren't the best. I had no idea how to navigate this. What little I had learned from my family to help Mitch through his grief was an unhealthy example. I tried not to expose him to my grief and only addressed it when I had my emotions stuffed in enough to not, at least as I saw it, cause him further pain. I didn't want him to feel responsible for solving my pain. I didn't help him learn that it is okay to express difficult emotions. Instead I would cry into my pillow, cry while I showered, cry in my car, anything to be "steady" for him. In my mind I see us crying together at some point, hugging each other. However, I don't know if that actually happened. The inability to be present and focused was real. I think maybe my hope is that I gave him an example at some point that openly grieving and talking about Maryne was okay. My fear was that my grief would be fully displayed and would damage him in some way. So, I did what I thought I was supposed to do. I tried to be "strong" to be able to support him so he would be okay. That's the joke here. I ran around pretending to be okay. I didn't want to burden anyone with my not being okay. I'm certain friends around me knew I wasn't, and Mitch as well. By putting on my mask every day, I might as well have given him one too. He learned to mirror me, with, "I'm okay." Neither of us were. My thoughts on how I thought I was supposed to be makes me hope that other people find healthier ways to grieve and be better examples. My example didn't help Mitch be able to open up about how he was truly doing.

One source of help, a suicide support group, came from my friend, Nola. I was able to go to a handful of meetings. I offered it to Mitch to come with me and offered for him to talk to a therapist, but he ended up not trying either. He felt that a therapist wouldn't be helpful unless they had experienced the same trauma. I respected his choice, even if I didn't like it.

I found it helpful to be around people in the survivors of suicide group who experienced the death of a loved one due to suicide. Not everyone had lost children, but hearing their stories was comforting. They knew my pain. I wasn't asked questions or expected to be okay. Other people were there trying to process what had happened. Some were there who had years to work on it and now wanted to help others with it, and others were like me, new to the experience.

At Maryne's services I answered requests from friends who wanted to know how they could help me. I'm grateful beyond words to my other anchors, my good friends who listened, and my intuition that led me to say, "I don't know what I need, but call me in a month. I know I'll need my friends." I'm grateful they listened! I am blessed to have truly caring friends that checked on me. They called, they were there for my birthday 10 days later, they joined me on walks, they listened to my sorrows and frustration for my daughter, trying to understand why everything had failed her. We enjoyed talking about everyday life. The real need I had was their companionship and compassion. I needed to be heard and feel connected. These ladies anchored me, helping me by not trying to fix me, and also just by being with me, were witnesses to my process of grief.

This is the question, how do we grieve? My daughter died nearly four years ago and I can see how I worked to figure out how to grieve. It was an existential crisis. Even with the support of friends, I felt lost, angry, and without purpose. Privately, I felt responsible for my daughter's death, and angry with myself for not rescuing her. Guilt is insidious and sliced me in pieces. I had never seen anyone grieve, that emotion wasn't displayed to me growing up or even in my adulthood when my grandparents died. There wasn't a plan to prepare or a process put in front of me. I felt like I was a child, falling into a hole, grasping for anything to help me from falling in. I read books about surviving after a suicide loss. I tried to feel a connection to my daughter, reading books she liked, listening to her favorite podcasts, listening to her music lists on Spotify, and talking to a psychic on her birthday. I took a course on happiness, I educated myself more about depression, anxiety, ADHD (Attention-Deficit/Hyperactivity Disorder), and BPD (Borderline Personality Disorder). I was trying to understand what had failed. I know there was no singular reason, it was what I refer to as the "Perfect Storm" that had occurred. I had frustration and heartbreak over and over because nothing was going to fix it. I was resisting the fact that my daughter was gone, no answers were ever going to bring her back. I could rationalize all the pieces along her life that led to her death, beat myself up for all the could-haves and should-haves. Hindsight is a bitch and didn't help me. I learned to let myself fall onto my knees and scream. I scream and scream at the unfairness, at the suffering, at the traumas my daughter experienced. And I scream for my own. I cry and scream until it feels better to be released from the emotions I held in. I understand that my sorrows need to be released and this helps me. It is primal and it is a primitive pain that I am expressing, exhuming from the depths of my soul.

My grief journey will never be done, just as I know I will continue to suffer. Life doesn't let up, it is in constant motion causing continuous change. I knew this but I didn't fully understand it. While I was in the first year of grief, the world moved on. COVID-19 pandemic closed my work and the world as I knew it in mid-March 2020. Mitch was in his senior year of high school. I was still deeply grieving for my daughter and the secondary losses, the dreams I had for her life in the future. Now adding to Mitch's and my grief was the losses of his experiences during his senior year. Something that had helped him have something to look forward to. If I had ever thought life was fair, life hit it home, NO IT ISN'T. For me, being home was helpful. It gave me time to reflect when I hadn't been giving myself time for it. It also provided time to scramble about looking to understand Maryne's death as I previously described. Maybe it provided an opportunity for Mitch to grieve also.

In May before Mitch graduated, he told me he was going to live with his dad. I hadn't expected to be an empty nester so quickly. I knew he was planning on going to the local Junior College. My mind was not happy with his choice and I knew I could block it, but he was going to live in a large house with more privacy, a pool, and a father who constantly traveled and who didn't mind if he had "kick-backs" at his house. No contest. I realized I needed to gracefully accept this rather than cause a problem that could put a wedge between me and Mitch. With sadness, I let him go and grieved this loss.

My friend Tanja reappeared in my life at this point. She was looking for a place to live locally and I certainly had space. This decision was a life-line for both of us. I was in need of something positive, a distraction, and companionship and she was also. We had lost contact, except on Facebook, since she and her family had moved out of state in 2009. Until about 2008, our families were close. We celebrated our children's birthdays together, went camping, swimming, walking, just having fun with our husbands and children. Interestingly, we had both recently divorced in 2019. February for me and October for Tanja. As we reconnected, I began to understand that not only is divorce one of the more difficult stressors in life, it is also something you grieve, the loss of the dreams you had for a family and a spouse. My daughter had brought up "narcissism" to me in 2018. The more I read about it, the more I understood why she thought her father had narcissistic traits and I began to understand his behavior. As Tanja and I opened up about our lives, I realized that Tanja's ex-husband (she says "wasband") had been highly toxic towards her. Besides the many things he did to mentally push her down, he had found ways to insert distrust into their daughters, resulting in parent alienation. She was grieving and struggling over the loss of relationship with her two daughters. Cut off from the girls she adored. Grief comes into life in many forms, death being the most recognizable. I have learned that grief includes all kinds of loss, loss and grief and intertwined pieces.

Tanja has lived with me for three years now. I can say with certainty that we have been anchors for each other. We have taught each other and worked towards understanding our traumas and supporting each other, expanding and opening to different views regarding life and healing. Together, we have both become wiser and mentally healthier. I helpied Tanja through her emotional pain from my experiences, and she helped me with her ability to have positive energy. Getting me out of my head and back into enjoying the pleasures of nature again. We are both seeing and owning our beauty and individual gifts we have.

As lucky as I have been not to have a family member die from COVID-19, I didn't escape another loss in 2019. I have worked and continue to work with children in schools. At that time my parents were in their 80s and with the uncertainty of how COVID-19 was spreading, how it may be in the future, and no vaccination, it had become difficult to help my parents with their arising health problems. My brother came out to help after our father had surgery. It became clear that our parents were going to need more assistance. We agreed they should move near my brother as he could help them more than what I was limited to. The day our parents got in the car with him to Montana was just one year after Maryne died, and the day that would have been her twentieth birthday.

Grief is loss and I grieved. The pain grief brings is not subtle. The expressions you have likely heard are true: pierced through the heart, a hole in your heart, your heart feels like it's been shattered. I had already been "torn to pieces," now my mind moved in to protect me and numbed me once again. The brain does protect us and mine numbed me to help me not feel. Otherwise, I don't see how I would have made it alive. This time my grief wasn't intense, my parents were safe and alive. The timing of their move left an imprint that I am now beginning to understand. The two years since their move, I have experienced depression. Not on the date of the move, but before summer ends. My mind seems to be preparing, knowing what is coming on the horizon. It's time, time to remember my daughter's death date. Time for Halloween when she experienced a significant trauma, her birthday, my birthday, Thanksgiving, and Christmas. All the fun events at the end of the year that were incredible and celebrated with family... now it amazes me I make it. Like most people having had a family member die, it's especially difficult the first year of holidays without loved one(s).

My grief has gotten better as I learn to live with it. One particular lesson I've learned, that has helped me and I have explained to other friends when one of their loved ones has died, is that grief doesn't shrink; we need to learn to grow our life again around our grief. Our life gets bigger around grief as we interact with others and have new experiences. I have learned to accept my life as it is, being present each day and continuing to grow. There is no "getting over it" for me.

Grief became a piece of who I am. This is learning radical acceptance. I continue to desire my beautiful daughter to be alive with me and I accept the pain of her absence. I accept that I am here and continuing to grow and hopefully thrive. I now have boundaries around the holidays as they come along. I decide how I want to celebrate or not. I don't accept guilt to pretend or put on a mask any more in my personal life. Someone can think I'm selfish, I see it as self compassion. When people are grieving, we need to let them find what tools, needs, and boundaries are necessary for them to grieve the way they need to, not how we think they should. I have the need to do what is right for my emotional and mental well-being. I hope that our culture is beginning to be able to give each other grace, and that we understand we all have different experiences as none of us can expect people to grieve the same way as another. I hope for understanding of how grief stays in our bodies and minds; it is a universal human experience. I tried finding many different ways to heal, and I will continue to heal. I will also continue to grieve until I am no longer breathing. Through talking about my daughter, about my grief, and being heard and not having someone try to "fix" me, this is what helps me. That connection I experience with other people.

Donna Lamson Matthews
Sacramento, CA

I am a phoenix.
I have been burned into ashes,
And I am growing again.
I am not perfect,
The scars of life are inside me.
I am all of life: pleasure and pain, joy and death.
I am whole.

~ Donna Lamson Matthews

 The Story in Review

"Mental health killed my daughter," Donna stated when I first interviewed her for her story. She goes on to say "Mental health needs to be checked up like physical health." I couldn't agree more, and it is worth stating for this review. You will find more resources available to you in the Part IV Resource section.

Unless you have experienced it, it is hard to know the true pains of losing a child or losing a loved one to suicide. The closest I found to Donna's pain is that expressed by Brené Brown in *Atlas of the Heart* for the description of anguish. She writes:

> Anguish is an almost unbearable and traumatic spiral of shock, incredibility, grief, and powerlessness. ... [It] not only takes away our ability to breathe, feel, and think – it comes for our bones. Anguish often causes us to physically crumple in on ourselves, literally bringing us to our knees, or forcing us all the way to the ground.
>
> The element of powerlessness is what makes anguish traumatic. We are unable to change, reverse, or negotiate what has happened. And even in those situations, where we can temporarily reroute anguish with to-do list and task, it finds its way back to us. ...
>
> It's often hard to find a way back into our bodies after experiencing anguish. This is why so much effective trauma work today is not only about reclaiming our breath, our feelings, and our thinking, but also getting our bones back and returning to our bodies.
>
> When we experience anguish, and we don't get help or support, we can find it difficult to get up off the floor and reengage with our lives. We go through the motions, but we are still crumpled. ...
>
> There's another alternative to not addressing the trauma of anguish– we can convince ourselves that we're okay and keep ourselves upright by hanging our crumpling anguish on rigidity and perfectionism and silence, like a wet towel hanging on a rod. We can become closed off, never open to vulnerability and its gifts, and barely existing because anything at any moment could threaten that fragility, rigid scaffolding that's holding up our crumpling cells and keeping us standing. [47]

Donna's story powerfully mixes in so much raw expression, learnings, and wisdom. The following highlights her story using the **Healthy GRIEF Framework**.

Gather: Donna's story, although all focused around the loss of her daughter Maryne, has a number of "Gather" moments. These included the tragic day with her daughter and the decision to remove her from life support, when her son moved out, and when her parents moved out of state.

Relate: Studies indicate that the most stressful grief occurs for parents who experience the death of a child. Donna's gamut of emotions included numbness and loss, sadness and depression, guilt over not "doing enough" or protecting her daughter, and feeling "without purpose." If you are someone you loves is contemplating suicide, please refer to the resources found in Part IV.

Involve: Donna has engaged in various activities over the four years since her daughter's passing including shopping, getting out in nature (walking, hiking, and kayaking), listening to her daughter's music and podcasts, and interacting with her housemate.

Ease: A critical point Donna makes through her story is finding others who weren't trying to fix her or expect her to be okay. Various formal and informal activities and support included therapy, attending a suicide support group, talking to a psychic, reading books about surviving suicide loss, educating herself through courses (on happiness, depression, anxiety, ADHD, and BPD), and reconnecting with an old friend who became her housemate. *Donna's story is classified as* **traumatic grief**. *As she noted, trained professionals have been a key part of her journey.*

Focus: The divorce is final, her son has moved out, her parents are settled in another state, Donna's continues enjoying her housemate, and she will forever live with Maryne's loss. As noted by Donna, it's not about "moving on" because you will never "move on"; it's about moving through. Using her story as a motivator to help others, Donna has joined the Breathe for Change[48] team, where she receives training in social-emotional learning strategies, mindfulness techniques, and yoga practices. These tools are designed to enhance the well-being of educators and bring positive transformations to school communities.

A Son's Grief:
The Power of Grace

The greatest gift we can give those who are no longer here is to live our lives to the fullest, letting go of the false narratives that tear us down and hold us back.

In 2012 I was stationed overseas in Japan. That summer I went home to visit family and attend our annual family reunion. I was grateful to be back home and was having an amazing time catching up with my family.

While there, my uncle pulled me to the side and said that he had something very important to tell me. He told me that my mother had been diagnosed with cancer and that she only had a few weeks left to live.

Due to the fact that death had been a consistent occurrence throughout my life, I believe at that moment (out of instinct) my heart began to harden. I numbed myself by burying those feelings down and accepted what he had to say. My mother had been dealing with a terminal illness for most of my life so there was always the idea in the back of my mind that this day was coming. Perhaps because she had defied the odds for so many years I had given in to hope, or perhaps denial, to give my heart some peace.

I spoke to my mother that evening and she confirmed what my uncle had said. She told me that she didn't want me to worry about her while I was overseas, seeing as there was nothing that I could do. I informed my military leadership in Japan of the situation and they were truly amazing. They made it so I was able to spend extra time back home.

Unlike my father, grandmother, or sister who had all passed away suddenly and without warning, I was presented with the opportunity to spend time with my mother, asking her things about her life. She also asked about mine and we had the opportunity to learn so much about one another. There were some beautiful moments, but there were also some difficult ones. They primarily consisted of the days when her pain medication would have a negative impact on her mental state. I did my best to simply focus on being grateful for the time I was given and refilled my cup by spending time with friends.

Eventually, I was told I needed to go back to Japan. My mother understood and told me that it was okay. I still remember that final morning. My girlfriend at the time had come to take me to the airport and I was running very late. As I said goodbye to my mother she just held me. While I wouldn't allow myself to think it, I believe that she knew that this would be the last time that she would see me so I just stayed there and held her until she was ready to let go. I'm so grateful that I did that. We then rushed to the airport for the flight that I was sure that I was going to miss. To my shock and surprise, not only did I make the flight, they told me a free business class seat had opened and gave it to me. That had never happened to me before and hasn't since.

A couple of months went by and I was back in Japan doing my usual morning routine which consisted of calling my mom and girlfriend to check in. I called my mom but got no answer. I then called my girlfriend and was greeted with hysterics. She told me that my mother had passed away.

My mind began racing a million miles a minute. I did my best to maintain my composure while asking my supervisor if I could speak with him outside. Once away from everyone else, I began to break down. I just didn't know what I was going to do. I didn't have my passport and I needed to get home. He reassured me that everything was going to be okay. Amazingly, the same day I got that phone call supplies were being delivered to the ship. They were able to get me on the supply ship which took me to Singapore where I was able to fly home.

Once home, we buried my mother and I began the process of moving on. I attempted to simply bury down the feelings associated with the loss, but, as I stated before, that did not work out.

One specific event let me know the extent to which her loss was affecting me. I had finished my tour in Japan and had just been stationed in Ventura, California, where I was adjusting to life back in the States. My aunt (who was truck driving at the time) was working nearby and invited me out to lunch with her. I hadn't seen her in a long time and was excited to spend time with my family.

We met up at a truck stop and when I laid eyes on her my heart jumped. She resembled my mother so much that for the briefest of moments, I thought that she had come back to life. This of course was immediately followed by the harsh realization that that wasn't the case. The tearing away of that hope tore a hole in the walls holding back the feelings I had buried and it took all of my strength to maintain my composure during the lunch.

Once back in my room I broke down and felt more miserable than I ever had in my life. It was the first time in my life that I had consciously wanted my life to end and I'm quite sure that if I had access to lethal means, I would have gone through with it. Lucky for me that wasn't the case and I woke up the next day with the wall firmly reestablished. TV talk show host Phil Donahue once said, "Suicide is a permanent solution to a temporary problem." For me, this was absolutely the case.

That was my rock bottom and you know what they say about hitting bottom: there's nowhere to go but up. I'm so grateful that my life did not end that day because I had no idea at the time all that the future had in store for me including the birth of my son which happened shortly thereafter.

In 2015 I began my healing journey which consisted of several self-help books, seminars, and workshops, as well as working with both a life coach and therapist. Throughout this inner work journey, I identified a pattern from my childhood. It was a pattern around my response to loss.

This began with my father, whose loss weighed heavy on me. I remember being at his viewing and smiling. This was my favorite person in the world at that time and I was smiling. Even laughing at times. I now know this was due to my inability to properly process the emotions I was experiencing. I don't believe I ever cried. It's as if I refused to believe it. The same thing happened with my grandmother, who we lived with for a time.

The next loss was my younger sister who passed away at 17 from spinal meningitis. Her loss deeply affected me, especially considering my last words to her were, "Stop pretending, you're making mom worried" (referring to her sickness).

These words echoed in my mind for years and the guilt from them made it very difficult to properly mourn. Outside of the few seconds after they gave us her diagnosis, I did not cry. I remember at that moment my older brother (seeing my pain) attempted to embrace me and I pushed him away. I then just focused on burying the emotions back down.

As an act of self-preservation, my mind and heart made the unconscious decision that this pattern was the best course of action to keep the vessel going. Bury, move on, repeat. That was until the loss of my mother. Even on a conscious level, I knew that I wasn't ready to address that loss, as I was still attempting to process the loss of my sister.

I then attended a workshop that completely changed my life. While attending the workshop we performed an exercise where we sat knee to knee with a partner. My partner was a sweet and beautiful human being named Janet. We had been partnered for a couple of days and had built great trust with one another.

In the exercise, we were told to pretend that our partner was someone we needed to speak to. I chose my mother. Perhaps it was the great environment the organizers built or the motherly love that came from my partner, but I allowed myself to fully let go and immerse myself in the exercise. I told my mother how sorry I was for being in Japan while she was dealing with her sickness. I let her know how much I loved and missed her, and most importantly I allowed the pain to be seen, acknowledged, and began the process of letting go. I've never cried so much in my life and it was extremely liberating.

The exercise concluded with the loving embrace of my partner followed by the support from the rest of my team. I experienced what felt like a thousand-pound weight lift off of my shoulders. I felt more love in that experience than I had ever felt in my entire life and it helped me realize that I was both afraid to love as well as be love for fear of being hurt, which affected so many relationships in my life.

My childhood experiences made me keep people at a distance. I'm naturally very introverted and this experience taught me the power of community and letting people in. Being in the military and growing up as a male in the environment I grew up in made me feel as though I had to constantly keep my walls up and mask on.

Throughout the course of that event, I learned the power of safe spaces. I know safe spaces get a lot of criticism, likely from those who have yet to experience their benefits. My belief is that they are not places to live but places that we all should visit from time to time. Life is so much more pleasant when you let go of unnecessary burdens.

The final element that has helped me most on my healing journey has been the power of grace. I remember having so much resentment towards my father for abandoning me and my siblings, as well as towards my grandmother for keeping us from my mother. Once I was able to release that anger and instead show empathy and love and step into their shoes, I was able to acknowledge that my father felt his being in our life was doing more damage than when he wasn't in it. It was an act of love that I wasn't able to comprehend as a child.

My grandmother took us in when my parents were no longer in a place to do so. She was an older woman who was dealing with illness, constant family drama over us, and three children who despised her despite keeping us fed with a roof over our heads, teaching us discipline, and loving us in her own way.

Dr. Wayne Dyer introduced me to the concept that there are no justified resentments. It brings to mind that old saying that holding on to anger is like holding on to a hot coal and expecting the other person to be burned. The best thing we can do is let it go and let it heal. We must have that same level of empathy towards ourselves. I needed to understand that I was worthy of both my mother's and sister's love and forgiveness and that nobody who loves you wants you to suffer. I believe that people hold on to the pain of their guilt as penance. I know that was the case for me.

The greatest gift we can give those who are no longer here is to live our lives to the fullest, letting go of the false narratives that tear us down and hold us back and instead holding on to the reality of the love and cherished memories of beautiful moments shared. With all of this in mind, have patience during your grief journey and understand that it is indeed a lifelong journey and not a destination. Let go of the thoughts and feelings that don't serve you. Don't suffer in silence; find solace in community. Finally, understand that you are worthy of love, grace, joy, and inner peace.

Timothy Wallace,
San Diego, CA

The Story in Review

Timothy's story is a powerful journey through losses to the pit of suicidal ideations and on to recovery and self-love.

 Cultural: To quote Timothy, "Being in the military and growing up as a male in the environment I grew up in made me feel as though I had to constantly keep my walls up and mask on." At a few points in his story, Timothy indicated the need to "maintain composure," specifically in front of this military leader upon the news of his mother's passing, and with his aunt.

 Toxic Positivity: At his father's viewing, upon his passing, Timothy recalls smiling and laughing, yet never cried, "as if I refused to believe it." Although, as Timothy noted, this may have been an inability to properly process the emotions at a young age, it's an example of expressing positive emotions to cover up effectively processing feelings.

 Mind: Through therapy, Timothy identified a pattern from his childhood related to loss. Out of self-preservation, the pattern was "Bury, move on, repeat" leading him to keep people at a distance.

 Gather: The critical points in Timothy's story were when his uncle told him about his mom's cancer diagnosis and her final passing which also brought up unresolved thoughts and feelings about the loss of past family members.

 Relate: So many emotions are rolled up in Timothy's story. The psychological rollercoaster of emotions and thoughts included "hardening of the heart" due to the news of his mother's diagnosis, "mind began racing a million miles a minute," numb, burying feeling for "self-preservation," anger, resentment, guilt (over sister's passing) and holding onto it as a penance, hitting rock bottom ("If I had access to lethal means that I would have gone through with it."). With support, Timothy found his way through acceptance to healing by learning self-love and compassion; showing empathy towards others; and knowing that he is worthy of love, grace, joy, and inner peace.

Involve: Learning from the experiences of his father, grandmother, and sister who had all passed away suddenly and without warning, Timothy was presented with the opportunity to spend precious time with his mother including seeking additional time off of military duty. To quote him, "I just stayed there and held her until she was ready to let go."

Ease: Support Timothy sought and received throughout his grief journey included asking for time off from his military supervisor, "refilling his cup" by spending time with friends, self-help books, seminars, workshops, a life coach, and a therapist. Timothy referred to "the power of safe spaces." "Safe spaces" is a term similar to that described in the chapter "Ease" of "holding space" for someone. More specifically, according to the Oxford Dictionary," it means "a place or environment in which a person or category of people can feel confident that they will not be exposed to discrimination, criticism, harassment, or any other emotional or physical harm."

Focus: There are so many points of wisdom in Timothy's story which is why he has used it as a platform to help and heal others through his own forthcoming book, *I'mperfect Masterpiece Playbook* about self-acceptance and living a driven purpose lifestyle. Core learnings from the manner he is living in his "new normal" is self-love, forgiveness, living in grace, showing empathy and love to others, and standing in the power of community and letting people in. Personally, Timothy gives some of the best hugs.

A Daughter's Grief: One Last Fire Bell for Father

My grief is not as strong as I envisaged it would be.

*M*ost people have experienced grief relating to death at some point in their life, and the death of a loved one so close is heartfelt and difficult to cope with. For me, I feel I was already grieving before he died because he had very mild dementia so the person I knew and loved had, and was, diminishing in front of my eyes. This man was my father, who passed away just a few weeks before writing this.

I was so proud of my father, yet I could no longer go to him for help and support; instead I had become that for him. The easiest way to deal with the situation was to treat him as he used to be, chatting to him about our shared passion for the Fire Service. He served for 32 years finally retiring as a senior officer and I worked in the Fire Control Room (taking emergency calls, working radio dispatch etc) for 12.5 years. We worked together during my years in the service and, like any other of my colleagues, I called him 'Sir' in accordance and acknowledgement of his rank.

My passion went further back than that to when I was a little girl and Dad would take me to the fire station with him when he was off duty. I would get to sit in a fire engine and wear his (very oversized) fire helmet and fire boots. I loved seeing the fire engine leave the fire station and hear the fire bell being rung by one of the firemen riding on it to a fire. (Yes, I am that old!) When we were sharing those memories I would get a glimmer of the man he used to be.

On other occasions, we would share eye contact that spoke volumes (much more than any words) and which was often a mischievous sparkle in his eyes.

His physical death brings with it another type of grief – a finalisation of a life well lived (he was 95-years-old), and a realisation that it's the end of an era and I will never see him again. My memories will serve me well.

Huna, a spiritual belief system, came to my rescue as I studied it for over 20 years. In the chapter "Life After Divorce" I share more about taking a workshop about *Huna* and the Ancient Teaching of Hawaii. I have many more skills and techniques at my disposal which enabled me to deal with my father initially being hospitalised and then his final demise.

Huna is ultimately about spiritual empowerment, and through my experiences and knowledge I was able to make sure that my father was looked after by my spirit guides, especially when I was not able to be with him. My guides kept him safe and I was comforted by the fact that they would also keep me informed of his condition and any changes.

My spirit guides also assisted with his transition to the other side. Knowing all of this gave me the strength I needed to help my mother and my sister during this time. I spent most of the day with my dad on the day he died and for that I am grateful. When I checked in with my guides they told me it was time and on that basis I visited the hospital much earlier than I would have done normally.

The Hawaiians do not believe in goodbye and they say *A hui hou* which means "Until we meet again." Additionally, they do *ho'oponopono* with the person who has died which cuts the *aka* (sticky connection) cords which allows the person to be set free from the emotional ties of the bereaved. *Ho'oponopono* is an invaluable tool, and is also known as the "forgiveness process." I have done *ho'oponopono* with my father and I've guided my mother and sister through the process too.

My grief is not as strong as I envisaged it would be and I believe that comes from having *Huna* in my life. (It's how I live my life!) *Ho'oponopono* gave me the opportunity to say everything I needed to say to my dad so I could set him free. I'm not holding him here with my grief. My grief is not overwhelming and he would not want me to be 'making a fuss' so I shall live the rest of my life being proud that I am his daughter and celebrate those character traits I see in myself that I know came from him.

Stella James
Frome, UK

The Story in Review

Through decades of learnings, Stella's story emphasizes the power of living a life of self-discovery which allows her to more easily approach life's challenges.

 Gather: The critical points in Stella's story are when her father first started showing signs of dementia, his hospitalization, and his final passing. It's not uncommon to grieve the loss of one's mind long before their body says "goodbye." This is a form of *anticipatory* and *disenfranchised grief*.

 Relate: Having only lost her father a few weeks before sharing her story, Stella is still in the early stages of her grief journey. However, her story is powerful because she has done significant work to release the past traumas, triggers, and limiting beliefs that would have otherwise led her down a longer journey through grief. (Read her additional story on her healing journey in the chapter "Life After Divorce.") Most of her emotions were positive and reminiscent. This includes a pride in her father, a loss of not being able to go to him for help yet she was that for him, positively reminiscing about their days at the Fire Service, noticing that grief has not been overwhelming, and taking time to celebrate her father's character traits she sees in herself.

 Involve: One activity mentioned in her story is taking the time to connect and reminisce with her dad in the last days of his life.

 Ease: Although it has only been a few weeks, Stella strongly relied on the following to support her through this end-of-life process: the ancient Hawaiian *Huna* techniques (discussed more in the chapter "Life After Divorce") including leaning on her spirit guides, and *ho'oponopono* to release emotional ties with her father.

 Focus: Stella said it best in her last sentence, "I shall live the rest of my life being proud that I am his daughter..." May you glean from Stella's narrative the ability to face loss with grace and ease (both honoring the loss with sadness), honor the life that special person had in your life, and continue living knowing you are better having had them in your life.

In Summary

*"Perhaps they are not stars in the sky, but rather openings where
our loved ones shine down to let us know they are happy."*

– Eskimo legend

*What's your story? What's your first recollection of the death of someone you knew?
How did others (authority figures) respond to it? What did they teach you about death?
What beliefs did you create about yourself or the world based on these past experiences?*

Our responses to death and dying are profoundly shaped by the **culture** we emerge from and the beliefs, values, and attitudes we hold. These elements intricately influence our thoughts, feelings, actions, and reactions of the **mind** when faced with the challenging path of death and grief. Two stories mention *suicidal ideations*, one of which specifically mentions *mental health*. One story brought forth the view held by Dr. Gabor Maté that mental health issues are not just individual problems, but are often symptoms of a larger systemic problem.[49] For further suicide support, refer to the chapter "Hotline Resources" in Part IV. While these stories have not yet delved into the physical aspects of grief, we will explore this further in upcoming chapters.

    Toxic positivity, a concept scrutinized in select stories, emerges as a pivotal theme. When examining positivity, our aim is to discern when it helps or hinders the grieving process. In my personal account, I channeled positivity naturally to honor my father and unite with others during his celebration of life – this proved to be a healthy approach. However, I also used positivity to shield myself from my authentic emotions, a manifestation of toxic positivity. Timothy, too, employed smiles and laughter as a deflective tactic, while Donna employed positivity to convey that she was "okay" so as not to "burden others." In essence, while these tactics may serve as valuable short-term coping mechanisms, they become "toxic" when they obstruct the path to healthy, long-term grieving.

Our journey through the **Healthy GRIEF Framework** was a unique experience for each individual. Here's a concise summary of the framework's key components:

Gather: When confronting the death of a loved one, the "gather" moment – marking either the *end* or the commencement of a new phase – can encompass numerous stages, such as diagnosis (e.g., cancer, ADHD, BPD), health decline (e.g., dementia), major health incidents (e.g., heart attack), hospitalization, removal from life support, or the moment of passing.

Relate: The spectrum of emotions experienced, particularly in the case of sudden child death due to suicide, is vast. Some of these emotions, organized according to the *SARAH* acronym, include shock, numbness, confusion, sadness, depression, loss, anger, rage, guilt, pride, celebration, grace, and self-love.

Involve: This stage encompasses various phases, each reflecting the importance of allowing oneself time to grieve. This may involve connecting with a loved one before their passing, caregiving, planning a celebration of life, or managing estate and financial matters.

Ease: Access to formal and informal support played a significant role, including therapeutic modalities like NLP, Time Line Therapy, and Hypnotherapy, as well as the guidance of life coaches, therapists, support groups, psychic readings, educational resources like self-help books and podcasts, the collective strength of friends and coworkers, and spiritual practices such as *Huna* techniques, including *ho'oponopono*.

Focus: Evidences of transitioning into the *"New Normal"* phase included forgiving oneself and others, fostering self-love and love for others, acquiring knowledge and skills to support individuals facing similar challenges, launching businesses to aid others through similar difficulties, and the authoring of books aimed at guiding and inspiring others (one of which you are holding in your hands now).

May you discover stories within these pages that resonate with your own journey. Take note of their wisdom and incorporate their lessons into your own narrative of healing and growth.

Healthfully grieving when your loving relationship is no longer.

INTIMATE RELATIONSHIPS

"The best and most beautiful thing in the world cannot
be seen or even touched - they must be felt with the heart."

~ Helen Keller

The second most common form of grief we will nearly all experience is the loss of an intimate relationship. This is often referred to as having or causing a "broken heart." However, given our reflection on grief and how it settles in the body, be careful how you describe it. Your body is listening!

As humans, we are social creatures. We are not meant to live in isolation. In the next chapter, we will explore griefs associated with other forms of relationships. We'll look at break-ups, divorce, reconciliation, and finding love again with my own story, those of my clients, and others, along with some research and statistics, all before exploring the grief cycles associated with failed intimate relationships and how you can move through them healthfully. In this chapter, we are only focusing on intimate relationships.

In the first story, we get a male's view on losing not only his girlfriend but his best friend in a tangled web of relationships. Read about how William's painful experience sparked a powerful coping skill. Rachel walks us through the pain of coming home to an empty house and discovering infidelity. Find out what plays a big part in her road to recovery, and what she's doing now with her story. Based on a 2018 Facebook post, we walk through the process of reconciling a marriage after her husband's affair. Her messages ring loud and clear of a certain view society places on individuals and marriage following infidelity. Next, is my own story about my first divorce. This reflects on the internal and external pressures of marriage and divorce while finding love (and me!) again. We close with Stella's stories of her first two failed marriages to intentionally finding, meeting, and marrying her soul mate! It's a beautiful journey of finding her way back to "resurrecting" herself.

Each story ends with a review of how culture, mind, and body have influenced their approach to decisions and responses to other's choices in their relationships. We then explore the **Healthy GRIEF Framework** to help summarize their unique paths to hope and recovery. Find a story or more than resonate with your own journey.

Breaking Up:
Writing Out Grief

I like to think of grief as a time of mourning for the person I was and the person I imagined myself to become.

This tale begins at the start of the 90s when my best friend invited me to a water park in San Dimas, California. I've never been to a water park, so I was very focused and listened to the other guests who were getting their waterslide orientation. Of course, my friend insisted we try out the highest tower. I'm not sure why he picked this moment, but he casually told me that he was now dating my girlfriend. At first, I thought he was joking and when I asked him if he was serious, he nodded in the affirmative.

This news really confused me because I wasn't aware that my girlfriend and I had broken up at the time. Sure, there was this odd tiff we had a couple of days earlier, but I didn't even know what it was about. It came out of the blue and I was so upset I asked her to drop me off and I was still in that cooling-off period. We rarely argued so I needed time to process and the invitation to get away seemed like a really good idea at the time.

So, once I realized this wasn't a joke, I found myself being asked to step up to the front of the line. I felt numb. This was one of those times when you can feel your blood pressure drop. Your mind is racing but everything is a blur, you can't make out exactly what you're thinking or feeling, it's just too much all at once. I could hear them give instructions for crossing my arms and legs, but then, as I went over the edge, I flailed and experienced a very painful rush of water in my most delicate of places.

This was my brother, even closer than a brother, and he was giving me the news that made absolutely no sense. We had met at a random college party, and became inseparable and indistinguishable from one another – like a two-headed coin that you never knew which end was up when you regarded us by our pop culture acumen, unceasing creativity, and warped sense of humor. To say we finished each other's sentences was a poor example of how alike we were.

When I met this incredible girl at a graduation party my first thought was "What was I going to do about my best friend?" As it turned out, my new girlfriend had a sibling so we conspired to set them up because she was dating a real dud at the time, so we pulled some strings and everything just sort of worked out. Now the dynamic duo was a fearsome foursome, and I didn't think life could get any better.

On my best friend's birthday, I borrowed some equipment from the AV department and did a secret documentary where I recorded people relating favorite stories about my best friend. I added a shot of me giving blood in his name and even stalked him a little with a long-distance lens while he was walking to class. He absolutely loved his birthday gift; so much so that he wanted to do one for his girlfriend, so he asked her sister to help. I got a call from them to see if I could help with the final scene and I agreed. While they sat in lawn chairs in fancy dress, they both admitted to the camera that they were not being completely honest with her this past week. They weren't off doing the errands they had claimed but rather doing this... I suddenly rush into frame and stated candidly that they were not having an affair, but in fact, producing this birthday video... for you.

That's where my immediate thought went when I tried to accept what my best friend was telling me. Is that really where it started, or did it begin much earlier? I had no idea it had gotten so bad between me and my girlfriend as we rarely discussed how we felt. I asked my friend a few questions, but, overall, I really didn't know what to say. I wasn't angry. I was confused.

The next day I was angry, but, for some reason, I was angrier at my girlfriend who hadn't taken the time to make it clear that we were no longer a couple. It wasn't reasonable anger; it was me just lashing out. We had a chalkboard in our apartment, and I did my impression of Bart Simpson writing many times what I thought of my now ex-girlfriend.

I believe that's how my path of healing began. Writing down my thoughts. They didn't have to be rational or even true... just whatever was passing through my consciousness at the time. Like catching a bee in a glass. While it's violently buzzing around, you get this sense of relief when you release these things that should never get too comfortable in the recesses of your mind when you're in pain.

Since everything I enjoyed doing would either remind me of my best friend or my girlfriend, I couldn't engage in activities that usually brought me pleasure or comfort. The only way to move on was to completely change the script. It also didn't help matters after receiving a call from her sister who told me she was no longer dating my best friend a full week later.

The phone call reminded me that my situation was not unique and there were plenty of souls out there who have experienced much worse than me. I mean betrayed by your own sister is about as Greek tragedy as it gets. However, I do not think it is comforting to know it could be worse, but it does put your pain in perspective.

I think that's what snapped me out of my ruminating over what went wrong. I stopped trying to affix blame on whose fault it was or what I could have done to prevent it. Letting go of what happened was something I needed to do for my own well-being. When I really thought about it my best friend and I may have been similar in personality, but our lives were very different. I was a divorced college student with two young children and my best friend had no such obligations. It made sense that if given a choice my girlfriend would choose him over me, someone she could start a family with.

Accepting this realization did not make the pain go away. I still found myself mourning the loss of both their daily companionship and starting over after the vacuous holes left behind by their absence was no small order. Every burger joint, arcade, and beachfront reminded me of the adventures we used to have. Dealing with loss isn't just lamenting what was, but it is also letting go of all the unwritten experiences that have now been taken from you. I think that's often where most of the unreconcilable pain comes from – our imaginations.

Grief, stress, and anxiety all come from the same place. What you think or believe will happen is rarely as bad as what does or could happen. When I started to look for new places to hang out, I realized that it was more than likely my best friend would be there – as they say great minds think alike. Visualizing a new future is not easy when what's familiar is such a good fit. As it happened, I opted for the college library, a place that neither my best friend nor girlfriend visited very often.

There I poured myself into my process. I decided creative writing was a perfect distraction from the constant churning in my stomach that made sleeping and eating nearly impossible for weeks. By utilizing my imagination to produce creative explorations into fiction, it was no longer spending time trying to assess what went wrong or how I could repair what was lost and can never be replaced.

I cannot stress enough how important it is to keep your imagination in check. By focusing on my stories, I was able to take all my denial, anger, bargaining, depression, and acceptance and pour all those emotions into a collection of short stories.

By the time I was finished with the last story, I had already made some new friends which in turn allowed me to explore new sides of myself that I'd never experienced before. I like to think of grief as a time of mourning for the person I was and the person I imagined myself to become. So often we do not realize how much our life goals shape who we are, so when those dreams die, we also lose a piece of our past selves as well as our future selves, our potential if you will.

However, one of our most recognizable advantages as the human species is our ability to adapt. So, when one door is inexplicably closed, you can either continue to waste your time trying to open that door or you can move on with your life and start trying some new doors. No matter what happens in your life, you always hold the rudder of where your vessel is heading. You always choose what to focus on and what's more important.

There was a time when I did attempt to broker peace between us, but neither was having it, so I let them go. Investing in myself through my writing was what kept me from wallowing in sorrow. When I used my creativity on projects that interested me, I found I was spending less time allowing my imagination to fuel my anxieties and fears.

30 years later, while going through a second divorce, I decided to use writing as a distraction and creative outlet to focus my imagination again. I formed a

premise that those stories I wrote back in college could still be relevant today as a sort of nostalgic look into the vanishing world we call the 90s, hence the title of the book, *Planet 90s*.[50]

One thing I noticed was that a lot of my writing tried to imagine the future. I think that is how I was healing, by imagining a new future me without my best friend and girlfriend and what I discovered was an expansive world that still had a lot to offer me. The other thing I noticed was that the stories encapsulated all the raw emotions I was experiencing at a time of loss. I believe writing them out in this way really helped in processing these strong emotions, which eventually allowed me to acknowledge them and let them go. This is essentially how journaling works best.

Grief is a necessary process to shed the old you to become the new you. You cannot grow in life if you stay on a path that no longer leads to growth. Letting go and moving on is essential to becoming the next best version of yourself.

So, grieve as they do in New Orleans where they celebrate the passing of life by cherishing all that what life has to offer. When you focus your creative energies on opening those new doors, that's when life really starts to get interesting!

William Kovacevich
Murrieta, CA

The Story in Review

Let's explore William's grief journey.

Culture and **Toxic Positivity**: William's story highlights a significant issue – men also experience emotional turmoil during and after failed relationships. Unfortunately, societal norms often compel men to conceal their feelings and project an image of stoic composure, which can be a harmful form of toxic positivity.

Mind: Within William's narrative, we observe the beliefs he formed about himself and the world. For instance, he wrestled with the notion that it somehow "made sense" for his girlfriend to choose someone else, given his divorce and two children. This reflects the human tendency to seek meaning in events to alleviate emotional pain. William found comfort in channeling his energy into creative writing, effectively keeping his imagination in check.

Body: William briefly touched on the physical toll this ordeal took on him. He described a "constant churning" in his stomach, which interfered with sleep and appetite. Psychosomatically, the stomach is often associated with "digesting ideas." Drawing from Wendi Jensen's book, *The Healing Questions Guide*, we can explore this mind-body connection through a series of questions.

1. What will it take to recognize and release unnecessary burdens?
2. What will it take for me to digest new ideas, suggestions, and criticisms with ease?
3. What is blocking me from knowing I am capable?
4. What will it take for me to see beyond the worry?
5. What will it take for me to allow new ideas to flow through me effortlessly?
6. What will it take for me to see myself and others as equal?
7. What will it take for me to allow things to happen easily?

8. What value is there in making things so hard?

9. When will I finally accept that it does not all depend on me? What will it take to understand what part is mine and what is not?

Note: These questions invite introspection. Not all questions will resonate, yet they offer insight into how our bodies communicate with us on a subconscious level.

 Gather: The pivotal moment in this story occurs when William's best friend reveals that he's dating William's ex-girlfriend.

 Relate: As a writer himself, William channeled his emotions through his words. He journeyed through a range of feelings, following the *SARAH* model, from numbness and confusion to upset and anger, from stress and anxiety to denial and depression. Eventually, he reached the stage of letting go of what happened and accepting it.

 Involve: William adopted various action steps to process his grief, such as looking for new places to hang out (so he wouldn't be triggered) and pouring all his energy into creative writing.

 Ease: As an introverted individual, William leaned towards writing as an outlet for his emotions, given that the person he would typically confide in had become romantically involved with his ex-girlfriend. However, he did forge new friendships that allowed him to explore different facets of himself.

 Focus: Over nearly three decades, William continued to express himself through creative writing, culminating in the publication of his book *Planet 90s*. This experience contributed to the development of coping skills that he would later apply during his second divorce.

Divorce:
Life After He Left

My husband did me a favor.

The day that altered my life forever. I didn't see it coming. It was a Friday evening, September 12, 2008. I had just gotten off of work after a hard day at the salon. I picked up my kids, we walked into our home, looked around, and realized that all of my husband's things were gone. He was gone. I stood there in shock. My kids were crying. We were all processing what was going on. My oldest son was 11 years old, my middle son seven, and my youngest six.

I stood there, looking around and so many emotions were running through my mind. Anger, frustration, confusion, panic, worry – what am I going to do? I have three kids, a job, and a mortgage to pay. How am I going to do this?!

In that moment it was a moment of a new normal. And the next several months would be the beginning of figuring it all out.

I started to call his phone and he didn't answer. Over and over I call all night with no answer. I called my sister and parents. The kids and I cry ourselves to sleep in my bed.

Over the next few weeks I found out that my husband was having an affair with a woman at work and left us to be with her.

This was something I never imagined would happen. Our marriage was a struggle from the beginning. We were high school sweethearts. Young and not very smart in relationships. But I never expected him to leave us.

I, as a child and into my late 30s, struggled with being good enough, worthy enough, smart enough. I had poor self esteem and lacked self confidence.

My friends and family were all in shock that he was gone. Just the day before we celebrated his 33rd birthday. We had a surprise party for him. My parents and friends were a great support. I am very grateful that I had uplifting people around me. It was still a very hard road to healing and recovery.

Loneliness consumed me. Over the months after he left I started down a path that led me to a deep depression. I laid in bed most of the time unless I had to go to work or get the kids to school. I started going out to the bars to fill a void, which led me into an even worse depression. Doing a daily task was a chore and took a lot. The way I reacted to the situation was not a healthy one.

My husband and I ended up getting a divorce. We did not get along at all. There was so much anger, bitterness, and unforgiveness built up. It was very hard on our children. I ended up losing our home to foreclosure.

As time passed I was at rock bottom. The pit and lowest of lows. I had a really awesome boss and friend I worked with who asked me to go to church. I kept telling them I was fine and didn't need church. Until one day I was crying and couldn't stop. My boss asked what she could do for me. I said, "I don't know!" She replied, "When I don't know what to do, I go to the man upstairs," as she pointed to the sky. I decided that day was the day I needed to go to church.

I texted my friend and she picked me up that Sunday for church. That day the sermon was all about having a choice between going down a path of distraction or going down a path that leads to life, truth, and the right way. I was crying my eyes out and asked my friend to go to the altar with me. That day I asked for forgiveness and forgave my husband and asked God into my life. I instantly felt a weight lift off my shoulder. That was the start to transformation, to the road to healing. This was about six months after my husband left. We still contended with having a civil relationship for our children. That never happened while they were kids. There were multiple times after I got saved that I had to forgive myself and my husband.

My healing was a process for a couple years. I went to a counselor to help me deal and heal. She gave me tools to help mentally and emotionally. I started going to church and reading my Bible. I plugged myself into a Bible study and did a lot of praying. I surrounded myself with people who were positive and would help me.

I was single for five years. In those five years I worked on myself and being with my kids. I focused on healing and growing.

I started to see myself and the situation differently. My husband did me a favor. As I said earlier we didn't have the best relationship, but we had three kids together so we stayed together. It wasn't healthy for the kids. And now looking back, it's been 15 years. Where he is in his life is not where I am or want to be. I have always had a big dream and a big vision.

If I could give myself advice 15 years ago it would be: this is a small part of your life that is going to be part of your story to help others. Love yourself first, avoid worrying about men and being lonely. Embrace the time you get to be with your kids and work on you. You get to take this time to grow spiritually, personally, and emotionally. It will all be worth it in the end. You're going to grow and learn and impact so many. Inspiring people to live their best lives and purpose. You're going to share your story to heal and inspire others. You're amazing and have an amazing life. You are going to love your dreams.

Rachel Best
Spencerville, OH

The Story in Review

Let's explore Rachel's journey ...

 Culture: Rachel's story raises a common dilemma: staying in an unhealthy relationship "for the kids." Many believe it sets an example of working through tough times, yet it may inadvertently teach children to endure suffering, adding pressure to struggling couples with children.

 Mind: Rachel had a set of limiting beliefs that hindered her progress including feelings of not being good enough, worthy enough, or smart enough as well as having poor self-esteem and lacking self-confidence. These had a significant impact on her emotional well-being and her emotional rollercoaster.

 Gather: The pivotal moments in Rachel's story include returning to an empty house, discovering her husband's affair, the divorce, and the loss of her home due to foreclosure.

 Relate: In addition to the previously-mentioned limiting beliefs, Rachel's emotional journey included confusion, panic, worry, anger, frustration, bitterness, unforgiveness, loneliness, deep depression, hitting rock bottom, and experiencing the lowest of lows.

 Involve: Rachel discovered that going to bars to cope with her emotional void was an unhealthy approach. Instead, she found comfort and support in attending church, reading the Bible, and engaging in prayer.

 Ease: Rachel found invaluable support from various sources, including her uplifting social circle, her deepening faith and spiritual practices, as well as guidance from a skilled counselor who equipped her with essential mental and emotional tools.

 Focus: Her "new normal" includes self-love, time with her children, spiritual and personal growth, self-forgiveness, and inspiring others with her story.

Reconciling Marriage:
No More Shame

It was in that moment that I knew.

It was December 27 - my "D-Day." The day I discovered the truth about my husband's affair. Yet that's only half the story. Half of it contains pain, heartbreak, discovery of the truth, and discovery of myself. Yet the other half is one of recovery, reconciliation, and restoration.

I am sharing this next chapter of my life on the anniversary of my D-Day to show that life after an affair can be beautiful again. It might be messy, hard, painful, frustrating, and scary but also warm, joyful, loving, and peaceful.

I have been holding back on sharing the rest because I wanted to protect it, nurture it, solidify it before bringing it out into view. I wanted to be sure I can withstand the criticism and judgment. Because "stay" is the new shame.

So many women are suffering under the weight of the shame. The shame that society puts on us. The shame that has been brought on by our freedoms that we have been afforded in the last few decades. Those freedoms have led to a society where being just as powerful as men means we need to be cold, calculated, and aggressive. If we don't just up and leave we are weak, stupid, money hungry, and a number of other things.

I have seen it myself in many moms groups, someone posts about their husband cheating and 99% of the responses are:

☑ *Screw him!*

☑ *Take the kids and run!*

☑️ *Hire the best lawyer you can and rake him over the coals!*
☑️ *Drain the bank accounts!*
☑️ *Tell his parents!*

You get the point. Very few and far between are people taking a softer approach.

Infidelity is painful, devastating, selfish, unnecessary, and downright sinful. So yes, infidelity is certainly a good and viable reason to take a long, hard look at your relationship. Heck, it's even a viable reason for you to leave, but should that always be the default option?

I'm here to tell you it doesn't need to be. It doesn't need to be a cold, calculated severing of ties. It doesn't need to be vindictive, spiteful, hurtful. There is a space in between.

After my separation in January, I had to create my space in between. I needed to set boundaries that would allow me to process, grieve, heal, and quite frankly figure out my life.

I asked myself:

🙂 How do I go from sharing my life with someone to purposely keeping them on the outside?
🙂 How do I create boundaries with my husband when we had very few before?
🙂 What do I need from my husband right now?
🙂 How do we co-parent now that we aren't together?

I was also asking myself questions that weren't as easy to answer:

🙂 How did my best friend in the whole world become my enemy?
🙂 Why do I still want to run to him, for him to comfort me through this, when he is the one who caused my pain?
🙂 How will I ever trust him again?
🙂 And most importantly: Do I want a divorce?

I'm not going to lie; it was a struggle!

And here's the thing, I got it WRONG a lot. It was a whole lot of trial and error. There were many times I had to recreate my boundaries, fortify them, and in some cases let them a little loose. What I found was that this was a process of discovering myself in a lot of ways.

With time I started to heal, to gain strength and clarity. I discovered what I needed; I discovered my voice. I learned how to stand in my own power and bravely ask for what I needed yet be soft enough to give grace. This also led me to determine what I needed from my husband. I needed transparency, consistency, patience, kindness, softness, sympathy, understanding, respect, space, flexibility, openness, vulnerability.

And he did it. 100% of what I asked for, even when I would say yes and then change my mind. He was patient, kind, understanding, and loving. For months, he showed up for me, again and again and again.

Yet I was still unsure. I was still in my grief of what had happened, how badly he hurt me. I didn't realize this experience in a lot of ways had hardened me. I put up thick tall walls, peeking through the cracks to see the other side. To see him. I operated from that place of hiding behind walls for months. Until one day it came crashing down.

A panicked phone call about being rushed to the emergency room. As soon as I pulled back the curtain in the emergency room it was as if my wall had come crumbling down. He was covered in blood. Shaking from the shock. A dirty bloody rag wrapped around his hand. His finger in a cup behind him.

I took it all in. Then I saw his face. His eyes full of pain yet so happy to see me standing there. I saw his body relax when I walked in the room. I felt him fall apart when I held him.

It was in that moment I knew – I knew that I still loved him. That the love between us was worth trying to save. I finally allowed myself to really see all the effort he had been making for months. That is the moment when I made the CHOICE to rebuild my marriage.

I didn't do it for the kids. I didn't do it for the money. I didn't do it for security. I didn't do it because I was weak or stupid. I did it for LOVE. The love I had for him, the love he had for me. The love we shared. This is where Us 2.0 began.

And let me tell you, staying and working it out is HARD and not for the weak. So if you are reading this and you made the choice to stay or thinking of staying, I want you to know:

- ✧ You are NOT weak, or stupid, or any of the negative things you hear in your head or from others.
- ✧ You are AMAZING and STRONG and BRAVE and you are not alone.

There are many of us out there that are walking through this season. Most of us are standing in the shadows of infidelity trying to recover and rebuild in secret. I am bravely stepping out of the shadows of the shame and stepping into the truth that even with infidelity, marriages can survive, they can thrive, and can be even better than they were before.

I stand proudly, with my husband by my side, and say:

- ✧ I CHOOSE this.
- ✧ I CHOOSE a restored marriage.
- ✧ I CHOOSE love.

Forever, For Always, No matter what.

If you or someone you know has chosen to rebuild their marriage after infidelity, let there be NO MORE SHAME. Let's show those who are hurting and alone that they have our support as they navigate their hard and painful season.

Anonymous
Modified and adopted from a Facebook Post
Facebook User no longer active

The Story in Review

Although unable to track down the original author after a number of years following her Facebook post, I felt compelled to share. Let's explore why.

 Culture: The author's story addresses a significant aspect of our culture – the criticism, judgment, and shame that individuals often face when they choose to reconcile a marriage following an affair.

Toxic Positivity: While not explicitly discussed in the narrative, one can infer that the author might have concealed her true emotions behind a facade of fake smiles, normalizing her activities, and responding briefly with an "everything is okay" demeanor. This could have served as a shield against criticism, judgment, and shame, allowing her the space to contemplate the fate of her marriage. However, it may also have hindered her from seeking the guidance and support necessary during her decision-making process.

 Mind: The author takes us through the thought-provoking questions that guided her journey.

 Gather: The pivotal moments in her narrative revolve around "D-Day," the day she discovered the infidelity, and the day when she encountered her husband in the emergency room, ultimately choosing to reconcile their marriage.

 Relate: Throughout her journey, she navigated a wide range of emotions. She experienced criticism, judgment, and shame but also found inner strength and clarity. She discovered her needs and her voice, learning to assert herself and ask for what she required. She also extended grace, forgave, and ultimately found love along the way.

Involve: She took brave steps, including assertively communicating her needs in her relationships and making the resolute choice to rebuild her marriage and setting healthy boundaries. (See Part IV Website Resources for an eBook on Setting Healthy Boundaries.)

 Ease: The story did not specify any particular resources or means of emotional support the author sought during her journey.

 Focus: The central theme of her post revolves around the pivotal decision to rebuild her marriage. All ensuing actions served as indicators of whether they remained aligned with that initial decision. As she conveys in her narrative, making this choice can be an arduous and painful journey, yet it remains entirely feasible.

My Divorce:
Finding Me Again

It was less about finding my future Mr. Right, and more about finding ME again.

When he first extended an invitation to go out with him, I couldn't help but chuckle. Fresh from ending a previous relationship, I hadn't been seeking another romantic connection. Yet, as fate would have it, two years down the line, he found himself asking me the same question.

In those days, I used to unwind by going country western dancing with a group of colleagues after our work hours. It served as a splendid outlet for relaxation, physical activity, and socializing with my coworkers. It also provided me with the opportunity to two-step with other men without feeling obligated to embark on romantic entanglements.

And then, there was Kevin.

Tall, dark-haired, handsome, a captivating dancer, and adorned with an endearing smile, Kevin had not captured my attention when he initially proposed going out two years prior. However, on that particular evening, all of that changed.

In the following November, I was bestowed with the honor of being the maid of honor at my niece's wedding, a ceremony that took place on the eve of Thanksgiving (a tradition her parents had established decades before). Enveloped by the atmosphere of love and celebration, Kevin and I chose to embark on our own marital journey the next month, opting for an intimate home wedding on Christmas Eve (an echo of a tradition upheld by three generations of my family).

At the time, I was 32 years old. Although I cared deeply for Kevin, a question lingered in my heart: was I genuinely, unequivocally in love with him?

I distinctly recall a visit from a close friend of mine during our high school reunion, a mere four years prior to my current situation. With well-meaning intentions, my mother uttered something along the lines of, "Karen, why aren't you married yet like Jennifer?" While her phrasing might not have been precisely as I remember, I found myself incensed by her words. It felt as if I were being judged for being 28 years old and unmarried.

I had been engaged on two occasions before, both engagements I had ending for various reasons. And so, there I stood at 32, having finally tied the knot.

Six weeks after our wedding, my husband found himself ensnared in a hit-and-run accident while driving my car. This unfortunate incident led to his arrest for drunk driving, and he offered the suggestion of an annulment, deeply embarrassed by the whole ordeal. However, modeling my parents' enduring marriage of 55 years (at that time), I was committed to exploring every avenue to salvage our union. This conviction extended to even more profound choices – within two months, I confirmed I was pregnant.

During this tumultuous period, I made the conscious decision to halt my dancing activities. Dancing had been an integral part of my life since the tender age of four, and my involvement had only grown more substantial after joining a professional Polynesian dance *halau* (school or troupe) at age 14. Overwhelmed by my situation and a pressing need for self-care, I tearfully reached out to my *kumu hula* (hula dance director), explaining that I needed to take a break from dancing. My emotions were too raw to pinpoint exactly why I needed this hiatus, and it would take another seven years before I could articulate the true reason to her.

For a significant portion of my pregnancy, Kevin was incarcerated, serving his sentence for the events that had occurred just six weeks after our wedding, yet later finding that this was not his first DUI and he had actually been driving on an expired license. His release coincided with the birth of our son, Tyler.

Tyler became the radiant center of our lives, a source of immense pride and joy. However, Kevin's struggles and addictions shifted from alcohol to oxycontin, introducing further tension into our marriage. In a valiant effort to preserve our union, I exerted myself in every possible way, all the while nursing growing resentment.

One pivotal day, during one of Kevin's "looped out" states from oxycontin, he stumbled while holding our sleeping five-month-old son in his car seat. The seat crashed onto the front steps, causing Tyler to awaken, stunned yet mercifully unharmed. In that harrowing moment, a surge of inner strength seized me – a strength that had lain dormant until then. I was no longer willing to expose my beloved child to harm. Without hesitation, I initiated divorce proceedings.

I shared with a friend that if not for Kevin endangering Tyler's safety, I might have continued clinging to the relationship. Why? Because I believed it was my duty, as a "good woman," to persevere despite the mounting tensions.

Within the intricate dance of human relationships, few steps are as profound and convoluted as codependent behavior within failed marriages. During this challenging time, my closest confidante, Meesh, herself a therapist, introduced me to the book *Codependent No More* by Melody Beattie.[51] Through her compassionate guidance, I began to untangle the web of my relationship and consider new paths that I had once dismissed.

The notion of identifying as a "single mother" initially gave me pause, and I recoiled at the thought. In truth, this apprehension might have been lurking in my subconscious when I became pregnant with my son. At that time, I was aware that my marriage was faltering, and although I knew having a child wouldn't remedy the situation, a part of me still hoped it could. And so, my son became the shining outcome of my marriage, and I wouldn't trade those experiences for anything.

I am profoundly grateful to my close circle of friends, colleagues, and family who played pivotal roles during the critical transition from marriage to single motherhood when my son was just five months old. With their unwavering support, I navigated the tumultuous waters successfully.

Despite the chaos that surrounded me, I channeled my energy into completing my doctoral work. Just nine days before Tyler's birth, I submitted my dissertation proposal. Throughout my maternity leave, I managed to nurse Tyler while conducting 103 hour-long post-research calls for participants in my study on emotional intelligence and leadership. I earned my second master's degree, defended my dissertation, and proudly graduated with my Ph.D. – all before Tyler turned two. It's a period I reflect on with pride, though I wouldn't necessarily recommend it to others. Throwing myself into my doctoral work became a constructive outlet, a way to take control and find purpose amidst the turmoil of my divorce. It also provided a welcome distraction from the emotional upheaval. During this period, Tyler was primarily cared for by my mother and aunt. Luckily, Tyler and I have a very strong bond today and I was able to make up for lost time along the way.

Despite navigating the transition from marriage to single motherhood with relative composure, wrestling with the concept of "being single" was an ongoing struggle. I felt like a letter "D" for "divorced" was emblazoned on my forehead. At the time, my parents had celebrated over 55 years of marriage, and my oldest brother had surpassed 30 years. I began to feel "used" and "tainted," as if my status as a "34-year-old divorced single mother" rendered me unappealing.

This sense of self-doubt manifested in how I treated myself. I referred to my waistline with a dose of humor, dubbing it "my PPP - Proud Pregnancy Poundage." In truth, it was an excuse to let myself go. I ceased dancing, a practice that had been integral to my life since the tender age of four. I clung to the lingering post-pregnancy weight and found myself sinking into depressive tendencies. I even withdrew from country and line dancing, activities that were inextricably tied to the memory of meeting Kevin. The prospect of encountering him again was too daunting.

During this challenging phase, three essential friends played pivotal roles in my life. My steadfast best friend Meesh, also a therapist, offered a mix of love and honesty. She guided me in discovering myself and encouraged my growth. Another dear friend and colleague, Jenn, extended a listening ear during lunches, providing not only a space to vent but also facts, research, and counsel to help me remain focused, particularly in relation to Tyler's well-being. A third friend, Wendy, stands out for her remarkable gesture. In a moment of despair, she offered to go grocery shopping for me. My response was a despondent "nothing," reflecting my inability to muster the effort to decide on groceries. Unfazed, she texted back, "I'm at the store now. If you don't give me a list, I'm buying what I think you want and showing up at your house." The presence of friends like these – and many more – was instrumental in pulling me out of the depths of my post-divorce despair.

Wendy also played a pivotal role in coaxing me back into the dating scene. To this day, I suspect she orchestrated it intentionally. At that point, two years had elapsed since my divorce. Wendy contacted me, explaining that she had signed up for a Speed Dating event but couldn't attend. Since she couldn't get her money refunded, she suggested I take her place. My litany of excuses was met with unwavering determination. She took me dress shopping, arranged for a hair stylist, and practically pushed me through the door. While I was decidedly awkward and clumsy, this experience became the gentle nudge I needed to recognize that life indeed existed after divorce.

I also began seeing a therapist during this period. Our sessions were dubbed "Cleaning the mental closet to prepare for the next relationship," a term I've since used with my own clients. One exercise she had me undertake was to create a profile on a dating site. The purpose wasn't necessarily to dive into dating again but rather to examine how I chose to portray myself. Similar to crafting a resume highlighting my professional skills, this profile served as a canvas on which to paint a picture of who I was to a potential partner. Even the selection of pictures for the profile was a deliberate process. The experience was illuminating, leading me to make the profile public. This step motivated me to start taking better care of myself once more. I adopted a healthier, more consistent diet and invested in a treadmill that I used regularly. Pounds began to shed, and I felt and looked better. This transformation translated into increased happiness at work, at home, with friends, while dating, and most importantly, with my son.

As an added bonus, I would share my dating escapades with my close friends and my mother, eliciting laughter and camaraderie. I was having fun. The endeavor was less about discovering my future "Mr. Right" and more about rediscovering myself. Any romantic outcomes were secondary.

Just as I was contemplating a six-month subscription to Match.com, fate intervened and introduced me to Mr. Right. Surprisingly, he didn't hail from Match.com but was, in fact, my high school sweetheart, re-entering my life two decades later. More about that in the chapter "Death, Divorce, and Illness."

To this day, I still advocate for marriage, but with a more precise perspective. I champion healthy marriages, unions in which both partners are dedicated to growth, learning, and evolving together.

Dr. Karen Kramer
San Diego, CA

The Story in Review

Codependency played a significant role in this narrative. Codependency, often used to describe an unhealthy fusion, occurs when individuals in a partnership become emotionally enmeshed, leading to intertwined identities. Initially rooted in affection, this attachment can evolve into a stifling cycle of dependency, control, and bitterness. Codependent partners often sacrifice their own needs, aspirations, and boundaries in a desperate bid to maintain fragile harmony, perpetuating a toxic cycle of emotional entanglement. Such dynamics prevent personal growth, hinder effective communication, and erode the foundations of a marriage. Confronting and comprehending codependency requires embarking on a path of self-exploration and renewal. This journey involves unweaving the intricate threads that connect two lives and fostering healthier modes of connection, although not together.

Now, let's review the story ...

 Culture: External and internal comparisons to societal standards significantly influenced the narrative. These standards included societal expectations regarding the timing of marriage and parenthood, preconceived notions and stigmas of marriage and divorce, and societal definitions of a "good woman."

 Toxic Positivity: Two forms of toxic positivity emerged in the story. Initially, I isolated myself from my dance group, which had been part of my life for nearly two decades, out of embarrassment over my failed marriage. Secondly, I employed humor about my "Proud Pregnancy Poundage" (PPP) as a coping mechanism, rather than attributing my weight gain to a lack of self-care.

 Mind: In addition to adopting limiting beliefs shaped by cultural norms, I was confronted with codependent behaviors and felt judged by others for not aligning with perceived expectations.

Body: The most notable physical change involved weight gain. Although I initially attributed this to reduced exercise and childbirth in my 30s, I later realized that my weight had subconscious roots. Referring to *The Healing Questions Guide*, these are some questions I would have asked myself back then related to "Overweight":

1. What will truly cause me to feel more secure about myself?
2. What part of me am I still rejecting? What can I do to accept all of me?
3. What am I trying to protect myself from? Is this a legitimate concern? Does the extra weight really protect me from anything?
4. What will it take for me to feel safe in my body and release any false need for protection?

All of those questions resonated with me at that time in my life. They were a window into the world of how my body spoke to me at the subconscious level.

Gather: Several pivotal shifts marked the transition from one phase of life to another. These included significant events like Kevin's accident shortly after our marriage, the decision to remain married, the final decision to divorce, and the divorce itself.

Relate: The emotional journey spanned feelings of numbness, embarrassment, shame, and being used. It also included moments of feeling dirty, furious, and angry, leading to depressive behaviors and despair. However, as the journey progressed, it brought forth a sense of power, strength, pride, fun, and eventually, laughter.

Involve: I undertook various action steps, including maintaining a regular and healthy diet, acquiring and using a treadmill, pursuing further education, and venturing into dating again by creating a dating profile.

Ease: I found support from a network of key friends, a divorce attorney for an uncontested divorce, a therapist, and a persistent friend who provided groceries. Friends and family also assisted with childcare.

Focus: Life after divorce involved accepting my identity as a divorced, single mother in my mid-30s; achieving a healthier mind, body, and attitude; and reentering the dating scene, eventually finding love again while rediscovering myself.

Life After Divorce: The Demise of the Relationship and the Resurrection of Me

We have been married 19 years this year and the future is bright.

I met and fell in love with Jim when I was just 18-years-old. I was young and very idealistic about the world, and I loved him to the very depth of my soul.

We were married when I was 19-years-old, and that's when life got in the way. I had no idea that married life would be such hard work. Our relationship was fine, but family emotional issues for Jim meant he often didn't go to work, either owing to physical or mental/emotional issues. I supported him as best I could but, financially, the lack of income from him was taking its toll. My income wasn't enough to support us both, and so I took on freelance work alongside my full time job.

We had pets too, so, as I was responsible for the money, I made sure everyone was fed and I came last. This resulted in me losing weight to the extent that I was close to anorexia. I didn't feel I could fix this, and so a decision had to be made. I decided to end the relationship as my health was already suffering and financially things were becoming harder.

I was very angry and also very hurt. Jim seemed unable to help with the situation and I couldn't do it on my own. All my hopes and dreams of our future together were dashed. I believed marriage was for life and there should be no divorce. I was heartbroken.

I felt I had failed. I looked to myself for reasons why it had not worked, asking myself: How could I have done things differently? What did I need to learn from this? What was the purpose of life? How could I make sure I didn't make the same mistakes again?

My anger motivated me to pick myself up and build a new life without him.

And then I met Alan, a man older than myself by 10 years. Despite some misgivings I married him. Needless to say, I should have listened to my instincts, but there was an element of emotional blackmail going on and I thought I could manage it. Little did I know that Alan also had emotional demons darker than I had imagined, and so I endured 11 years of emotional and, at times, physical abuse.

My life wasn't all bad and neither was he. Together we bought a house with a little garden; we had pets and I had my horses (I'm an equine professional). On the surface, my life looked pretty good and it was. I loved my life and my man, but hated his behaviour and how that made me feel.

The demise of the relationship and the resurrection of me as a person started when I signed up for a course on "An introduction in Counselling," which was going to help me learn skills for the job I was in and ultimately the profession I wanted to move into. After that, I signed up for a course in personal development followed by taking a certificate course in counselling.

I learned so much about myself and I was able to release some of the emotions that I'd been holding in for so long. I was beginning to feel better about myself.

I then went on a three-week residential course to train as an NLP Practitioner. There was no going back after that. I was truly able to see how toxic and unhealthy my relationship was and that nothing would change unless I made the change.

I decided to leave Alan. I was filled with fear for the future, my safety, and whether I would be strong enough to cope. I knew that counselling for myself would be necessary in order for me to heal and come out the other side. My ace card was my NLP training. Additionally, I had a very strong support network of people around me, including my work colleagues and my employers.

Here I was again. I felt I was destroying all my hopes and dreams that I'd had for our future, but I knew that life could be so much better even if it meant being on my own.

This time, breaking up our home was so much worse because I had to find new homes for all the animals. I used all the skills I'd learned from the NLP training and received professional counselling through my work, which helped me to break free of those self-imposed chains that held me in my relationship.

I no longer felt that 'I wasn't good enough' or that 'I deserved it' or that somehow it was all my fault.

The grief was huge. Loss of hopes and dreams, loss of a loved one (despite his behaviour) and loss of all my animals.

Then I went to Hawaii to take a workshop about Huna and the Ancient Teachings of Hawaii. That's when the real healing began. I learned skills and techniques which allowed me to finally lay to rest any negative feelings I had towards my ex and myself. I also really began to understand me, and to truly love myself.

One of the techniques I learned is known as *ho'oponopono*, and is an invaluable tool for situations like mine. It's also known as the "forgiveness process." This process taught me how to forgive myself and to forgive my ex.

The most important thing that comes from these teachings is to learn the lessons that life brings, which ultimately brings great happiness. Through *Huna*, I learnt how to set an intention and have it manifest. So I set an intention for the man I wanted to be in a relationship with. My list of requirements was a full sheet of paper long!

One year after writing my list, I met Ken. He was everything on my list! We are truly soul mates. We have been married before in a previous life, which we knew instinctively but it's also indicated in our astrological birth charts. We have been married 19 years this year and the future is bright.

Stella James
Frome, UK

The Story in Review

Let's explore the importance of healthyfully moving through grief.

 Culture: Stella's belief in the sanctity of marriage for life and the societal pressure to conform to the notion of a "good woman" staying married played a significant role in her story. Ending her first and second marriages left her feeling that she had shattered her dreams for the future.

 Mind: Stella's journey was marked by a series of limiting beliefs that initially hindered her ability to navigate grief in a healthy manner. These included "I came last," "I am responsible," "I'm not good enough," "I deserved it," and "It's all my fault."

 Body: While Stella mentioned that her first two marriages had a detrimental impact on her health, she specifically noted being "close to anorexia." Utilizing Jensen's *The Healing Questions Guide*, here are questions that could have aided Stella in exploring the underlying factors contributing to her physical presentation of anorexia. *(Note: These questions are generalized and not specific to Stella, though parallels with her story can be observed.)*

1. What value is there in hating myself? What will it take to learn to love me... every part of me?
2. What will it take to feel safe to be me regardless of whether it pleases my mother?
3. What will it take to have the wisdom to express my need for my mother to support me differently?
4. What will it take to feed myself emotionally with unconditional acceptance and loving affection?
5. How would my life be different if I stopped focusing on me and my supposed insufficiencies and redirect my attention to creating something beautiful or doing something for someone in need?

6. What will it take for me to really trust that I have what it takes to create an abundant successful life?

7. What am I resisting about growing up? What will it take for me to gain the maturity I need to move on and claim a productive life?

8. What lesson am I trying to learn by starving myself? Is there a more effective way to learn it?

9. What will it take to process my emotions in a healthy loving way?

10. What will it take for me to stop thinking I need to be punished?

11. What will it take for me to really gain control over my life?

 Gather: The most significant turning points in Stella's story occurred when she made the courageous decisions to end her first and second marriages.

 Relate: Alongside the identified limiting beliefs, Stella's emotional spectrum encompassed hurt and heart-break; loss of hopes and dreams, loved ones, and her animals; anger; and fear (of the future).

 Involve: Stella took several proactive steps to regain control of her life, including enrolling in courses and programs, obtaining certifications, and applying her skills in NLP and *Huna*.

 Ease: Stella found support through various resources, such as enrolling in counseling courses, obtaining training and certification as an NLP Practitioner, participating in a *Huna* workshop, practicing *ho'oponopono* for forgiveness, seeking counseling, and maintaining a robust network of people, including work colleagues.

 Focus: Stella's "new normal" emerged as she cultivated genuine self-love, forgave herself and her ex-husbands, and set intentions that led to meeting and marrying her third husband, with their marriage enduring for 19 years as of the time of this writing.

In Summary

"We are not held back by the love we didn't receive in the past,
but by the love we're not extending to the present."
~ Marianne Williamson

What's your story? What messages did you receive about marriage and divorce growing up? What expectations did you place on yourself (or by others) to marry (or not divorce)? Who (e.g., parents) or what (e.g., religion) imparted those beliefs, and who enforced them? What beliefs helped or hindered you in making decisions regarding creating and maintaining healthy relationships?

Our beliefs are often influenced by messages from our past, the people who imparted them, and the societal norms that surrounded us. This exploration invited you to probe into your unique narrative, consider its influences, and understand how it impacts your thoughts, feelings, actions, and reactions in intimate relationships. Furthermore, we discovered how grief can manifest within the body through these stories. If any of these stories resonated with you, I encourage you to reflect on the questions provided in Jensen's *The Healing Questions Guide* that correspond to the ailments, pains, or diagnoses discussed.

Let's do a quick recap on some of the themes that emerged in these stories.

Intimate relationships, especially marriage, hold a significant place in our **cultural** and societal fabric. However, this prominence has given rise to various ideologies and societal pressures that individuals often contend with, including:

◊ The expectation for men to suppress their emotions, contributing to a culture of toxic positivity

◊ Societal pressure regarding the timing of marriage and having children

◊ Prescribed gender roles for women within the context of marriage

◊ The often well-intentioned but challenging expectation to "stay together for the kids"

◊ Criticism, judgment, and shame often associated with attempting to reconcile a marriage following an affair

◊ The stigma surrounding divorce, whether imposed by external forces or self-inflicted

◊ Coping with the emotional aftermath of shattered dreams and the disruption of expectations for a future intertwined with marriage.

Toxic positivity can be insidious, with cultural and societal norms often compelling individuals to "suck it up" and present a facade of normalcy even when struggling. This could lead to isolation, self-deprecating humor, or artificial smiles that obscure true emotions, hindering the support one might need.

Unveiling your personal story may reveal a window into the **mind** of thoughts and beliefs, including limiting ones such as "I'm not worthy / smart / good enough," "I come last," "I deserved it," or "It's all my fault." Codependence was explored further in one of the story reviews.

Intriguingly, several stories point to the **body**'s response to grief, all centered around eating and digestion. One individual experienced *stomach problems* making eating nearly impossible, another struggled with retaining post-pregnancy *weight*, and a third came dangerously close to *anorexia*.

According to a study on the "Relationship of eating behavior and self-esteem with body image perception and other factors among female college students of University of Delhi," research has long linked low self-esteem to *eating disorders*, as individuals often engage in self-critical evaluations of their bodies, impacting their eating behaviors.[52] This includes distorted perceptions of weight and shape, leading to strict dieting or other harmful practices. These physical responses are diverse, each reflecting unique psychological scenarios related to grief. Some turn to food to fill emotional voids, while others control their intake as a way to regain authority over their lives. Depression may also lead to neglecting self-care, contributing to weight loss or gain. If grief is significantly affecting your weight or your relationships with food, I encourage you to explore some of the body-related questions posed in these story reviews.

The journey through the **Healthy GRIEF Framework** manifests uniquely for each person. Here's a brief summary of its key components.

 Gather: Significant moments include questioning stability to decisions about the future, the realization of a relationship's end, and the official divorce or break-up.

 Relate: Emotions span the spectrum, from confusion and numbness to feelings of shame, anger, fear, and heartbreak. Negative limiting beliefs, as previously mentioned, also play a role.

 Involve: Activities can either help or hinder the grieving process. Distracting behaviors, like overworking or jumping into another relationship, can be detrimental long-term. It's crucial to identify actions that promote healthy progress, such as setting boundaries, seeking education, or journaling.

 Ease: Support came in various forms, including friends, family, counseling, education, and personal development methods like NLP.

 Focus: The journey's destination varied yet included self-love, forgiveness, personal growth, and the ability to inspire others with their story. It might also lead to a new, healthier partnership or marriage.

As we close this section, I encourage you to reflect on your own unique narrative and the powerful influences that have shaped your beliefs and values surrounding intimate relationships. Consider the societal norms, family dynamics, and past experiences that have contributed to the tapestry of your thoughts, feelings, actions, and reactions within your relationships.

As you resonate with the stories shared and incorporate their wisdom into your own path, may you find inspiration, clarity, and strength in the pursuit of the healthiest and most fulfilling relationships. Remember, you are not alone on this journey, and there is a wealth of wisdom and support to guide you along the way.

"

As humans, we are social creatures. We are not meant to live in isolation.

These connections remind us that, in our most vulnerable moments, we are not alone on this journey through grief.

~ Dr. Karen Kramer

OTHER RELATIONSHIPS

"Those who loved you and were helped by you will remember you.
So carve your name on the hearts, and not on marble."

– C.H. Spurgeon

Apart from intimate relationships, our lives are woven with vast connections – friendships, family bonds, classmates, coworkers, and acquaintances – all of which ebb and flow in the course of our existence. In this section, we navigate three stories that illuminate the complexities of these varied relationships, exploring **family estrangement**, **ambivalent friendships**, and **moments of divisiveness**.

The opening narrative is a deeply personal account, an account of my brother and sister-in-law's seven-year separation from our family. The journey leads to a thoughtful exploration of the phenomenon of family estrangement, enriched by valuable research.

The second story is revealed through the lens of a client's ambivalent friendship with Cali. Within this narrative, we decipher the intricacies of uncertain relationships, and the single transformative question that discerns the nature of that relationship.

The final tale revolves around another client, facing the challenging decision of choosing between her health and witnessing the birth of her first grandchild. This story underscores the power of setting healthy boundaries while respecting the desires of others.

Each narrative is augmented by relevant research and additional insights aligned with the **Healthy GRIEF Framework**. As you explore these stories, seek resonance with your own experiences, drawing wisdom from their journeys to enrich your own path.

Family Estrangement: Coming to Peace Before Going to Pieces

Life is too short to let past resentment stand in the way of letting someone you love know you truly love them.

My brother Ed married his second wife, DC, in 1999. I flew home after spending two to three months working in Brussels, Belgium, to attend their wedding. While we were all happy for my brother, there were certain things that felt "off."

My brother had divorced his first wife a little over a year prior, after a 22-year marriage, and he quickly entered into this new relationship. As time went on, we began noticing certain aspects of DC that raised eyebrows. For instance, there was a picture in my office that included my entire family, along with my brother's first wife and her children and grandchildren. On one visit, DC remarked how she disliked the picture and didn't want it in my office. At the time, I found it odd, but in hindsight, it seemed to be a sign of things to come.

I was the youngest of three children, with Ed as my middle brother, 16 years older than me. Our close-knit family, spanning three generations on family land, made it all the more exciting for me to build my own home next to my brother's. I completed my home and moved in during April 2000.

Then came the summer of 2000.

My brother was helping my mom design the cover for her upcoming book, based on her clairvoyant experiences. DC, a devout born-again Christian known for freely sharing her strong opinions and beliefs, took it upon herself to call my mother. She told her that her book was "wrong" and referred to her as the "Devil's Spawn." My mom hung up, and DC was angered.

Later that day, my older brother Gene visited my parents on his way home from work. He called to speak with Ed, who wasn't home. DC answered and chose to tell Gene that he needed to be separated from his mother because of her "evilness." During this conversation, my dad, sensing something was amiss with Gene's conversation, turned on the phone voice recorder to capture the conversation. Unfortunately, the tape lasted only three minutes, and DC heard the "Beep, your recording has ended" message. She hung up, furious.

Soon after, Ed and DC showed up at my parents' house. While my dad, older brother, and niece were in the kitchen, DC confronted my mother in the living room with Ed standing in the corner. My mom, a foot shorter and in her mid-70s, slapped DC after being berated in her own home. They left, with Ed calling my mom later to say he wanted nothing to do with his mom.

This marked the beginning of the family rift.

In response, I defended my mom through an angry email to my brother. He fired back, and our exchange – typical of two introverts – was certainly not our finest moment. Meanwhile, I was adjusting to living next to my brother after building my home, and now they were isolating themselves from the rest of the family, except for sporadic communication with my older brother's wife, Dale.

One day, DC called me, screaming threats about running my mom over with her car if she saw her on the street. Why? She had heard from Dale that my mom had made some negative comments on her wedding ring. It was an absurd and toxic situation. Everytime I engaged in another family tension, I found my shoulders becoming more and more tight as if I was carrying the weight of the world.

On another occasion, Dale told me that DC was calling me a "spoiled brat." DC, with a view from her kitchen window to my laundry room door, saw my dad helping me set up my washer and dryer, assuming they had been paid for by my parents. In reality, I had purchased them myself, and my dad simply enjoyed helping. My response to Dale was that how DC chose to perceive me was her issue, not mine.

As I navigated these challenges, I was also pursuing my doctoral program and working on a dissertation about emotional intelligence and leadership. My studies helped me gain perspective on the family drama, and I wrote a paper titled

"Coming to Peace Before Going to Pieces." Recognizing that I had been trying to repair the relationship with my brother for years, I realized I needed to stop taking action towards them and just send them love without expectations.

It also provided me with an opportunity to step into my brother's shoes. He must have been caught in an awkward position, torn between defending his wife whom he loved, married, and shared certain opinions with, and his own mother, a choice that could potentially threaten his marriage within a year of tying the knot. I also sensed that the separation must have been a source of sadness for him. We were once a tightly-knit family, and as his younger sister, I had even built my home adjacent to his. Imagining his predicament, I recognized that his behavior might have been an attempt to preserve peace within his marriage rather than harboring negativity towards his family. Despite the heated exchanges we had through email during the initial ordeal that culminated in the summer of 2000, I empathized with my brother. However, I also recognized that I needed to continue living my own life, which I did.

I married my first husband in December 2001, and my brother was noticeably absent. My first child arrived in December 2002, and once again, my brother wasn't there. In 2003, as I navigated a divorce, my brother's guidance and brotherly support were conspicuously absent, a void that he had filled in past relationships. Although he still resided next door, his presence felt remote. Every time I stepped out of my front door or visited my mailbox, their house served as a reminder.

My aunt lived at the top of the hill, just above my brother's home. She looked after my son when he was around two years old. One day, while I was pushing my son downhill in his stroller after picking him up from my aunt's, I spotted Ed and DC doing yard work in their front yard. Summoning my courage, I pulled up beside the fence so they could see their two-year-old nephew (my son). They briefly glanced in my direction and then retreated into their home. Once again, I was crushed. I felt abandoned, hurt, and infuriated. This was 2004, and four years had passed with no communication.

They weren't there to share in my triumphs either. As I graduated with my second masters degree and then my doctorate, their absence was palpable. They missed celebrating my son's birthdays as he turned three and four. During this period, I sought comfort in therapy to help me navigate my first divorce and manage the estrangement from my brother.

By 2007, seven years had slipped by without communication. As my soon-to-be second husband and I deliberated over who to invite to our impending wedding, I harbored a strong desire for my brother's presence. While I couldn't control his response, I couldn't let another significant life event pass without extending an invitation. So I did, and to my delight, he was the first to respond with a resounding "Yes." Our family hadn't interacted with Ed and DC for seven years, and although I was elated, uncertainty loomed.

On the morning of my wedding, a wardrobe mishap surfaced. My stepdaughter realized she had left part of her bridesmaid dress in my closet. With everyone either on-site or en route to the wedding, my brother Ed was the only potential family member still at home on our family land.

Summoning courage, I dialed my brother's number, my heart racing. As if the seven years hadn't lapsed, our conversation flowed pleasantly. I apprised him of the situation, directed him on accessing my home, and locating the item. I don't think I breathed again until I hung up the phone.

That day marked my reunion with my brother. It was a day when our family was whole again, Ed and DC attending the wedding.

Yet, the underlying tension persisted. A tension that had its origins seven years prior, but we chose to ignore. Certain subjects, such as religion and politics, were avoided to maintain family harmony. This continued after the wedding as our family worked to reunite.

DC maintained an email newsletter that regularly circulated among friends and family, featuring her political and religious opinions. Somehow, I found myself added to the mailing list. For the most part, I brushed it aside or deleted the emails. Some contained amusing cartoons or quotes. Then came a divisive political issue on the ballot. In her newsletter, DC made an offensive statement against a minority group, a comment I found deeply disturbing. I had overlooked and deleted her emails for long enough. I decided it was time to exit the list and composed a brief, polite response. I consulted my older brother Gene and Dad before sending it. The essence of my email was: "Please remove me from your newsletter list. I enjoy your humor, so you're welcome to keep me on that list. Love, Karen." Despite their strong advice against sending it to prevent family strife, I went ahead. Their caution irked me, as it felt like my voice was being stifled for the sake of overall peace. So I hit send.

As anticipated, DC was offended and chose to launch a personal attack on my character, veering far from the topic of her newsletter. Fortunately, I was in a better emotional state, allowing her insults to slide off me. In the end, she removed me from her mailing list.

For years, we trod carefully around DC, meticulously avoiding touchy subjects that might cause another family rift. In retrospect, it was an unhealthy environment. Even my children didn't want to be around her.

In July 2012, my father passed away. Ed's first wife, Sherry, provided immense support to our family, including her son (my nephew), who lived next door to my parents. When it came time to decide who to invite to my father's celebration of life, we knew DC strongly opposed Sherry's presence. I engaged in discussions with my older brother and mother, leading to a unanimous decision: "Anyone who wishes to honor Dad is welcome." This unequivocally included Sherry. As the event's coordinator, Ed tried to persuade me to exclude Sherry and his two step-sons. I stood my ground, repeating the statement I had crafted earlier, "Anyone who wants to honor Dad is welcome."

Then came the day, a month after my father's passing, when my 18-year-old cat passed away. Grieving my cat's loss and mourning my father's demise (as described more in the chapter "My Father's Passing"), I called my mom to share the news about my cat. Before I could, she informed me that Ed had approached her, objecting to my decision to invite his ex-wife to the celebration of life.

Consequently, both my older brother and mother had decided to rescind Sherry and my nephew's invitations, honoring Ed's wishes. I erupted in anger. I yelled, screamed, cursed, hung up on them all – my mom, both brothers, DC – observed by my then-husband and my three youngest children. It was far from my finest moment.

Upon reflection, I attributed my outburst not just to my grief but also to years of built-up anger and resentment towards Ed and DC. These feelings were rooted in the 12 years that preceded it – all the unresolved pain and anger stemming from the events since 2000, the bitterness of my silenced voice, all in the name of "preserving family peace." All of it erupted on that single day.

To honor my father's memory, we eventually smoothed over the situation. I don't quite recall the details, but I believe my mother played mediator. The celebration of life went well, except for an incident where DC confronted Ed's ex-wife, declaring she didn't deserve to be there. Fortunately, I wasn't present at that moment; otherwise, I might have needed bail money later.

As a family, we continued to tread carefully around one another. Then, in 2018, Ed and DC built a house in Sedona and moved away from the family property. I broke down and cried the day I saw their U-haul leave. Despite the turmoil of the previous 18 years, I mourned for the brother I used to have in my youth and more that he was no longer physically living next to me.

In 2022 my oldest brother and mother passed away within two weeks of each other (as described in the chapter "Double Death and Dementia"). In April, we organized a combined celebration of life at my home. While coordinating the event with Ed and DC, my sister-in-law Dale, and my nephew, I was resolute in my stance: "Anyone who wishes to honor Mom and Gene is welcome." I was equally clear that if anyone felt uncomfortable attending or if tensions arose, they would be excused from (or asked to leave) the event.

The day before the celebration of life, I intended to call my brother to let him know that I was inviting his ex-wife. However, before I could let him know, Ed faked a cough and claimed he was unwell, conveying their inability to attend. Initially, I was infuriated for about five minutes. My brother wasn't going to attend the celebration of life for our mother and older brother! Yet, the realization dawned on me that their absence meant we wouldn't need to walk on eggshells around them, and Ed's ex-wife, Sherry, could be present without apprehension.

In that moment, I recognized that I had been complicit in perpetuating a dynamic that prevented my mother from meeting her three great-great-grandchildren. Since Ed's divorce from his first wife, he had severed ties with that side of the family. Our family had failed to openly include them in various events in honor of my brother's wishes.

I resolved that I didn't want the younger generation to inherit the tension that had plagued our family for nearly 25 years. The burden of Ed and DC's issues was not mine to bear, and I was determined not to perpetuate it. I was committed to using all my influence to reunite the family.

Following my call with Ed, I contacted Sherry and urged her to invite her entire family. The celebration of life was a precious occasion. Regrettably, my mother and older brother never had the opportunity to meet the younger generation from that side of the family. The gathering included eight members from that side, including my mother's three great-great-grandchildren. This was the generation I wished to shield from the family turmoil.

However, one nephew chose not to attend. The past dynamics had wounded him deeply. I later conversed with him, taking full responsibility for my role in that strained relationship. I acknowledged that by not advocating for the side of the family Ed had distanced himself from, I had tacitly aligned against them. That was a mistake I was committed to rectifying.

Within a month of my mother and older brother's passings, Ed disclosed his early-onset dementia. It felt like I was losing my brother all over again. And conversely, I questioned whether I had ever truly regained him. At present, Ed and I exchange occasional texts and calls to check in on each other. We express our mutual love, a sentiment I genuinely mean. Life is too short to let past resentment stand in the way of letting someone you love know you truly love them.

Dr. Karen Kramer
San Diego, CA

The Story in Review

Estrangement, the long-term rupture of a familial relationship, is a phenomenon that affects a substantial portion of the population. Research indicates that over 27% of adults in the United States – equivalent to more than 65 million individuals – have experienced family estrangement, either as initiators or recipients.[53] It's a prevalent issue, and many of us have encountered it within our extended families or social circles, including my own, which compelled me to share my story.

My narrative, however, doesn't solely focus on my brother and sister-in-law; it explores the unique dynamics that characterize estranged families including the various roles all members played. Dr. Joshua Coleman, a renowned psychologist and best-selling author of the book *Rules of Engagement*, underscores the commonality of estrangement, especially following divorce or the introduction of a new significant other. [54]When someone dear suddenly distances themselves or severs ties, it becomes imperative to possess the tools and a playbook for outreach – knowing exactly what to say, or not say, and when to halt these efforts.

In the following sections, we'll delve into the profound importance of navigating the grief associated with family estrangement, as seen through the lens of the topics discussed in this book.

 Culture: Family estrangements often stem from a multitude of factors. In this story, the core of this rift lies in the divisiveness which began due to religious and political differences. These belief systems, meant to bring people together, have historically led to conflicts and wars.

  The **Mind** and **Toxic Positivity**: To maintain an uneasy peace in dysfunctional family dynamics, individuals often adopt beliefs, values, and attitudes steeped in toxic positivity. Unhealthy family relationships are often marred by the patterns displayed in my story: reactions to offensive comments, treading lightly around contentious subjects, wearing a façade of a fake smile during divisive conversations, and being silenced by other family members to prevent disagreements.

Body: In this story, my emotional turmoil manifested predominantly in shoulder pain – a common response to stress. If you resonate with this physical response, you may find the following questions, based on Jensen's *The Healing Questions Guide*, helpful:

Frozen Shoulders:
1. What will it take for me to ask for help instead of expecting others to show up the way I need them to?
2. What value is there in being over-responsible? What would be a healthier approach to life?
3. What baggage am I carrying that is not mine to carry? What will it take to let it go?

Shoulder Problems:
1. What will it take to tend to my responsibilities with more grace and ease?
2. What will it take to learn how to set healthy boundaries regarding my responsibilities and the responsibilities of others?
3. What will it take to start attracting the assistance I need?
4. What will it take to do what is required and fulfill all my desires?
5. What will it take to express myself wisely and freely?
6. What will it take to trust that things really are easier than they appear?

Right Shoulders Problems:
1. What situations am I being the authority over that I am really not supposed to control?
2. What will it take to meet the pressing requirements and meet my inner needs as well?
3. What will it take to return others responsibilities back to them in a kind way regardless of how they react?

Left Shoulder Problems:
1. What will it take to allow others into my world?
2. What will it take to notice those who want to help me and all the available support I am receiving from the Universe?

3. What will it take to ask for help and trust that others truly want me to succeed?

4. What will it take to stop believing I have to do it all on my own?

Shoulder Tension:

1. What benefits do I receive by *taking on too much*? What will it take for me to stop thinking this is a healthy way to cope with my life?

2. What will it take for me to allow others to help me?

3. Whose burdens am I carrying that should be borne by them or by God?

4. What will it take for me to learn how to say no when no is the right answer?

Note: References to the Universe or God are intended to be replaced with whatever form of one's word or phrase for their higher power.

Gather: This family estrangement journey comprised distinct phases such as a family rift, an episode of anger, and a decision to forgo an important family event.

Relate: Navigating this estrangement yielded a rollercoaster of emotions and thoughts. There were moments of feeling hurt, devastated, sad, and utterly lost, as if abandoned. At other times, a defensive and angry stance emerged, giving way to bitterness, frustration, and a boiling sense of resentment that eventually exploded. Amidst this tumultuous journey, there were fleeting moments of confidence, often mixed with apprehension. Joy arose at the prospect of reconnection, but it was accompanied by the lurking fear of potential consequences.

Involve: In the pursuit of resolution, several steps were taken to navigate this complex journey. These steps encompassed a commitment to pursuing understanding through education, engaging in therapeutic processes to heal and grow, and cultivating the practice of sending love without expecting a response. Additionally, efforts were made to extend invitations to reconnect with loved ones without undue pressure, all while establishing and clearly communicating personal boundaries and the associated consequences. When deemed necessary for one's well-being, adjustments were made to the amount of time spent with certain family members, ensuring a balance between self-care and familial relationships.

 Ease: Resources played a crucial role in navigating family estrangement. They included educational opportunities, therapy and counseling, and support from colleagues, friends, and family.

 Focus: The aftermath of the estrangement brought forth a fresh perspective, characterized by forgiving myself and others, setting healthy boundaries, reuniting family without placing undue expectations on family members, and expressing messages of love to my previously estranged brother.

Ambivalent Friendship: From Best Friend to Frienemy

I'm free to be me!

C ali and I have shared a bond since our adolescent years, a friendship that traces back to when we were both just eight. Our personalities diverged – I was reserved while she embraced her uniqueness. Nevertheless, our connection deepened, an unusual pairing of souls. We stood as a striking contrast, with her donning dark, somber attire that obscured half her face, while I adorned pastel hues and a perpetual smile.

From high school graduation to college adventures and diverging paths beyond, our communication endured. Standing as each other's maids of honor, we celebrated milestones and faced life's heartaches together. Our firstborns arrived in quick succession, and we lent strength to one another during the somber farewells to our parents. Amid divorces, our shared history provided an anchor. Decades manifested, rich with a collection of shared experiences, a testament to our unbreakable bond.

Then, a disconcerting shift took place in July 2020. While I traversed through work-related journeys, news of a family loss reached me. I made a brief Facebook post to share the news. Soon after, Cali texted, acknowledging the news from my online presence. Caught in the midst of travel logistics, my response was terse, unintentionally causing offense. Her swift retort caught me off guard, an accusation of hurt from something I said. There I was, struggling with family loss, stranded at the airport, now burdened with deciphering the cause of my best friend's ire.

I sifted through past messages, realizing she hadn't responded to any of my texts over the preceding four months. Our exchanges typically comprised random quotes, lighthearted images, and humorous memes, without immediate expectations of replies. We both led busy lives, but the absence of any response was an anomaly.

Recollections of events that took place during her silence resurfaced. My birthday, an event held via Zoom due to the pandemic, had united friends across the country. Cali was among them. Could her discontent have stemmed from jealousy, perhaps of my myriad friendships or travels?

Cali, a social worker, had challenged my evolving thoughts as I expanded my skills and experience in NLP. Her influence grew as my work with clients flourished. Did this evolution provoke her reaction?

As I attempted to decipher my offense, I confronted the perplexing quandary: when, where, and how had I hurt her? Although she expressed availability to console me over my family loss, I hesitated to engage until resolving our underlying issue. This dance persisted for six months, with minimal communication.

At last, a lengthy conversation surfaced, unearthing the source of her affront – an incident that happened nearly a year prior. I had complied with her request for a financial breakdown of the aid I had extended over the years. However, her displeasure stemmed from my spreadsheet detailing the transactions. Money had always been a sensitive subject for Cali, complicating even her requests for help. My intentions were to enable her gradual reimbursement, and my lack of haste was mistaken as indifference. Thus, her withdrawal began.

Christmas arrived, accompanied by a strained atmosphere that led me to propose skipping our customary gift exchange. This suggestion, however, only fueled her vexation. A pattern had emerged – each action or utterance seemed to stoke her indignation. The perplexing shift in our relationship weighed heavily on me.

In another visit, we attempted to mend our fractured relationship. Months later, I battled COVID-19, igniting heated text exchanges. My attempts to protect my health and utilize alternative treatments were met with her concern and criticism. Amid personal attacks, I invoked "I agree to disagree. I love you," before cutting off communication. Months ensued with silence.

Her final act was unfriending me on Facebook after misconstruing a post about a relationship that had nothing to do with her. The realization dawned on me – a friend of over four decades was slipping away. Looking back, I saw a longstanding pattern, with Cali often holding the dominant role. My transformation into a confident woman threatened the equilibrium.

I emerged with clarity. While I treasured our connection, I established boundaries and demanded respect. An NLP journey bolstered my self-assurance, attracting healthier relationships. The prospect of mending our friendship rests on her willingness to evolve as well. This newfound autonomy, liberated from the need to please, empowers me to authentically embrace my identity. This led me to attract new and healthier friendships. I'm free to be me!

Anonymous Client
Details changed for anonymity

The Story in Review

Before delving into the intricacies of adult relationships, it's vital to comprehend why it's crucial to recognize the type of relationship, particularly when these bonds sour.

In a revealing interview with motivational speaker Tom Bilyeu, author, teacher, mentor, and entrepreneur Vanessa Van Edwards emphasized the significance of adult relationships and acknowledged that some do lose their spark.[55] She astutely categorizes negative "friendships" into two distinct types: toxic and ambivalent.

Vanessa Van Edwards presents a straightforward yet powerful question to distinguish *ambivalent friends*: "Are you ever doubting that they are genuinely happy for you?" If the answer is "yes," it may indicate that they aren't authentically supportive of your happiness. Ambivalent relationships, as Vanessa further expounds, are characterized by uncertainty about where you stand with the other person and whether you genuinely enjoy engaging with them. These connections demand more energy and pose greater risks to our psychological well-being.

An article by organizational psychologist Adam Grant highlights that ambivalent relationships can be even more toxic than negative ones, often triggering stronger physiological responses under stress.[56] For instance, merely reminding individuals of their ambivalent relationships led to higher heart rate reactivity compared to thinking about negative relationships. Another study indicated a correlation between ambivalent relationships and increased coronary artery calcification among older married couples.

Psychologists Bert Uchino and Julianne Holt-Lunstad's research reveals that ambivalent relationships can detrimentally affect health, surpassing the negative consequences of purely toxic relationships.[57] An accumulation of ambivalent relationships has been linked to higher rates of depression, stress, and overall dissatisfaction in life.

Michelle Duffy, a researcher at the University of Minnesota, conducted a survey among police officers, shedding light on the unique challenges posed by ambivalent relationships.[58] These connections left officers in a state of perpetual uncertainty, requiring constant vigilance and mental effort. Unlike toxic relationships that are often easier to identify and sever, ambivalent ones lead us to second-guess, worry, and struggle with boundaries, draining our emotional energies. Furthermore, individuals with a higher number of ambivalent relationships experienced elevated heart rates.

Let's apply these insights to the case of my client's relationship with Cali, which unmistakably falls into the ambivalent category.

Culture: One cultural element that strained their relationship revolved around differing opinions on COVID-19 vaccines and medications – an issue that became highly divisive in the United States at the time.

Mind: My client's experiences with Cali closely mirrored findings in studies on ambivalent relationships which included feeling persistently judged, regardless of her actions.

Body: While my client did not explicitly mention physical manifestations of her interactions with Cali, previous research indicated that ambivalent relationships can lead to an increased heart rate and heart artery calcification. To address this, let's explore questions from Jensen's *The Healing Questions Guide* on "Hardening of Arteries":

1. What will it take for me to loosen up and soften my approach to life?
2. What value have I created in seeing life in such a gloomy, negative way? What would be a healthier and happier approach to things?
3. What will it take to reclaim my ability to feel and express love?
4. What do I feel so threatened by?
5. Who do I need to forgive for the pain and suffering they have caused me?
6. What will it take to be released from all the injustice I feel that has been placed upon me?
7. What will it take for me to feel more secure about money?
8. What do I need to do to increase my understanding of the laws of the Universe?

Gather: The initial shift in the relationship occurred when Cali expressed offense about something my client did, leading to a breakdown in communication. Following incidents formed a repetitive cycle of disconnection and reconnection.

Relate: Although there were a number of emotions present throughout her journey, my client only shared some of her emotions during this cycle which included shocked, stunned, and hurt. Since she was already going through emotional release work with me, she more easily cycled through some of the other emotions (such as anger) so it wasn't as present in her story.

 Involve: My client consciously opted not to engage in unnecessary worrying about Cali's unfounded offense, which became a significant positive step.

 Ease: The primary resource supporting my client was her work with me as her NLP Breakthrough practitioner, focusing on the release of triggers and limiting beliefs tied to her relationship with Cali including releasing the need to be a people pleaser.

 Focus: In her "new normal," my client was committed to establishing and maintaining healthy boundaries by articulating her expectations to Cali in a kind and honest manner, asserting her need for respectful treatment.

Divisiveness: Happiness, Health, and Grandchildren

I was grieving the loss of what was to come.

It's not often that my daughter Molly makes impromptu visits, but on this particular evening, both she and my son-in-law Stephen dropped by unexpectedly. I had a feeling something was afoot, and my intuition proved correct.

Sure enough, Molly leaned in and shared, "Hey, we forgot to give you your Mother's Day present last month." It was a grandma mug. I was going to be a grandma for the first time! I was overjoyed!

Promptly after, my daughter added, "Everybody needs to be boosted and vaccinated at least two weeks before the baby is born."

Though it was already 2022, the specter of COVID-19 vaccines still lingered. The pervasive notion that vaccination was the only way forward persisted. My decision not to be vaccinated was no secret, but I never imposed my perspective on others. My health was my priority, and the impending birth of my first grandchild compelled a weighty choice – whether I'd be present to welcome him into the world.

Undeniably, my well-being was crucial, and I chose to stand firm in my decision. Regrettably, this choice meant I wouldn't be able to hold my grandchild. A friend had undergone a similar ordeal, being deprived of her grandchild's presence for a year.

I harbored no resentment toward Molly's wishes. Indeed, had I been in her shoes, adhering to mainstream vaccine information, I'd have likely made the same call. My choice, however, seemed to cast a shadow over her baby's health.

With uncertainty prevailing, I threw a baby shower, compartmentalizing my mixed emotions as friends and family rejoiced. Amidst congratulations, I watched my daughter's radiant pregnancy glow, all while confronted with the knowledge that I wouldn't hold my grandchild.

The day after the celebration, I wrestled with grief. For hours, I remained in a profound melancholy, unable to rouse myself from bed or nourish my body. My decision was unwavering, but I mourned the loss of expectations. The day I'd envisioned – holding my grandchild upon his arrival – had slipped away. And the timeline of our reunion remained uncertain.

A friend suggested I'd grow angry, but anger seemed misplaced. Angry at whom? For making a choice concerning my health? Angry at her decision for her child's well-being? It wasn't about anger; it was about battling with the sadness stemming from my choice and the loss of an expectation I once had to be there when my grandchild was born.

Yet, I failed to share my turmoil with my friend, masking my emotions due to the fear of judgment. This suppression was toxic positivity in disguise, as I failed to communicate my need for acceptance without solutions.

Two weeks prior to the baby's due date, Molly's text about vaccinations arrived. It was an opportunity to articulate my stance:

"I honor and respect your wishes while also honoring my own health choices. I also continue to stand by you setting and holding the boundaries you feel are most important to safely protect the baby. Therefore, I look forward to a future opportunity when I may get to see and hold the baby knowing that it will not be soon after he is born. I look forward to pictures, videos, and even FaceTime (when possible) to watch him grow up. Although I dearly look forward to the time I can meet him in person, I am at peace with the decision. I love you, Stephen, and the baby very much, and look forward to virtually celebrating his arrival. Love, Mom. P.S. This is not intended to influence your decision. I honor you and the decision. This is only intended to let you know my choice."

With no response expected or received, time rolled on. On the day Molly was hospitalized, I was left out of the loop, further intensifying my marginalization as an estranged parent. When I discovered the birth through another relative, emotions ran high. Hurt, sadness, and jealousy intermingled. I knew my decision was right for me, yet the special day was bittersweet.

I clung to the notion that a year would pass before I saw my grandson, but Molly had not communicated her intentions. She reached out one day, her request for information leading to a surprise visit on my birthday. Tears of joy flowed as I cradled my grandson for the first time. He was almost three months old. It was an unparalleled gift, a moment to treasure.

Luckily, my interactions with my grandson increased. COVID-19 and vaccines remained unspoken. Not all stories conclude as mine did, and I'm grateful for the path my journey took. My steadfast decision, Molly's understanding, and the eventual reunion enriched our bond. I cherished my autonomy and counted myself fortunate that we navigated this chapter with respect and love.

Joyce*, Anonymous Client
Details changed for anonymity

The Story in Review

To fully grasp the importance of navigating grief in the context of divisive relationships, let's begin by summarizing the work done on setting healthy boundaries, which is crucial when relationships become challenging.

From social unrest, political divide, and conflicts over COVID care, setting and maintaining healthy limits with others has been a hot topic in 2020 onward. During this time, I did a number of speaking presentations and interviews on tips to navigate healthy boundaries with friends, families, and others.

Boundaries are the limits we create to maintain autonomy and dignity in our relationships. It helps to create the emotional safety that allows us to feel relaxed and trusting in our closest relationships. For any healthy relationships to survive, both parties need to establish, maintain, and respect boundaries.

Here is an overview of six quick tips on how to establish, maintain, and respect boundaries.

1. *Clarify Wants*: Identify what you do want by finishing the phrase, "I have the right to ..." An example may be " ... to say no."

2. *Remove Roadblocks*: Explore what may prevent you from getting what you want including potential limiting beliefs such as "I'm not enough."

3. *Tune your GPS*: Get clear on your relationship "Dream Makers" and "Deal Breakers."

4. *Prepare for the Conversation*: Tips encompass timing the conversation, maintaining a calm and respectful tone, employing "I" statements, providing specific details, and focusing on the future.

5. *Consequences and Coping*: You will be tested. Identify and articulate the consequences, and arm yourself with coping strategies when you employ the consequences.

6. *Follow Through*: Stand firm with your agreements.

These healthy boundary tips are those I shared with my client to help her through her situation with her daughter Molly. Refer to Part IV resources to obtain the full tips to navigating setting healthy boundaries. With that, let's review her story.

Culture: My client's experience is influenced by prevailing cultural and societal beliefs regarding COVID-19 and vaccines. She aptly describes the prevailing sentiment as follows: "If you didn't get a vaccine, you were evil, you were wrong. Vaccines were the way to go."

 Toxic Positivity: In coping with these cultural pressures, my client encountered toxic positivity in two distinct ways:

During the baby shower, she adeptly compartmentalized her mixed emotions while receiving congratulations on becoming a new grandmother. This strategy served her well in the moment, allowing her to maintain composure.

The day after the baby shower, when her friend was present, she concealed her true emotions for fear of judgment or unsolicited attempts at "fixing" her, rather than allowing herself to be heard and understood.

 Mind: The pivotal moment in her story was marked by a significant decision: choosing not to get vaccinated. This decision involved a thorough consideration of consequences, including the belief that she may not have the opportunity to see her grandson for at least a year.

 Gather: The most prominent shifts in her narrative revolved around the day she received the news of becoming a grandmother, juxtaposed with the requirement of getting the COVID vaccine to see her grandchild.

 Relate: Throughout this journey, my client experienced a range of emotions and thoughts, including mixed excitement about being a grandmother with sadness about her trade-off, deep depression and sadness, feeling marginalized and jealous, and finally thrilled with "happy tears."

Involve: My client proactively addressed this challenging situation through a series of strategic actions. She made a heartfelt decision that resonated with her values, even though it brought about some sadness. She effectively communicated this decision to her daughter and continued to stay actively engaged throughout the pregnancy, including hosting a baby shower. To maintain her connection and involvement in her grandson's life, she consistently requested pictures and videos, ensuring a meaningful connection despite the circumstances.

 Ease: Throughout this challenging process, my client found valuable support through her work with me as her NLP Breakthrough practitioner. This assistance facilitated the rapid release of triggers and negative emotions tied to her decision.

 Focus: As of the latest update, my client is thrilled to have the opportunity to see and hold her new grandson having only waited four months before her daughter extended her the opportunity. Her patience paid off.

In Summary

"Don't let the behavior of others destroy your inner peace."

– Dalai Lama

What's your story? What type of relationships do you have with your immediate and extended family members? Are there any that are unhealthy or estranged? What role do you play? Does that role help or hinder the ultimate goal of the relationship? Do you have any toxic or ambivalent friendships? What makes it so? Are there any decisions you are making in your life to "keep the peace" with others? What will happen in a year, five, or 10 if you do nothing to change those relationships?

In this section, we explored three distinct stories, each addressing various aspects of relationships. These narratives revolve around **family estrangement**, **ambivalent friendships**, and **divisiveness**. Each was further reviewed with statistics, research, and/or steps to better understand and process through these relationships challenges.

 Culture: It's imperative to recognize how culture can significantly influence our relationships. For example, in two of the stories within this section, the central conflicts revolve around differing viewpoints concerning COVID-19, vaccines, and health. These cultural disparities can either bolster or hinder the connections we share with others.

 Mind: In the stories presented here, a prevalent theme emerged – individuals feeling judged for their choices, whether they align with societal expectations or not.

 Body: Undoubtedly, unresolved grief can manifest in physical discomfort, leading to additional complications. This theme came to the forefront in two particular stories, shedding light on the adverse effects of shoulder tension and hardening of the heart arteries.

As we navigate these intricate stories, it became evident that the **Healthy GRIEF Framework** manifests uniquely in each case. Here's a concise overview:

 Gather: This phase encompassed various scenarios, such as an incident prompting one or both parties to alter their behavior or make decisions, action taken by one party (such as not attending an event, blocking communication, or unfriending on social media), or firmly upholding a decision (even when it's known that the other party may not approve).

 Relate: The emotions encompassing the spectrum of feelings similar to those associated with SARAH. However, these stories also included holding mixed feelings at the same time – thrilled and scared, happy yet apprehensive, and excitement and jealousy, as examples.

 Involve: The stories presented here also highlight several constructive action steps taken by individuals challenged with complex relationships, including making decisions or setting boundaries in alignment with personal well-being, minimizing unhealthy interactions, and extending invitations rooted in love without expectations of reciprocity.

 Ease: Individuals found support and assistance from various sources, such as education, colleagues, family, friends, and therapy. Another powerful resource was working with an NLP Breakthrough practitioner to help quickly release the triggers, limiting beliefs, or rising negative emotions associated with the other party.

 Focus: The "new normal" that emerged from these experiences included forgiving oneself and others, respecting each other's decisions, extending love and fostering openness, maintaining healthy boundaries, and living life autonomously.

As you explore these stories, may you discover parallels in your own journey and glean valuable insights to enhance your personal growth and relationships. Take note of these lessons and integrate them into your own narrative.

Healthfully grieving when who you were is no longer.

IDENTITY

*V*arious life transitions can trigger feelings of loss, where individuals may find themselves struggling with a sense of identity they once held or experiencing a profound sense of emptiness and purposelessness while striving to forge a new identity. It's crucial to emphasize that the theme of "loss of self" or identity is central to this book, as it can potentially lead to significant health issues.

Dr. Gabor Maté, physician and author of *The Myth of Normal: Trauma, Healing, and Illness in a Toxic Culture*, (Yes, his subtitle did influence the title of the book you are reading now.), in an interview with podcaster Rich Roll, talks about a phenomenon that is gaining more attention through research and slowly finding its way into the mainstream medical industry.[59] Here's an excerpt from the interview that truly caught my attention.

There's a rise in autoimmune disease. Autoimmune diseases are conditions where the immune system turns against itself. It starts destroying the immune system, which is meant to protect us, [and instead] turns against the system and starts destroying our bodies. Examples are rheumatoid arthritis, scleroderma, lupus, chronic fatigue, multiple sclerosis, Crohn's disease, ulcerative colitis, chronic psoriasis, autoimmune eczema, and one could go on.

This is rising in our society. And not only is it rising in our society, as the globalized economic system takes over more of the world, it's rising internationally. And it's rising particularly amongst women.

When I looked at the people who develop autoimmune disease, it's always related to stress and, particularly, people's coping styles. So people with autoimmune disease typically repress their emotions. They don't know how to be in contact with their healthy anger. They tend to suppress their real selves to fit in with society and with their families. And essentially, when people don't experience their healthy anger, the anger doesn't go away; it gets suppressed, and turns against themselves.

Our emotional apparatus is very much connected to our immune system. In fact, they're part and parcel of the same system. When our emotions turn against us, our immune system can turn against us as well.

In this society, because so many people are not allowed to be themselves, they have to kind of suppress who they are in order to survive and fit in, we're getting more and more autoimmune diseases.

This is not just a theory. More and more research is growing to back this up. Psychiatrist, and trauma researcher, Dr. Bessel van der Kolk supports Dr. Maté's findings in his own book *The Body Keeps the Score: Brain, Mind, and Body in the Healing of Trauma.*

And, in case I haven't grabbed your attention yet, check this out! A comprehensive 30-year study involving over one million individuals has unveiled a robust correlation between individuals suffering from stress disorders, such as PTSD, and a heightened susceptibility to developing autoimmune conditions, including arthritis and Crohn's disease.[60] While the connection between severe life stress and autoimmune diseases may seem intuitive, scientific exploration into the direct link between stress-related psychiatric conditions and specific immune-related ailments has been limited. The extensive observational study tracked one million participants in Sweden, with over 100,000 diagnosed with stress-related disorders, matching them with an equal number of unaffected subjects. The findings revealed that those with diagnosed stress-related disorders were 30 to 40 percent more likely to develop one of 41 different autoimmune diseases, such as rheumatoid arthritis and psoriasis, underscoring the impact of stress on immune function and marking a significant milestone in research on this association.

Grieving healthfully is not just a "nice thing to do;" it can help you live!

Brené Brown writes, "To form meaningful connections with others, we must first connect with ourselves."[61] Connecting to ourselves starts with grounding ourselves in who we are. With that, let's jump into the stories …

The first story is my personal journey from stepping out of the corporate world and into entrepreneurship. This came with my challenges in identifying who I was again.

Mike's cliffhanger of a story comes next about the drudgery of working a superhero job. His wake up call came at a painful price yet one which allowed him to create a life by his design.

The third is Jan's story of stepping out of the structure of the corporate world and onto the "freedom" of retirement. She walks you through her journey to finding who she really is.

Chad leads the fourth story with his proud narrative of childhood trauma and hard life experiences leading him to question who he really was. Backed by facts that plagued his early years, Chad's story is an inspiration.

Fifth is Dr. Z's story of her descriptive journey into menopause and middle-age. Hear her shed light on and disrupt the stories culture places on women.

Michelle's story rounds out this section with her narrative about her father. Who is she as the roles she once held to be true reversed?

Let's dive into some rich learnings...

Corporate Gal to Entrepreneur: Harmonizing the Freedom and Flexibility to Be Me

Focus on what you do want, not on what you don't.

W hen I started college, I wasn't entirely sure about my path. My dad's advice was clear, though: "No matter what you want to do, get a degree in business. It will take you anywhere." And so, that's exactly what I pursued.

I didn't limit myself to just business, though. Intrigued by the interplay between people and systems, I explored other potential minors like child development, sociology, psychology, and human resources. Anything that could help me understand, what I still refer to today as, "people within systems, and systems within people." This desire for understanding led to a slightly longer college journey at San Diego State University than anticipated.

The day after I graduated, I began my first full-time job at the Center for Creative Leadership (CCL). This non-profit educational institution aimed to advance leadership understanding, practice, and development for the greater good. My initial role was behind the scenes as a Program Coordinator. Yet, my aspiration was to facilitate leadership programs in the classroom. Thankfully, I had mentors who believed in me and presented opportunities to excel.

With their support, I progressed to management roles and eventually became a Program Manager for CCL's flagship Leadership Development Program. My role included overseeing leadership training facilitators, facilitating in the classroom, leading small groups, conducting one-on-one executive coaching, and designing custom leadership programs worldwide. I enjoyed traveling and facilitating programs in places like Belgium, Spain, Singapore, and Japan. I collaborated with organizations like United Way, Boeing, Nike, Google, and American Express.

In 2007, I remarried and became a mom and stepmom to five kids, spanning preschool to college. Balancing family and work became more complex as my husband wasn't keen on my extensive travel due to our younger kids' needs.

The economic downturn in 2008 impacted CCL, prompting me to reapply for my program management role I had had for 10 years. And at that time, I did what I thought I should be doing and continued to climb the corporate ladder. I threw my hat in the ring again for a modified version of the position I'd had for 10 years. And then, after talking with my husband, I realized that the additional responsibilities of the position were not conducive for our current lifestyle. He didn't like me traveling to begin with, and this position was going to ask me to do more of it. So I declined reapplying.

Later, I came to realize that my true passion lay in managing people, projects, and programs – all of which were notably absent from my current role. This realization left me feeling like I had lost touch with my identity. Letting go of the role I had once been so proud of, a role I had diligently climbed the metaphorical ladder of success to achieve, left me wrestling with an existential question: "Who am I now?" I found myself in the process of redefining my place within the organization.

In the spring of 2009, the economic repercussions of the 2008 downturn prompted CCL to implement both voluntary and involuntary layoffs. The organization extended severance packages and offered employees the option to reduce their work hours. Given that I no longer held a prominent "role of importance," a gnawing fear that I might be let go from the organization took root within me. To proactively address this, I opted for a reduction in my work hours, accepting a 60% schedule. While this choice meant earning less, it also meant that I could retain my position and continue contributing to the organization.

During this transitional period, I was on a quest to redefine my role within the organization. A term I picked up from one of my colleagues in North Carolina resonated with me – I felt like a "JDT," or "Just a Damn Trainer."

The reduced workload presented me with an unforeseen opportunity to spend more time at home with my children. As both a mother and stepmother to five kids, spanning an age range of four-to 21-years-old, I observed the parallels between leadership in the corporate world and leadership in the realm of family dynamics. This period of increased presence allowed me to connect with my own children and their friends, witnessing how they navigated the challenges life threw their way. It was a valuable vantage point from which to reflect on the intersections between executive leadership and the intricate dance of parenting.

In July 2009, I found myself presented with the rewarding opportunity to facilitate CCL's Young Women's Leadership Program, tailored for girls entering their junior and senior years of high school. As the five-day program drew to a close, a profound and visceral experience moved me to tears. It was in that moment that I made a resolute decision – this was my calling. I wanted to be a guiding force in the success of our youth.

Just two weeks later, I eagerly enrolled in a certification program offered by Teen Wisdom Inc., embarking on a journey to become a certified teen girl life coach. Within a mere five months, I had established and launched my private practice. My original intention had been to operate my practice during the 40% of my time that was not allocated to CCL. However, the fervor and dedication with which I approached this new chapter, CCL was demanding 80-90% of time even though I was only compensated for 60%. This unbalanced equation left me battling with a mounting sense of stress and frustration.

One morning, as dawn's light crept in, I awoke with an epiphany – I had dreamt of composing a letter of resignation addressed to the organization that had been my professional home for nearly 17 years. The realization struck me profoundly. Sharing this revelation with my husband, his response encapsulated the truth I had been avoiding: "It's about time! You've been unhappy for a year." My nocturnal vision had been stirred by my bedtime reading – a passage from a book titled *Ladies Who Launch*.[62] Its wisdom reverberated through my thoughts: "Focus on what you do want, not on what you don't." The truth was evident – my discontent had grown from the incongruity between my quest to rediscover my identity within the organizational framework, my endeavors to build my private practice, and the inadequacy of my compensation for the reduced time I was devoting to the cause.

And so, after dedicating nearly 17 years to CCL, I took the bold step of submitting my letter of resignation. Although I continued my association with CCL as adjunct staff for another 13 years, facilitating leadership programs, this transition afforded me the liberating freedom to cultivate my private practice. In less than a year, my reputation grew, establishing me as the premier life coach for both teenage and young adult individuals, regardless of gender, in San Diego.

Yet, as I ventured beyond the corporate realm, a new chapter in my life presented an array of challenges. As I embarked on this transformative journey, I found myself challenged with questions of identity and purpose. The feeling of being adrift resurfaced – who was I now that the mantle of "Program Manager" no longer defined me? This period also prompted introspection on my role as a "stay-at-home mom." What kind of mother was I becoming? Did this new path align with my true self? As I pursued the final stages of my certification for my private practice, I was also left pondering how to categorize my evolving professional identity. These contemplations underscored my quest for self-discovery.

Despite the birth of my private practice, I found myself with pockets of time that needed filling while I nurtured my growing business. The landscape of parenting experienced a notable shift for me, my children, and my husband. Our youngest trio remained at home, ushering me into roles I had never anticipated – chauffeur for school and sports, grocery shopper, chef, tutor, and so much more. My life pivoted toward ensuring my children adhered to schedules and met responsibilities, creating an intricate framework of obligations. Having leaped directly from college into the corporate sphere and only becoming a mother at 33, I had long considered myself part of the corporate world. This new chapter, however rewarding, posed questions about maintaining my intellectual stimulation beyond my home and family.

I also recognized a sense of isolation stemming from the absence of the vibrant social connections I had fostered in my corporate career. While the newfound autonomy of working independently had its perks, I also acknowledged the need to proactively build a structured schedule. However, this choice inadvertently distanced me from the camaraderie and connection that a traditional workplace offers, leaving me coping with feelings of loneliness and frustration.

To bridge this gap and satiate my desire for external stimulation, I immersed myself in my children's school and sporting events. Donning the mantle of Room

Mom, I assumed responsibilities on the school's PTA Board and embraced various roles that beckoned. I found myself assisting in one son's drama class and taking on the mantle of a team mom for another son's water polo team. Through these engagements, I finally began to taste the social connection I had been missing. While I invested my organizational and leadership skills in these voluntary roles, they also served as a means of fortifying my sense of purpose in my newfound identity as a "stay-at-home mom."

Balancing my roles as a mother, entrepreneur, volunteer, and wife proved to be another intricate challenge I encountered. For instance, in my role as a coach for teenagers and young adults, the optimal times for sessions often clashed with my responsibilities as a mom – the afternoons, evenings, and weekends. This dichotomy led to considerable tension, exacerbated by my husband's expectations for my availability during non-working hours. He, like me, believed that leaving my corporate job would grant me more leisure time at home. Yet, in reality, my commitments had increased, not diminished. In response, we devised a structured schedule, dedicating specific time slots – such as Wednesday nights and weekdays until 5 pm – to work, aiming to achieve the elusive equilibrium between my professional and personal life. This scheduling strategy, now known as my Ideal Schedule, has since become a cornerstone of my coaching practice. In shaping this approach, I drew inspiration from Randi Zuckerberg's book, *Pick Three*, which advocates for prioritizing three essential aspects of life and focusing your energy on them.[63] As Oprah wisely put it, "You can have it all, you just can't have it all at once."

Another formidable obstacle I confronted was the intricacies of marketing. Having never viewed myself as a marketer – a role the corporate environment had always provided – I struggled with a sharp decline in self-assurance. The challenge lay in articulating who I was and what I offered. I leaned on a business support group and immersed myself in two business networking groups to navigate this unfamiliar territory. Despite my husband serving as our primary financial provider, I placed immense pressure on myself to not only establish a viable business but also ensure its profitability. Fortunately, my husband's unwavering support and reminder that building a business demanded investment of both time and money were crucial in bolstering my confidence to embark on this venture.

A pivotal point in my transformation involved reconciling my identity as a teen life coach with my role as a parent. Struggling as a parent, much like any other, I was learning on the fly, managing my skills and abilities while stumbling along the way. Embracing my vulnerability, I harnessed it as a tool to convey to other parents that perfection was not my prerogative. Instead, I learned invaluable lessons from fellow parents, clients, and most importantly, my own children. My journey epitomized the idea that perfection was an unattainable ideal. Amidst this realization, I gained profound insights into the pitfalls of striving for perfection during this period.

Through this transformative process, I encountered numerous instances of feeling lost, besieged by pressure, and overwhelmed with frustration. The compulsion to "know it all" and "do it all" weighed heavily on me, magnifying the sense of disconnect I felt from my husband who failed to understand me. Nights spent shedding tears in the solitude of my bathroom or beneath the covers became a frequent occurrence.

Simultaneously, my body began to express the stress of this transition. Persistent aches, including lower back issues and tension radiating through my shoulders, emerged. In response, I found myself resorting to regular use of flexeril – an average of two half-pills weekly – often relying on it to facilitate sleep. A decade later, through the transformative power of NLP (Neuro Linguistics Programming) work, I was able to release the burdens that had accumulated during that period, including the notion that I needed to bear all responsibilities single-handedly. It wasn't until two years later that I realized I had consumed a mere one-and-a-half pills from a full bottle of flexeril over that two year span.

Emerging from these trials, a new equilibrium became my "new normal." The task of harmonizing flexibility, freedom, and balance across my private practice, motherhood, and wifely duties came to define this phase of my life. A stark contrast to the rigid 9-to-5 structures of my corporate job, my newfound identity encapsulated these diverse facets. With unwavering determination, I succeeded, culminating in the opening of The VillaVision Wellness and Retreat Center – a testament to my resilience and the journey I had undertaken.

Dr. Karen Kramer
San Diego, CA

The Story in Review

Let's review why navigating grief in a healthy manner was paramount in this narrative.

Culture: Cultural and societal beliefs surrounding identity significantly influence our choices. In my case, it entailed reconciling what it meant to excel as both a dedicated stay-at-home wife and a driven entrepreneur.

Toxic Positivity: Within this narrative, there were moments of toxic positivity. One facet manifested when I imposed unrealistic expectations on myself, striving to "know it all," "do it all," and maintain a facade of perfection. During these periods, I concealed my genuine vulnerabilities, thwarting opportunities to seek the help and support I deeply needed. Another instance occurred when I felt misunderstood by my husband, leading to countless nights spent in solitude, tears staining bathroom tiles or lulling me into restless sleep.

Mind: Initially, this story was shackled by limiting beliefs that hindered the healing process, particularly the notion that I must perpetually "know it all," "do it all," and embody unwavering perfection.

Body: Throughout the narrative, I alluded to moments when my lower back ached or when I described my shoulders resembling earrings. (See the Story in Review the chapter "Family Estrangement" for questions regarding shoulders.) To address these physical manifestations, I turn to Jensen's *The Healing Questions Guide*, presenting a series of questions associated with lower back issues:

Backache:
1. What value is there and blaming others for the lack of emotional support I feel I did not or am not receiving? What would be a healthier and more empowering outlook?
2. What will it take for me to receive emotional support I seek from within, rather than seeking it from others?

3. What will it take for me to delegate some of the responsibilities I am currently weighed down with?

4. What will it take to convince me that I am capable to handle what is being expected of me?

5. What is it I want to escape from? What is a better option?

6. What will it take to get the rest and relaxation I need so I can continue with what needs to be done?

7. What sexual emotions are coming up for me that need my attention? What will it take to attend to my sexual needs in a productive and healthy way?

Back Problems:

1. What value is there in believing I am alone or separate from those I love or from God? What will it take to feel more connected?

2. How would my life be different if I could trust I was supported by God? what will it take for me to get in alignment with God so I can receive the divine support I crave?

3. What am I afraid of losing? Is it true?

4. What value is there in believing I need to do everything on my own? What would be a healthier and more interdependent outlook?

5. What support is available to me that I am resisting or denying because I believe I have to do it all on my own?

6. What will it take to convince me that I no longer need to protect my heart?

7. Who was pressuring me? what will it take to address the pressure honestly and productively?

8. What am I hiding behind my back in fear of being exposed? what will it take to be more honest with myself and others?

9. What am I trying to get rid of?

10. What value was there and believing I do not deserve support or that no one will support me?

11. What will it take for me to learn how to effectively manage my emotions?

12. What value is there in attempting to control or dominate over others?

13. What value is there in being over-dependent on others?

14. What will it take to convince me that I am capable?

Lower Back Problems:

1. What is out of balance in my life? What will it take to bring it back into balance?
2. What support am I afraid I am not receiving or will not receive?
3. What is interfering with my ability to experience more harmony in my life?
4. What will it take for me to tap into a more abundant and hopeful outlook?
5. What will it take for me to align with what is required to receive divine support?
6. What can I do right now to nurture myself?
7. What will it take to receive the financial support I need right now?
8. What will it take to have the courage and wisdom I need to overcome the obstacles I am facing?
9. What value is there in fearing success? What will it take to overcome the fear and step out of my own way?
10. What do I need to connect to that I am currently disconnected from?
11. What will it take to release some of the aggression I am feeling right not regarding my present responsibilities?
12. What sexual guilt needs to be healed?
13. What will it take to come into complete harmony with my sexuality?
14. What value is there in beating myself up? What will it take to address myself with more loving kindness?

 Gather: Although the story has various phases, the pivotal shift lies in my transition from corporate employment to establishing my home-based business.

 Relate: Throughout this journey, a myriad of emotions and thoughts coursed through me, including fear and a noticeable drop in confidence. I struggled with feelings of unhappiness, loss, and loneliness, and the weight of stress and frustration often left me challenged to find my footing. Eventually, I harnessed my vulnerability as a means to connect with other parents who, like me, faced imperfections in their journey.

Involve: To facilitate this significant transition, I took concrete action steps that included immersing myself in relevant literature such as *Ladies Who Launch* and *Pick Three*. I also engaged actively in my children's school and extracurricular activities, fostering a social network, a renewed sense of purpose, and quality time with my kids. Crafting an ideal schedule became instrumental in supporting the mounting demands of my new venture. (See Part IV for your free download.)

 Ease: Various resources bolstered my transition, notably my husband's unwavering encouragement and support. Joining a business support group and networking within entrepreneurial circles proved invaluable. Simultaneously, I maintained connections with my corporate relationships while cultivating new friendships with parents from my children's social circle. Furthermore, my involvement in the NLP community provided a nurturing space.

 Focus: The "new normal" I forged embraced flexibility, freedom, and balance, skillfully harmonizing my private practice, my roles as a mother and wife, and carving out precious moments for self-care.

Career-Life Transition: Leaping from Sky to Soil and the Life That Followed

This was my all-in moment, my chips pushed to the center of the table. The stakes couldn't have been higher, and I was the sole player in this game.

*Y*ou know how in superhero movies, the hero zips across the sky, fearlessly facing danger? That was my day job. Seriously, as a helicopter paramedic, it was like I got to live out a blockbuster movie script daily. I'd soar through the air, swoop down, save somebody's life, strike a pose, and fly away. Slipping into that uniform, I felt like I was donning a cape. For a moment there, I was invincible.

But hey, even superheroes have an Achilles' heel. Mine wasn't a villain with a sinister plot; it was the gnawing reality of lives I couldn't save. Picture this: you rush to a car wreck only to find out you're too late to save a kid. Or you enter the bedroom of a four-month-old infant who is "vital signs absent" from Sudden Infant Death Syndrome.

Then there was the stark reality of encountering the devastating effects of societal challenges – homeless psychosis, drug overdoses, rape, and other forms of violence. Those experiences weren't just chapters in my job description; they were burdens I carried in my psyche long after the calls ended.

And it wasn't just the high-stakes rescues that weighed on me. As a base supervisor, I got tangled in this web of endless paperwork and office politics. Trust me, managing a team of ego-driven medics is way more difficult than managing a multi-car pileup, and a lot less fun! It felt like I was caught in a never-ending cycle, oscillating between the high-stakes excitement of rescue missions and the soul-crushing drudgery of managerial tasks that few other medics ever have to deal with.

To shake off the cobwebs, I had a little escape hatch – a side hustle. Outdoor experiential team building and adventure race training. When I wasn't leaping out of helicopters, I was scaling rocks and guiding folks through the wild. It was my version of taking a breather, a slice of normal in a life full of extremes.

So there I was, one seemingly routine Saturday morning, setting up a rappelling exercise for an adventure racing client. The sky was a spotless blue, the air was invigorating, and my trusty border collie Fred accompanied me. It felt like another good day in a life built on taking risks to help others.

But then, in the blink of an eye, my reality shifted. I found myself with my foot wedged between two rocks, my balance lost, and an unavoidable headfirst fall from atop a 35-foot cliff. The distant whirring of helicopter blades seemed to echo in my ears, a stark reminder of the life-and-death scenarios I had faced in the skies.

In that critical moment, a tidal wave of adrenaline washed over me. Though my career had prepared me for all kinds of emergencies, this was different. For the first time, I was the one in peril. There was no room for error; no time for doubt.

Instincts kicked in. I jumped from the cliff to avoid a much harsher fall. Not just dodging physical harm but leaping toward a future that, despite its complexities and emotional weight, I wasn't ready to give up on.

The landing? Let's just say I wouldn't recommend it. I felt the jarring crunch before the pain even registered – radius, tibia, L4 vertebrae, all busted. Then, lights out. When I came to, it was Fred's worried eyes and wet tongue that pulled me back into consciousness.

When I finally snapped back to reality, Fred's eyes were locked onto mine, almost as if he were asking, "You good?" But I was far from good. I was smack in the middle of nowhere with bones in pieces. And here's the kicker: no one would even start wondering where I was for hours. It was a harsh dilemma: stay put and risk... well, who knows what, or summon every last bit of grit to make it back home.

I chose grit. I'm talking about teeth-gritting, jaw-clenching determination. Step by agonizing step, I limped back to my cottage. Fred was my four-legged cheerleader, nudging me along the way as if to say, "Come on, you got this."

Once I hobbled through the door, my wife and her sister, an ICU nurse who knows a thing or two about medicine, saw my state and their faces said it all. Next thing I know, I'm in an ambulance speeding to the ER, lights and sirens in full swing.

Post-op wasn't fun, but it gave me something I hadn't had in years: time to think. You know, we all wear these badges of 'busyness' like they're medals of honor. But lying there in that sterile hospital bed, the medals didn't mean jack. I was 'Mr. Hero,' living the dream – or so it seemed on the outside. In reality, I was being consumed by the job. The emotional toll, the politics, the constant grind, the endless "always-on" cycle – it was a price tag I didn't want to pay anymore.

It was a switch, flipping from "Life's just fine," to "Whoa, I need a change, and I need it now." This wasn't a setback; it was a wake-up call from the universe, loud and clear. Something had to give.

So, there I was. I made a choice that even my closest friends and family had trouble wrapping their heads around. I sold my house, and the cottage with the cliff that changed my life, and "retired" from my years-long career as a paramedic – the cape, the helicopter flights, the life-and-death moments – I traded it all for 164 sprawling acres of raw, untamed wilderness. And let's not forget the abandoned sawmill that sat in the middle of it, weathered and worn, yet filled with untapped potential.

People thought I'd gone off the deep end. Heck, I wasn't a builder or an architect; my hands were more accustomed to medical equipment than hammers and nails. But it wasn't just about putting up walls and a roof. This was my shot at crafting an entirely new chapter, a life designed on my own terms. I wasn't just building a new home for my wife and me; I was constructing a future where the risks, rewards, and responsibilities were all mine to bear. This was my all-in moment, my chips pushed to the center of the table. The stakes couldn't have been higher, and I was the sole player in this game.

Tool belts replaced trauma kits. Power drills took the place of defibrillators. Sure, I tripped, stumbled, and sometimes flat-out face-planted, but each time I got up I was learning, growing. I was becoming the architect of my own destiny, one plank at a time.

Fast-forward 22 years, and here we are. The sawmill? It's more than wood and nails now. It's a symbol, a tangible proof of a life rebuilt by hand. Am I happy? No, I'm thrilled. Life threw curveballs, and yeah, there were hiccups and roadblocks. But each one was a lesson, a stepping stone to something better.

So, what's the big takeaway? Don't get stuck in a life that looks good on paper but feels empty in your soul. Sometimes you've got to shake things up, take that leap of faith, even if it scares the living daylights out of you. I found out the hard way that capes and helicopters aren't prerequisites for being a hero. Sometimes, all it takes is the courage to say, "This isn't working," and the willpower to do something about it.

And the superhero dream? That's evolved. I don't need to soar through the sky to feel like I'm flying. By taking charge of my own path, I discovered something far richer – a freedom and fulfillment that no uniform, no title, and certainly no nine-to-five grind could ever give me.

Mike Caldwell
Denholm, Quebec

The Story in Review

Let's explore Mike's "cliff-hanger" of a story.

Culture: Mike's story illuminates the challenges of the cultural definition of "success" – the nine-to-five J.O.B. In addition, Mike stated, "We all wear these badges of 'busyness' like they're medals of honor."

Mind: ... Yet this success and busyness came with some unsettling drawbacks once his "superhero cape" was removed during off-hours – the emotional toll, the endless paperwork and office politics, the soul-crushing drudgery of managerial tasks, the constant grind, and the endless 'always-on' cycle. Even the adjectives Mike chose to describe his experience gave a window into the beliefs, thoughts, feelings, and behaviors that played out on a daily basis, so much so that he had a "little escape hatch," his side hustle.

Toxic Positivity: Giving up his job and his home was a choice his closest friends and family had trouble understanding; to others, Mike was giving up on what others deemed as symbols of "success."

Body: From Mike's cliff fall, one of the areas he broke was his back, L4 vertebrae, specifically. Although the following is not specific to Mike and his story, you might find some of the parallels from Jensen's The Healing Questions Guide interesting.

Lower Back Problems:
1. What is out of balance in my life? What will it take to bring it back into balance?
2. What support am I afraid I am not receiving or will not receive?
3. What is interfering with my ability to experience more harmony in my life?

4. What will it take for me to tap into a more abundant and hopeful outlook?

5. What will it take for me to align with what is required to receive divine support?

6. What can I do right now to nurture myself?

7. What will it take to receive the financial support I need right now?

8. What will it take to have the courage and wisdom I need to overcome the obstacles I am facing?

9. What value is there in fearing success? What will it take to overcome the fear and step out of my own way?

10. What do I need to connect to that I am currently disconnected from?

11. What will it take to release some of the aggression I am feeling right now regarding my present responsibilities?

12. What sexual guilt needs to be healed?

13. What will it take to come into complete harmony with my sexuality?

14. What value was there and beating myself up? What will it take to address myself with more loving kindness?

Broken Back:

1. What will it take for me to start dealing with things in a whole new way?

2. What can I do to align with God and the laws of the Universe [or whatever version of divine source is] so I can feel more supported?

Fourth Lumbar / Firth Lumbar Disc (Lower Back):

1. What will it take to believe I have the right to live a joyful, productive and successful life?

2. What can I alter in my belief system that will eliminate the idea that I was not created for joy?

3. What value is there in believing that I do not have what it takes to succeed? What will it take for me to believe I am capable?

Gather: The major shift in his story was his "wake-up call from the Universe" fall from a 35-foot cliff.

 Relate: Mike's emotional rollercoaster included moments of feeling gnawed by uncertainty, often stuck in a never-ending cycle of soul-crushing drudgery that left an emptiness in his soul. It was a devastating journey, laden with burdens that sometimes scared the living daylights out of him. He found himself tangled in the throes of an agonizing emotional wake, tripped, stumbled, and sometimes flat-out face-planted. However, as he summoned his willpower and courage, he discovered the thrill in persevering. Despite the emotional toll it took, he couldn't deny the sense of triumph that came from conquering the challenges that twindled like waves of adrenaline, turning what once was soul-crushing into a testament to his resilience.

 Involve: Selling his house and cottage and starting new on vast land in the wilderness.

 Ease: Critical support roles in his story included his trust border collie Fred, as well as his wife and sister-in-law.

 Focus: Mike's journey to his "new normal" involved closing his chapter as a helicopter medic and supervisor to a new chapter where he created life by his own design. In the end, it gave him "freedom and fulfillment that no uniform, no title, and certainly no nine-to-five grind could ever give."

Retirement:
Redefining Life

*I can now give myself permission...
there is no hurry in my life.*

Most people look forward to the day that they can retire. When I met the requirements to retire from my management position at a technology company, I was happy! But, the actual activities related to retirement were negative because of the way that it was handled by the company. I'd had a very successful career; growing and moving up through a variety of companies and positions. I traveled the world, managed people internationally, led several highly visible, and high impact projects. I was a good manager and received positive feedback from my peers and people on my team. I worked hard on those projects, including creatively looking for answers, and requesting team members to work on activities that would result in successful results.

On my last day, because I worked with people around the world, I literally walked out of the building I worked in all by myself with no one to wish me well, thank me, and inquire about my next steps. The company was very flat; meaning there were few people at each level. I knew very few of my peers outside the projects I led. On the day I retired, my direct manager (who was in a different office location) assigned someone to collect my computer. It was pretty lonely.

The next day, week, month were wide open; no meetings, no travel. My friends and family congratulated me, but I don't think they understood this significant change. All they saw was my new "freedom" to do whatever I wanted to do. They certainly didn't understand the grief of suddenly losing the structure of my job, the friends I had made at the company, the loss of the benefits of my job (i.e., travel, both global and local), and the feeling of questioning my "new" role in life without those things. And, of course, getting a firm understanding of my financial situation and what I could realistically do. No regular paycheck, no upcoming bonuses, and what should I do about health insurance? I was definitely on my own, sometimes having to work through bureaucratic procedures as I moved from the support my company provided to doing it by myself. It was a significant change to my life pattern and I realized that I needed to step up and help myself move on. No one else was going to do it for me.

I am single and live alone, and felt that aloneness, but I continued to act as if everything was great with my new "freedom." I talked about things I wanted to do and places I wanted to go. But, I found that my confidence declined and I became worried/fearful about doing some of the things I had done when I was working; traveling alone to other countries, for example. I was able to take my first global trip with friends and that helped build my confidence back up, although I am not nearly as confident as I was when I was working.

Luckily, I had been seeing a counselor, and she helped me. I was depressed and feeling guilty that I wasn't busy, busy, busy every day. Instead I was sleeping more, and doing unproductive things, i.e., watching TV! Because of the depression, my level of concentration dropped, making it difficult to enjoy one of my favorite activities; reading. I stayed in my house, not going out to exercise, see friends, water my plants, etc.

I didn't consider this "grace time" to work on redefining my role in life. I just felt depressed and lonely.

I finally realized there were three things that were important to me, even more so in my new role: family, creating art, learning and continuing to grow. I reached out to my daughter in another state and arranged to spend more time with her and my grandkids on a regular basis. I started volunteering at my grandson's school and looked for other volunteer activities. (I had worked in food banks and worked in an international feed the hungry organization.) I took a workshop to develop my artistic capabilities; and that led to a workshop in Scotland. In addition to the workshop I spent time there exploring the culture, food, and sights in Scotland by myself!

I finally did reach out for help; reconnecting with my friends and sharing my situation. They were supportive of my new activities and encouraged me to continue to develop my art and my travel, in fact inviting me to travel with them on an extended trip to France.

While I was redefining my life, my friends were also going through some of the ups and downs of their lives. I stayed involved enough to provide friendship and support for them too. It helps to know you are helping others.

Another thing that brought me strength was to share my art with other artists and people. I started an art group that had over 60 members, and through that was commissioned to do a public art project in another country. By word of mouth, I was asked to make things on commission, and my art is now spread in several states!

I still experience times when I am lonely and nonproductive. I now give myself permission to take a nap or read all day, knowing that there is no hurry in my life. I can always do things tomorrow.

If I was to retire again, I would develop a stronger support system with family and friends. Having a counselor was so important and helpful. Taking my time, and realizing I had the time, to adjust to losing the working, managing, leading, traveling, confident person I'd been.

Another thing that was very helpful was to not dwell on the past. I wiped that side of my brain clean and opened it up to new things. My creativity improved significantly, and while I am still working on other adjustments, I can take my time and do it on my own schedule.

Jan Ghilain
Phoenix, AZ

The Story in Review

Ah, the joys of retirement... Or is it? Let's dive into the complexities...

Culture and **Toxic Positivity**: Our society often follows a structured path – education, college, job, success, and, finally, retirement. Yet, it rarely teaches us how to gracefully transition out of these roles. Retirement should be a period to look forward to, but what happens when it doesn't match our expectations? In Jan's story, cultural norms and toxic positivity played a significant role. Her friends and family congratulated her, but they failed to grasp the profound impact of this change had on her. There was an unspoken societal expectation that she should be ecstatic about reaching this point in her life. Jan felt isolated and trapped by the need to conform to this cultural norm, forcing herself to act as though everything was splendid when, in truth, she was struggling with the transition.

Mind: Jan's beliefs, hopes, and expectations about retirement initially hindered her. The abruptness of her retirement, devoid of any transitional celebration or well-wishing, left her feeling adrift. She lost the structure of her job, the camaraderie of coworkers, and the job benefits that had given her life meaning. Her entire identity, activities, friendships, and sense of purpose were deeply intertwined with her career. Managing income and health insurance on her own created anxiety, eroding her confidence. She struggled with guilt for not staying busy every day, as she had during her working years.

Gather: The pivotal moment in Jan's story is her retirement day.

Relate: Throughout this journey, Jan experienced a range of emotions and thoughts, including worry, fear, loneliness, depression, and guilt for not keeping herself busy, and a decline in confidence. She even questioned her newfound role in life.

Involve: Jan's story underscores the importance of recognizing both positive and challenging action steps during a grief journey. Depression-related activities initially occupied her days, and while these can align with the early stages of grief, professional support is essential if they persist. With guidance from her counselor, Jan identified three core priorities in her new life: family, artistic expression, and personal growth. This realization led to several transformative steps, including reaching out to her daughter and grandkids, volunteering, developing her artistic skills through workshops, and exploring new cultures and experiences on solo travels. She found purpose in helping others and nurtured her artistic talents, ultimately starting an artisan group. Jan now grants herself permission to savor leisurely activities, such as napping or indulging in a good book. These action steps are similar to the Japanese *Ikigai* as described in the chapter "Focus."

 Ease: Jan's journey was supported by her counselor, friends who traveled with her and helped rebuild her confidence, and the reconnection with her family and new friends. Volunteering, joining an artisan group, and engaging in various activities played a significant role in her transformation.

 Focus: In her "new normal," Jan emphasizes three core aspects – family, artistic expression, and personal growth. She now embraces life on her terms, cherishing the freedom to take naps or lose herself in a book without any rush, thoroughly enjoying what "retirement" looks and feels like to her on her own terms.

Who Am I?
The Chad Gaines Story

Loss works this way. It's a big ball of tangled up feelings.

*E*very year in America, more than eight million people suffer from trauma and PTSD (Post-Traumatic Stress Disorder). Most live with this nightmare in silence. Let me share two stories with you here. It's a story of darkness that was turned into light. The other story is also about darkness, only without the light at the end of the tunnel, so to speak. Let me explain. This is a story about two boys, cousins. Both young boys live with alcoholic dads. One was four years older than the other, both boys had mothers in the house growing up.

The only real difference from the outside looking in was that one mother was physically abusive while the other was not. In my research of both stories, I concluded there are some similarities. In my research, I wanted to focus on what was really the difference between the two boys growing up in the same households. Each had different mindsets for their future. In deeper research, as adults, both cousins served time in prison. What are the effects from being in an abusive family? At what point will these children who have turned into adults now be affected by their abusive childhood? What would be impacted by their past? I had many questions at that time.

Those questions would become my drive and my lifelong work to find out. I've come to know thousands of horrific stories. Some ended up in prison, others committed murder. FBI profiler Robert Ressler, in his 1992 book *Whoever Fights Monsters*, reports that "40% of the serial killers interviewed reported being physically beaten and abused in their childhood, with 70% reporting they had 'witnessed or been part of sexually stressful events' as children."[64]

Back in my 30s, I would interview both cousins and what I found was shocking. I asked each cousin the same six questions. I asked the older cousin in an interview: "Why did you start drinking as an adult?" His response: "I probably started drinking because my dad was an alcoholic." In my second interview, the younger cousin at that time was 32-years-old. The difference I noticed was that one was a heavy drinker and the other cousin gave up drinking. The next question: "Why did you stop drinking?" His quick answer to my question: "Because my dad was an alcoholic."

The questions were the same. The answers were the same. The clear difference was the ways of thinking they had. Both boys, now men, lacked education, both were told they would never amount to anything growing up. Based on the previously-mentioned statistics, how is it that the older cousin is up for release from prison in February 2047 while the younger cousin dealt with more physical abuse as child? In 2001, the younger cousin's step-dad was murdered by his mother. So, my mind wandered to a place where I thought on my drive from the prison to my home, how did the older cousin get to be 60 years, while the younger cousin endured a stabbing, beatings, a broken nose, being set on fire, and the murder at the hands of his mother, could go on a different path in life?

My name is Chad Gaines. In the story you just read, I was and am the younger cousin. In 2001, when I was 28 years old, my mother killed my stepdad, in a small farm town in northern Indiana. For me life was about survival and outliving her. In 2004, I was honored as one of the "Ten Most Outstanding Young Americans" in the country. In 2023, I wrote a book about my story, *Who Am I? (The Chad Gaines Story)* which is now becoming a major motion picture.[65] I don't speak about those things to boost about a book or a movie, or even the TV series they just wrote. I tell you those things to help you understand. If you are still breathing, you still have the chance to do great things. Don't let your circumstances or other people tell you there is no way out for you.

When something horrific happens to you...

Suddenly you have no choice but to live in a world you don't recognize anymore. Inside the violence of the mind, you can't escape. It feels dark even when it's daylight. Lonely even when you are surrounded by people. Only existing. Unsure of your identity. You can see life going on right in front of you. You even try to reach out and touch that world. But you can't. Yet. Or ever.

People out there are just living their mundane lives and seem to not have a care in the world. You sometimes try to live in that world too. At least briefly. This involves fake smiles and pretend interest in small talk. It's exhausting. So you choose to isolate instead. It's much safer than being with people who don't understand how my mother is just footsteps behind me. Always.

"I'll fucking kill you, you little son of a bitch." Those words play in my mind over and over, thousands of times a day!!

It would be nice to switch places with them. And not have your loss constantly replaying in your mind. All those anxious thoughts ruminating. It's a rude awakening when everyone just keeps moving. Laughing. Making plans. While you are suspended in time. A time you will never escape from. I was just going through the motions seven days a week. I had pain so deep that you can't even exactly pinpoint where it was coming from or when it started. Invisible to others on most days. But it was there. And it always hurt. It chased me, like my mother once did all those years ago.

People will say, "they are always with you." But where? It feels so long ago since you have heard their voice say anything. Most days it almost feels like you have been abandoned to roam this unrecognizable world alone. And on the other end, feel guilty for trying to move forward without them.

Loss works this way. It's a big ball of tangled up feelings. Somewhere between that crust in your eyes and a fishhook in your big toe. And it takes as long as it takes to move through these confusing emotions. It takes patience. Lots of self-care and being kind to yourself. Mostly self-control, which I lack on most days. Because grief is a lonely journey where you are the only one who truly understands how this trauma feels.

As a life coach now to many people around the country who are dealing with the long-term effects of trauma and PTSD I can tell you, the more I speak on stages around the United States, that my story is opening countless other adults to share their stories to help the healing. Now, let me tell you how this has affected my life. Even years after my mother's death, back in 2017, I still carry the horrific flashbacks with me. We lived in a farm town in Indiana in the 1980s. I never really experienced anything but violence in my childhood.

However, now as a 50-year-old dad and husband, I can tell you what it's like to jump off two stories from a boat into the Pacific Ocean off the coast of Honolulu. I can tell you what it's like to walk on a movie set and the excitement that comes with it. I can also tell you what it's like to feel small and less than zero on some days when I wake up.

All our lives we will encounter grief, shortcomings, heartbreak, and small victories. It's called life, and we can't get out of it alive. I think when I became aware of the memory loss was somewhere between 2018-2019. Sometimes at work I caught myself writing down simple drink orders or I would forget the order within the 50 seconds it took me to get to the soda machine.

As time went forward, I would lose my balance and run into tables that would lead to big leg bruises. By the spring of 2018, I would forget lines of a book I was reading. Even people who I worked with every day for a few years, I would lose their names somewhere in my brain. I'd spend many hours focusing on reading name tags to remember some of my friends. I have even left my keys in my P.O. Box at the post office more than eight times. I would dismiss it as I'm just getting older, I guess. My brain wouldn't process conversations I would have with my guests at work.

For me, I believe 2020 opened the flood gates to how my memory loss was affecting my mental health. After being laid off due to COVID, I became isolated from nearly everyone. I didn't want to go out or talk to people. I didn't know how to explain it, how I was a public speaker, but that light was losing its brightness.

I listened to music for about 14 hours a day to fight off what I was hearing in my head. I wasn't sleeping at night. I would only sleep when it became daylight outside my window. I made 12 trips across the country and back that year, I could barely tell you about three of them.

That's when I realized I needed to write my story before I forgot everything about my life and everyone I knew. I've met a lot of wonderful talented people throughout the world. I wanted to tell them how much I appreciated them coming and going in my life.

It took me nearly six years to write *Who Am I? (The Chad Gaines Story)*. One lady told me it didn't take me six years to write my story, but rather it took me 50 years to write my life story. I cried a lot while writing in the middle of the night. I wrote about what it was like after my dad left our home in 1979, including the beatings, the stabbing, and the alcohol abuse I witnessed as a young boy and teen. I also went into detail how my mother killed my stepdad in 2001.

It was very disturbing to write about my mother killing someone. I was embarrassed and full of guilt. It only began with my stepdad... After 2001 my mother moved in with my grandmother. That's when everything changed, and people started to die inside of their home. I had quite a few reasons to give up and put a gun to my head and pull the trigger. Fear did take control of me many times. The embarrassment made me feel I would never amount to anything. I found it's best to control those triggers by having a daily routine for everything! I have a wonderful wife who studies daily to understand my thoughts, feelings, and the effects of my C-PTSD (complex post-traumatic stress disorder). As a motivational speaker on stage, I explain life to being like the sport of Football. Life is about blocking and tackling. Blocking out your fears and tackling the opportunities. These skills can be applied to anyone's life. I give the middle and high schools I speak to the same message: life is going to hurt! In fact, it's going to uppercut some of you right in the mouth.

I give it to them straight because they deserve to know that. The wonderful people I get to work with or share a stage with are the same people my mother once told me I would never meet. When I came across this idea to write a chapter for Dr. Karen Kramer, I felt it was something I honestly had to do. The impact of these stories here inspires me to continue with my work worldwide.

Chad Gaines
San Francisco, CA

The Story in Review

Grief can sometimes be intertwined with trauma. In this book, I've chosen to explore the nuanced aspects of grief, focusing on situations that may not be universally classified as "traumatic" by others but can still leave us deeply affected. However, as you've seen, some stories intersect with trauma, as in the case of suicide in the chapter "Loss of a Child."

It's important to recognize that your response to trauma is uniquely your own. Your experiences, along with their duration and frequency, can influence how trauma symptoms manifest in your life. Chad's story introduces the concept of C-PTSD, or complex post-traumatic stress disorder. Let's begin by distinguishing it from the more well-known PTSD (post-traumatic stress disorder).

PTSD is typically linked to a single traumatic event, such as a car accident, natural disaster, assault, war, medical crisis, or attack. Whereas C-PTSD arises from *complex, relational, and developmental trauma.*[66] It often develops during early stages of life, involving repeated incidents within a supposedly safe relationship, as seen in Chad's story, where child abuse played a role. C-PTSD encompasses all the symptoms of PTSD but differs in its impact on the nervous system, particularly concerning attachment.

Living with C-PTSD can lead to reckless behavior, feelings of hostility, or dissociation that disrupt daily life. It may result in a sense of lost spirituality or overwhelming shame.

If you're not familiar with C-PTSD, it may be because there's ongoing debate within the mental health community about its formal classification. Mental health professionals following DSM-5 criteria would diagnose it as PTSD. Nevertheless, some experts advocate for C-PTSD to be recognized as a separate diagnosis in all manuals, apart from PTSD.

In Chad's case, categorizing his experiences and behaviors was helpful for better understanding his actions and reactions. Drawing from sources like *The Myth of Normal* and *The Body Keeps the Score*, which emphasize looking beyond labels to uncover underlying causes, let's consider both perspectives – the C-PTSD diagnosis and the underlying factors – as we explore the complexities of Chad's inspirational journey from tribulations to triumph.

So let's dive in ...

Culture: Cultural and societal beliefs about identity significantly influence the choices we make. In Chad's case, his identity was deeply entwined with the social stigma surrounding unspeakable acts committed by his mother and his cousin's incarceration.

 Toxic Positivity: Chad aptly describes his experience in this passage: "People out there are just living their mundane lives and seem to not have a care in the world. You sometimes try to live in that world too. At least briefly. This involves fake smiles and pretend interest in small talk. It's exhausting. So, you choose to isolate instead. It's much safer than being with people who don't understand..." This is an example of fake smiles and pretend engagement with others rather than being his real authentic self.

 Mind: Similar to childhood abuse trauma and C-PTSD, Chad's story is fraught with a myriad of values, beliefs, and attitudes rooted in the quest for safety and survival. One of Chad's most striking statements was, "I feel like I would never amount to anything." Fortunately, with support, he was able to challenge that belief and now leverages his story to make a positive impact on others.

 Body: Chad briefly touches upon how his life experiences affected his mental health, including his struggles with sleep and equilibrium. Let's explore questions related to memory loss from Jensen's *The Healing Questions Guide* to better understand the potential correlations with his story:

Memory Problems:
1. What will it take to create stability in my life as I experience this present transformation and restructuring of my usual way of thinking and doing things?
2. What will it take for me to relax and allow this life overhaul to fall into place?
3. What past traumatic event is coming to the surface to be healed? What will it take to heal it?

4. What will it take to be brave enough and skilled enough to safely revisit past experiences that are interfering with my ability to remember?

5. What nutrients are missing that are necessary to feed my brain?

Please note that these questions are intended to prompt reflection on underlying subconscious programming that might manifest as memory problems and do not necessarily imply that these topics are specific to Chad.

 Gather: The most significant shifts in Chad's story, as described more fully in his book Who Am I?, revolve around pivotal moments like the day his mother shot his stepdad. However, as Chad elucidates in this story, many of the outcomes he faced can be traced back to his experiences of childhood abuse. In his book, his most profound transformation occurred when he emerged from incarceration and decided to make a change in his own life.

 Relate: In addition to the previously mentioned limiting beliefs, Chad's story is replete with a range of emotions and thoughts, including feeling suspended in time, confusion, fear, hurt, anger, deep pain, guilt, and embarrassment.

 Involve: A notable action step in Chad's story is his commitment to maintaining a daily routine.

 Ease: Chad's most significant source of support is his loving wife, who diligently studies daily to understand his thoughts, feelings, and the effects of his C-PTSD. Congratulations to Chad and his wonderful wife, who tied the knot in Hawaii during the writing of this book!

 Focus: Chad's "new normal" encompasses a multifaceted role in which he helps others as a life coach specializing in trauma and C-PTSD, serves as a motivational speaker, and recently authored the book *Who Am I? (The Chad Gaines Story)*, which is being adapted into both a movie and a TV series. Find out more about Chad, his story, his work, and the various ways he is inspiring others, go to www.gaineschad.com.

Middle-Age and Menopause: Disrupting the Story

We owe it to all women to disrupt the story that being a middle-aged and menopausal woman is the end for us.

/ sat on the bleachers watching my son play water polo, blood trickled down my legs and landed on my flip flops. Shame paralyzed me. If I got up, the crowd behind me could see the back of my skirt where I was certain there was a blood stain. If I stayed, the blood would eventually drip onto the pool deck. After a minute of debating the pros and cons of my situation, I stood up, pulled down the t-shirt to cover my butt, and walked behind the bleachers with my thighs pressed together making shuffling steps toward the women's room. I grabbed a pile of paper towels and shoved them in the crotch of my soggy underpants. I didn't even bother taking out the two blood-soaked tampons that I had inserted into my vagina. I sidestepped to the parking lot and drove home.

At the age of 48, my body began to rebel. I no longer had control over it the way I had in the decades before. Suddenly, my waist grew thicker, which I didn't think was possible since I never really had a waist. Even at my thinnest, and I've purposefully been skinny, I'd never had a flat stomach. The bloating didn't help; I now looked like SpongeBob SquarePants. My Crossfit body turned to shit even though I still worked out the same number of days and amount of time with the same intensity. I had back fat spilling out over and under my bra. I started wearing bottoms with only elastic waistbands. My fingers swelled. I had chronic headaches. I became bitchier. I lost whatever patience I had, especially with my husband. I'd scream in my head, "Do you have to breathe around me?" I had zits and chin hair. In the middle of the night, I'd wake up in the middle of the cool night drenched in a pool of sweat. During this time, my depression and anxiety got so bad I finally went to see a psychiatrist. I took the PHQ-9 questionnaire to see how depressed and anxious I was, and I scored 22 out of 27 (I've always been an overachiever). I was prescribed four times the amount of Prozac I was taking before. Throughout this time I had a regular period that would sometimes be heavy like that day at the high school pool watching water polo.

What the f#%k was wrong with me? This wasn't menopause. I knew it wasn't menopause because I needed to stop having a period for twelve consecutive months. That is the clinical definition of menopause. So is this just part of what getting older looked and felt like? Was this what "middle-age" for a woman was? If I were to believe our cultural stories, this was exactly what happens to older women. Look around. Where are the stories told by middle-aged women? I don't see images of women like me – wrinkles, graying, brown spots. Instead, I saw commercials and ads for anti-aging creams, plastic surgery, and cosmetics. All of these came with the promise that if we bought these products we would look like the unlined models selling us the products. Marion Wright Edelman said, "You can't be what you can't see." So, I felt I had only had two choices: 1) buy the products and get surgery to look younger, or 2) retreat and keep quiet.

So, I chose the second option. Afterall, how could I talk about my body, along with my brain, going crazy? Who would believe me that I'd walk in a room forgetting what I went in there for? We've been told throughout our lives that our bodies are something we should be ashamed of. And don't you dare talk about your period. The only time you can have a conversation is when you start to have your period. You can talk to your mom or older sister or friends who have had theirs before you. Having your period is a celebration according to society. Based on our cultural stories, menstruating means we are women and are ready to physically bear children. But we don't celebrate menopause because it's the death of our usefulness, right?

Since we don't talk about the death of our menstrual cycles, we don't know that the crazy period (see what I did there) of hot flashes, dry skin and vaginas, depression, mood swings, and still having a period is perimenopause. What I experienced in silence and shame was a "normal" stage of my hormones transitioning to a point where I'd stop having my period.

To find out about menopause, we do searches on the internet. Here, we'll find facts like the definition of, symptoms and signs, side effects, and treatments for menopause. It's all very clinical. Or there are the "funny" memes about women and menopause such as "I'm still hot. It comes in flashes," Menopause, Menstrual cramps, Mental breakdowns... ever notice that all of your problems begin with Men?" and "Just so we're clear about this... I'm under no obligation to stay in the same mood for any length of time."

I believe the pivotal moment I started to grieve was when I was finally menopausal. Up until that point, the gaslighting and mansplaining about what menopause was kept me silent and alone. Now that I was menopausal, and not a perimenopausal freak (as I had been for the previous six years), I was pissed. That's why I write these stories. We need to disrupt the stories they sell and tell us about how women are defined by the ability to either have children or not. We are NOT just bodies for the pleasure and enjoyment of others and to create life. We should not be dismissed because we no longer have viable uteruses.

Contrary to popular opinion, menopause can be an exciting time in our lives. This is the time when we can write our story. We have more time than we had when raising families, working, making ends meet, driving to the grocery store once a week, and so on. We have more knowledge and wisdom. We don't put up with as much bullshit and we don't spend time with people or things that no longer serve us.

Since menopause, I don't have periods or pregnancy worries. My confidence and inner strength are on fire. I don't have mad mood swings because my hormones are stable. I have more energy for MY life. The number one person in my life is me.

Bottom line: I know, and I want you to know, there is another option besides buying a whole bunch of sh*t that promises eternal youth or keeping quiet and isolated. The third, and only option, is to tell your story – to tell the truth. We owe it to our daughters, sisters, friends... We owe it to all women to disrupt the story that being a middle-aged and menopausal woman is the end for us. When we tell and share our stories, we find sisterhood – a whole community of women who understand with empathy.

Michelle "Dr. Z" Zive, PhD, MS, RD

San Diego, CA

The Story in Review

Dr. Z's mission is to challenge and dismantle the narratives that women construct about themselves and others by drawing attention to and shattering these deeply ingrained beliefs. The information presented before delving into her personal story supports her mission by telling and sharing her story about something that is considered taboo.

Did you know that World Menopause Day is observed annually on October 18th? *I didn't!* Surprisingly, many people are unaware of this fact, and the reason behind this might be the perceived societal taboo surrounding the subject, as greatly illustrated in Dr. Z's narrative. She is not alone in her passionate pursuit, as other women refuse to hide in the shadows of aging, reject shame related to their appearance, and resist being confined to societal expectations regarding their bodies. Prominent figures like Justine Bateman [67](aged 57) and Sally Fields[68] (aged 76) are using their platforms in the media to challenge age-related prejudices.

Dr. Z's personal story effectively illustrates why this "taboo" topic is essential for the healthy process of grieving and navigating middle age for women.

Let's delve further into this narrative...

Culture: As highlighted both in Dr. Z's narrative and throughout society, media plays a significant role in shaping perceptions of "healthy" aging, often portraying the process as taboo or encouraging women to "fix" themselves through anti-aging creams, surgery, or cosmetics. This portrayal is compounded by instances of gaslighting and mansplaining regarding menopause, as Dr. Z attests.

Toxic Positivity: Toxic positivity permeates the journey of women facing menopause, manifesting in various forms, including humoristic memes of menopausal women. These seemingly light-hearted portrayals obscure the importance of this significant phase in a woman's development. Whether through memes, commercial ads, media representation, or societal reactions to aging, the message is clear: either attempt to reverse the aging process through products and procedures or remain silent, inconspicuous, and invisible. These implicit and explicit messages have a profound impact on the beliefs, values, and attitudes that women hold during the grieving process for the loss of youth and the embrace of middle age. Two key statements from Dr. Z's story underscore these toxic influences: "We've been told throughout our lives that our bodies are something we should be ashamed of" and "I had two choices: 1) buy the products and get surgery to look younger, or 2) retreat and keep quiet." Dr. Z's mission is to disrupt these limiting beliefs by drawing attention to and dismantling them.

 Body: Firstly, it's essential to acknowledge the natural bodily changes that women may experience as they approach perimenopause, embracing them as a normal aspect of this life transition rather than something to fear, shame, or attempt to "fix." These symptoms can be severe, and include bloating, brain fog, weight gain, muscle and joint aches, disrupted sleep, swollen fingers, headaches, zits, chin hair, night sweat, forgetting, hot flashes, dry skin and vaginas, depression, and mood changes. Not all women experience these, and some experience others. However, it's also important to explore how grief may manifest in the body, as Dr. Z's story offers an opportunity to do so. While headaches can be a natural part of this life change, they can also signify grief settling within the body. Using Jensen's *The Healing Questions Guide*, let's review the questions associated with headaches to gain insight into this potential correlation.

Headache:
1. What will it take to alleviate some of the stress I am feeling?
2. What fears and pressure am I placing on myself that are not even legitimate?
3. What am I resisting? What will it take to open up to the process of life?
4. What will it take to trust that everything is going to work out?
5. Is the effort I am putting forth worth the stress it is causing me?
6. What will it take to reverse the negativity and resentment and trade it in for positivity and mental freedom?
7. What am I trying to be the boss over that I need to just let go of?
8. What value is there and continuing to feed my insufficiencies? What

will it take to change my internal dialogue to include a loving and kind attitude toward myself?

9. Who do I need to forgive for hurting my feelings so I can feel better?

10. What ideas and information am I receiving that are incompatible with what I want to create?

11. What feelings am I trapping inside? What will it take for me to voice them in an effective way?

12. What will it take to remove myself from the chaos I perceive is happening to me and settle it as an observer rather than the participant?

13. What will it take for me to allow myself to laugh a little or do something fun?

 Gather: The notable shift in this story is her transition into menopause and middle age.

 Relate: The spectrum of emotions and thoughts encompasses feelings of shame, anxiety, depression, solitude, impatience, and frustration.

 Involve: Dr. Z's primary course of action, as demonstrated here, involves challenging the narratives told about women by both society and themselves. She accomplishes this by sharing her story and creating a platform where other women can shatter their limiting beliefs and become the best versions of themselves.

 Ease: Supportive resources include a psychiatrist and medication, while her most impactful contribution is the community of women she has cultivated to further disrupt the narrative by sharing their own stories.

 Focus: Dr. Z's "new normal" in the menopausal phase entails freedom from menstruation and pregnancy concerns, heightened confidence and inner strength, stable hormones with reduced mood swings, increased energy for her own life, and the prioritization of self-care and self-empowerment. Furthermore, as "Dr. Z, Doctor of Disruption," she has established a platform and community, Representation Rebellion (www.representationrebellion.com), enabling women to understand, empathize with, and share their own stories.

25 Years and Waiting: Time Altered and Standing Still

I lived with the fear and the tears and the pre-emptive grief that he was dying a slow and painful death.

The phone rang in June. It was a hot and sunny day. That was it.

That was when it started. The beginning of the end. You know what I mean. The end. The end of what I thought to be my hopes and dreams of an idyllic life. The end of my fairy tale. The end of my childhood dream of my father being invincible and living forever. I had my life built up in a certain way and never in my wildest dreams did I expect to get the call that I did. That was the day when the horrible villain grief came to call. Or at least that's what I thought at that time. I have since changed my mind about grief. At the time, it was really pretty earth shattering and suffocating. I thought that life was spinning out of control. I felt unbearably sad. I couldn't think. This news affected the rest of my life. I think a little differently about it now. More about that later.

"Your father has had a heart attack.You should stay put since you are nine months pregnant, There's no point in you coming until we know more."

Now, honestly, I was all over the map with my hormones, and I reacted exactly how you'd expect me to react. I was shocked and angry and resisted what I was being told until eventually I accepted the news. I lived about 20 hours away by car, had a 20-month-old daughter, and I was nine-months pregnant with our second child. (Adding a little detail: My daddy was only 53. He was a healthy and strong young man.) This can't be happening. Damnit! I don't have time for this. That was my thought. How can a strong man be going through this? This isn't what strength means, is it?

That was a pretty selfish thought on my part, wasn't it? And not the only time that I had it. You see, for the next few years, almost 25 of them, every single time I saw my dad, the possibility existed that it would be my last. I lived with the fear and the tears and the pre-emptive grief that he was dying a slow and painful death. He was suffering. Many other people didn't see it. He didn't often share it out loud to many people. I was privileged to have many conversations with him in quiet moments, usually on long drives, in backwoods, where he shared how he knew he was losing ground and losing pieces of himself.

My dad, Henry Joseph Gallant, had multiple medical issues. Among them was vascular dementia. He literally was living beyond himself in a way that he didn't always even know. I watched him change. Everyone who knew him and loved him had to negotiate with not knowing which parts of him were going to show up each day until the end of his life. It's a lot. And it happens regularly on this earth. There are many people who are shifting in their cognition daily and those around them lose pieces of themselves. It's hard to watch. Understanding how to support my nervous system, having therapists, coaches, counselors, pastors, colleagues, family and friends to process with over the years created a sense of safety.

Throughout 25 years, my dad had the opportunity to know all of his grandchildren and his great-grand-daughter Quinn. He witnessed so many moments. He read books. He told stories. He danced. He spent time doing the important things and being present even in the pieces that were missing. He was always there and he always will be. As I write this (and the tears flow), he is in the matchbox car found under the entertainment unit, in the deer I see crossing the road, in the bubbles floating, in the maple walnut ice cream, in the "You Are My Sunshine" tune that I hear.

With the knowledge that his days were numbered, or in his words, "his ticket was punched," changed how I viewed my dad from the time he was 53 until he died almost 25 years later. His identity became wrapped around and twisted incomprehensibly with diagnosis and pre-emptive grief and fear. Looking back, it is easy to see. During the time, it was a labyrinth of paths. His identity became wrapped in so many things.

The possibility of being stuck in a space of blame for the heart attack that caused the dementia that caused the kidney disease that caused the death... There are times, when I really think about it, I can see where I have been spinning my wheels about the future death rather than enjoying the ever-present moment now.

The grief that seemed so complicated to me may well have been all exactly as it was to be for the story of my life and my dad's, yet it became challenging to navigate. There was a worldwide pandemic with borders locked down and travel limited. I couldn't get to my parents as often as I wanted to. That caused greater distress.

The follow-up phone call came almost 25 years later and this time there was a knowing in me that it was the beginning of the end – the finality of the earthly journey. The journey through this grief was brought to a close in the pre-emptive part when I got the privilege of transitioning my father from this space on earth. It became an active grief in the midst of a pandemic, under lockdown, using a walker, and on medical supervision post-surgically for a hip surgery – for me. I got to go and be with my mom and dad during the active stages of his last days here on earth in his body.

Boy, did I experience so much in those last days, hours, and minutes. Everything that I had known shifted quickly. The times since then have changed as the days, weeks, months, and years have moved along. And all the emotions. At times, I wasn't sure they would move. There were times that I thought that I would die under the weight of it all. I recall time moving in a way that seemed to be altered and standing still. There were chunks of time that seemingly didn't exist anymore. Every encounter was somehow bigger. Every emotion had a greater depth. Such has been the path of this particular road with grief related to my dad.

When I reflect now, I can cry and laugh about it quite easily because I can see how my dad orchestrated my husband and me to finally getting some alone time "off" together following his death. Nothing like being quarantined for 14 days. At least that is the story that I tell myself and that's one that is way less traumatic than the actual story of how I survived those 25 years. Now onto resting my nervous system… It has earned it.

Michelle Petitpas
Windsor, Nova Scotia

The Story in Review

Anticipatory grief arises from various life experiences, where individuals mourn the inevitable future. Michelle's story encapsulates an *anticipatory grief journey* – the feelings of grief or loss that is felt before the loss actually happens – intertwined with profound love for her father as he endured "a slow and painful death" for nearly 25 years.

Let's review ..

Gather: The pivotal moment in her narrative occurred when she received the call about her father's heart attack and his eventual passing.

Relate: Michelle's emotional spectrum encompassed feelings of her world shattering, suffocation, and life spinning out of control. She described being in a state of shock, unable to think clearly, overwhelmed by unbearable sadness, tears, and distress. She also dealt with anger, resistance, fear, and a pervasive sense of safety.

Involve: During this challenging period, Michelle cherished the time spent with her father, uncertain of when that fateful day might arrive.

Ease: To help her through the process, she drew upon a network of supportive resources, including therapists, counselors, coaches, pastors, colleagues, and family and friends.

Focus: Michelle's "new normals" after her father's heart attack involved treasuring precious moments with him. And, when the time came, she facilitated his transition "from this earthly realm" at the moment of his passing. Michelle is no stranger to the world of grief and caregiving. She has harnessed her personal and professional experiences to assist others through her resources, including the Heal The Healthcarers Podcast (www.healthehealthcarers.com).

In Summary

"Have the courage to follow your heart and intuition. They somehow already know what you truly want to become. Everything else is secondary."

– Steve Jobs

Who are you? What shapes your sense of self? How has your identity evolved over time? What external influences have played a significant role in shaping your current self-image?

In this section, we dove into the intricate story of personal identity and the profound impact of grief. Our exploration began with an introduction to the foundational theories and research surrounding *autoimmune diseases*, shedding light on the profound loss of identity experienced by many, especially by women. Dr. Gabor Maté's insights served as a guiding beacon throughout our journey.[69] These insights set the stage for the five unique stories that delve into various facets of identity. The narratives emerge against diverse backdrops, encompassing transitions from **corporate careers to entrepreneurship**, **career-life transitions**, **retirement**, **childhood traumas**, the challenges faced by middle aged women, and the role of caretaking for a declining father – each leaving an indelible mark on one's self-identity.

 Culture: In this section, we encountered the expectations placed on women to seamlessly juggle the roles of stay-at-home wives and entrepreneurs. Definition of success by the likes of a 9-to-5 job were challenged when it dampers one's internal spirit. We explored the societal vision of retirement and the stigma surrounding unspeakable acts and familial incarcerations.

 Mind: We confronted the pressures of "knowing it all," "doing it all," and maintaining perfection. Doing the "right things" in regards to a career yet feeling empty inside was also explored. The absence of retirement celebrations and the sudden loss of job titles underscored these challenges. Furthermore, we came to grips with dwindling confidence, rooted in fear of navigating life beyond the corporate realm, along with feelings of guilt and unresolved trauma from one's formative years.

 Toxic Positivity: We witnessed the suppression of true vulnerabilities, hindering the ability to seek help and support. Well-meaning friends and family can place their toxic positivity by way of pressures on what they perceive as "right" and "wrong" for you. Silence became the refuge for unspoken emotions, isolating them in a world of "fake smiles" and superficial small talk.

 Body: Backaches, broken backs, memory problems, and other bodily tribulations mirror the emotional turmoil endured in these stories.

As we navigated these intricate stories, it became evident that the **Healthy GRIEF Framework** manifests uniquely in each case. Here's a concise overview:

 Gather: Key shifts included quitting jobs, retirement, starting businesses, transitioning into stay-at-home parenthood, leaving incarceration, and experiencing significant health challenges or losses of loved ones.

 Relate: Emotions run deep – ranging from confusion and shock to fear, guilt, and anger. Storytellers wrestled with feelings of inadequacy, questioned their new roles, and ultimately learned to leverage their vulnerabilities for connection and understanding.

 Involve: The coping mechanisms varied from reading and creating routines to reconnecting with loved ones, volunteering, developing new hobbies, and moving. Healthy boundaries emerged as crucial tools for navigating these journeys.

Ease: Support networks encompassed dogs, friends, family, therapists, and coaches. Participation in support groups, educational pursuits, and community engagement proved instrumental in healing.

 Focus: Embracing the "new normal" involved creating balance among different life roles, identifying priorities, building a life by their own design, and granting oneself the freedom to navigate each day on one's own terms. As they journeyed through grief, many became life coaches or experts on their personal grief experiences, inspiring others through various mediums such as motivational speaking, books, movies, or TV series.

The question remains: Which story resonates most with you, and what insights will you carry forward on your own path?

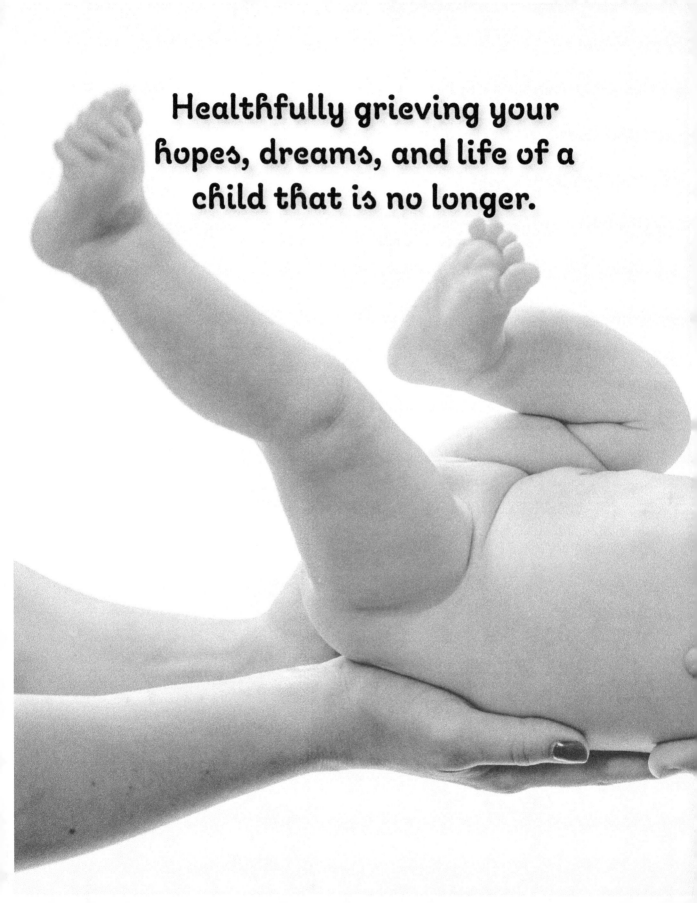

Healthfully grieving your hopes, dreams, and life of a child that is no longer.

MATERNITY

"Everybody is a genius.
But if you judge a fish by its ability to climb a tree,
it will live its whole life believing it is stupid."

~ Albert Einstein

One of the most miraculous aspects of a woman's body is its capacity to conceive and bring forth new life. Yet, within the realm of maternity, there exists a myriad of grief experiences, encompassing infertility, miscarriages, abortions, perinatal losses (ranging from stillbirths to infant deaths within 28 days post-delivery), and numerous others. In this section, we jump into the stories of two individuals, complemented by a heartwarming tale from my own life to conclude this chapter.

We embark on this section with Karen's poignant journey. Excited about their baby-to-be, Karen and her husband were confronted with the agonizing news and the unthinkable decision no parent should ever have to make.

The second narrative is through Nicole's eyes as she navigates her pregnancy. Unfortunately, she was confronted with a devastating discovery at month eight.

To conclude this section on a brighter note, I am delighted to share a poem I penned to my son on the day he left home – an experience that resonates with many empty-nesters.

May you discover stories that resonate with your own journey, gathering insights to enrich and augment your personal path.

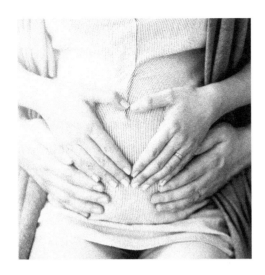

Pregnancy Termination: There Was No "Right" Choice

It was all wrong.

October of 2008 was a beautiful time. Four months pregnant with our second child, I was through morning sickness and felt strong. Our daughter would be three in a couple months and was aware of the pregnancy, she was excited – we were all excited. I was 39 and had always wanted to experience motherhood. I felt like the luckiest girl in the world.

Outside of my "advanced age," I had no reason to expect anything but a healthy baby, a healthy pregnancy. In my mind, the statistics were in my favor and I didn't have any trepidation. I chose to skip any invasive testing, initial sonograms showing normal development. At 19 weeks, we went in for our ultrasound. We didn't want to know the gender and we were clear with the technician, laughing in joy at seeing the head, turning away when he came to the middle of the body.

I couldn't see the technician, but my husband could. The technician was having a hard time getting a good "picture," rolling the ultrasound machine over my stomach. I was joking about the baby being shy. My husband says he noticed the technician's face, saw the intensity as he was trying to get a clear ultrasound. It went on for a while, I don't know how long. I didn't have any sense of trouble, even when the technician said he was going to get a genetic counselor. We were led to a room with lockers, a little table and a clock on the wall. My husband said that's when he knew something was seriously wrong and this was not the room we wanted to be in.

I met this counselor at the beginning stages of our pregnancy because of my age. I might have talked to him again during those first few months I can't remember. On this day I think I said it's great to see him again. Still not getting any foreboding feelings that I remember, but I could have also been in denial. He made eye contact, said he was glad he was at the hospital and able to come see us right away. He then confirmed our baby had down's syndrome. Although I was surprised, we had talked about this possibility. His next statement was that there were some issues in getting a clear shot of the baby's heart. It's not uncommon for babies with down syndrome to have heart issues – oftentimes they grow out of them, he said. But we needed to see a specialist, have further testing. It was a lot to take in, and at this point I'm thinking, ok, we can do this. We've thought about this possibility before and we felt like we could do it.

We saw the pediatric heart specialist within the next couple days. I'll never forget this man – quiet spoken, giving me the facts about a hypoplastic left ventricle, the most severe type. Only two chambers in our baby's heart. I had so many questions, it wasn't sinking in. I couldn't quite understand everything he was saying. So he drew on a piece of paper what a healthy heart looks like, explaining the functions of each area. Then he drew a picture of our baby's heart right next to it. I didn't totally lose it yet, I was waiting for the hope. He gave us the statistics of survivability, then surgeries, potential outcomes, all of which were for a baby without down's syndrome. The dual diagnosis certainly decreased the already minimal chances of simply surviving.

I went from denial to despair. Then back to denial. Give me a second opinion. A third. Give me the person who is going to tell me the diagnosis is wrong, the prognosis is wrong. The next few days are still a blur. Talking to the genetic counselor. Hearing our options. Getting spiritual counsel. Parenting our precious daughter. Having to make a decision between unimaginable and gut wrenching. There was no "right" choice. It was all wrong.

We chose to terminate the pregnancy. Our doctor supported the decision. Every medical professional I had contact with from that point on was empathetic, patient, supportive. So much of that week of surgery and physical recovery is lost to me. I have flashes. Befuddlement that the sun would come up. Holding so tightly to my daughter, parenting her, reading to her, distracting myself. We found out our baby was a girl. We named her Kayda, brought her remains to be cremated. We did not share in detail with people what happened, but our friends and family knew we lost our baby. Such a ridiculous term, "lost." I still feel that way, although I don't have a better one.

The following week we hosted Thanksgiving. It was my immediate family, their partners, and my father-in-law. I can't remember if I cooked, I know that everyone pitched in. No one knew what to do or say, I didn't know what I needed. There were plenty of "how ARE you"s, but I didn't have any words that I felt like I could say out loud. We canceled a vacation with friends we had planned for the following month, I knew enough to respect my process. I would take our daughter to the library, passing pregnant women, cursing under my breath. Resenting them, turning away from acquaintances before they could ask how I was. Angry at anyone who's life was just going on in what seemed like blissful oblivion.

I was involved in a meditation group at this time, my "sangha" or spiritual community. There were a few people there who I leaned on. One woman, a grandmother who was a dear friend, was so easy to talk to. Her unconditional listening gave me so much freedom to express the ugly. All these ugly feelings that were really unfamiliar to me. In those moments, just her way of nodding, looking right at me, let me know that I was ok and that maybe this was understandable to her. One day when we were leaving the center she asked me if I wanted to join her for lunch. I didn't answer, I just looked at her. I truly didn't know how to answer, I just felt blank. She took my hand and said, "Come." That was it. She took me to lunch. I don't know what we talked about but her certainty and gentle guidance to care for myself, to eat was so easy to be with.

A few months later my daughter and I started at a mommy and me preschool. These parents had all done the fall session together; we were new. One of the mom's announced at the beginning of class that she had just finished her first trimester and they were so excited to be having another baby. She sat next to me at snack time and I thought, of course. When I realized that I actually didn't feel any bitterness and I could look her in the eye, I knew that I was on my way to being functional. Of course, functional isn't thriving. I didn't recognize this at the time.

The most healing interactions for me were with people that didn't shy away from loss. One woman in particular, my father-in-law's girlfriend at the time, when they came to visit just came right up to me and looked me in the eyes and although I don't remember her words, the message I felt was that she understood this grief deeply. Most people didn't acknowledge that they knew I was no longer pregnant. It was just something that wasn't talked about. Although I certainly understood; I didn't know how to acknowledge it either. As friendships deepened, there were some people I spoke to of our loss, but I didn't give details to most. There is wisdom in that, I don't know that this story of loss is for everyone's ears. The deeper reason though is that almost unconsciously I still held on to some personal responsibility or fault in me.

I thought about our baby every day. We planted a tree with some of her ashes. We had a son the following year, healthy and huge. Life was going along with its joys and challenges. One night my husband and I were looking at some news about a baby born prematurely, at 22 weeks. The baby was surviving. It triggered so much grief for me, this miracle. My husband was confused by my reaction and when I told him I thought about our baby every day and why didn't we get a miracle? He had no idea I held this weight, that every day at some point in the day I felt the loss. This was not a shame on him moment – I hadn't shared my pain with him. It was an area in my life that just still felt broken.

Eight years later my life was still functioning but it felt like there was a film over everything. I didn't know why, but I knew I was not fully alive. I started doing breathwork with a facilitator and went on a seven-day retreat. I had three living children at this point and hadn't been away from any of my children overnight. Ever. It changed my life. It was a bit of a spiritual bootcamp and exactly what I needed. The part of my grief journey I never got to with Kayda was surrender and forgiveness. I just hadn't let go of the "why did this happen?" I hadn't let go of blaming myself for something I had no control of. I hadn't forgiven myself for making a decision that no one should ever have to make. I hadn't forgiven The Creator/God/Higher Power, as if this entity is outside of me. This was the missing piece for me. I needed a somatic approach to get me to surrender and let go. I needed the blessing of silence, of embracing the space between to find forgiveness. And every step along the way I have needed community. Unconditional listening.

Although I don't have any advice for that version of me, I do have assurance; you can't rush grieving. It's not efficient or neat, nor does it happen in any sort of order. Grieving truly is a journey. Let it change you. And I would say, you are exactly where you are supposed to be and you are loved.

I don't know that I could advise anyone either – other than to take time for yourself and listen. If you don't actively seek others who have experienced a similar loss, be open to them showing up. No human is an island – like all trials in life there are always folks along the path in front of, alongside, and behind you. Set your course to one day to have your pain be of service to another. My intention in writing this bit of my grief journey was to reach anyone who might relate to the experience, to support anyone in seeing a speck of light down the path. Perhaps just to see a crack where light could enter. And I received so much more from the writing, it somehow deepened the healing. I feel lighter having written it.

Karen S.

The Story in Review

Today, thanks to medical advancements, we not only have the ability to determine a baby's sex before birth, often accompanied by 3D imaging, but we also have optional noninvasive screenings to assess the unborn child's risk for specific congenital conditions. These genetic screening tests are recommended for all pregnancies but hold particular importance for women classified as having "advanced maternal age."

It's worth noting the terminology shift from "geriatric pregnancy" to *advanced maternal age,*" which now encompasses women aged 35 or older at their estimated delivery date. While statistically older maternal age does pose more risks, it's essential to acknowledge that there can be exceptions. For instance, my mom was almost 45 when she gave birth to me, and she experienced an uncomplicated pregnancy and delivery.

However, what happens when the genetic screening test results reveal a potential defect? This is a heart-wrenching decision that Karen and her husband had to navigate. Let's review their experience of grief and decision-making in this context.

 Culture: There's an existing cultural stigma surrounding abortions, which makes it even more challenging for parents faced with the gut-wrenching decision to terminate a pregnancy. However, their decision often arises from their deep love for their unborn child, as they want to spare themselves from inevitable suffering. Despite the local cultural norms, this decision was far from easy.

 Mind: Karen's story was marked by limiting beliefs that initially hindered her. She wrestled with denial, hoping against hope for an alternative diagnosis and prognosis. This denial is entirely understandable given the circumstances. Additionally, she carried a sense of personal responsibility and self-blame for her baby's condition.

 Body: Beyond the physical diagnosis, there were no significant physical aspects mentioned in this story.

Gather: The pivotal shifts in her story encompassed learning of the initial diagnosis, making the heart-wrenching decision, and ultimately terminating the pregnancy.

 Relate: Karen went through a complex emotional journey, what she referred to as "ugly emotions." This included experiencing denial and anxiously awaiting a spark of hope, feeling engulfed in a fog of activities that blurred events, encountering surprise and confusion, struggling with profound despair and a sense of being lost, facing a constant struggle to make the "right" choices amid overwhelming loss, harboring resentment and bitterness, wrestling with feelings of personal responsibility and fault and coping with a profound sense of brokenness.

 Involve: Throughout her recovery journey, she channeled her focus into dedicated parenting, seeking comfort in the care of her first child. She made the difficult choice to cancel a planned vacation to create space for her grieving process. Embracing mindfulness, she engaged in meditation, breathwork, and attended a spiritual boot camp. Writing this chapter for the book also became a meaningful part of her healing journey.

 Ease: Karen found support from numerous resources including doctors, spiritual counselors, meditation groups, breathwork sessions, and conversations with people who didn't shy away from discussing loss. She also found support in community and unconditional listening, as well as engaging in a seven-day spiritual bootcamp with a somatic approach to surrendering, letting go, and forgiving herself and others.

 Focus: Karen's "new normal" involves embracing surrender, letting go, and finding forgiveness for herself and others including not being triggered by pregnant women. She continues using her pain to serve others, such as sharing her story in this book.

"Who would want to hear my story?" That was Karen's first response when I gave her this opportunity to share with you. If this story resonates with you, I'd be happy to pass on your love and story with her by sending me an email at HealthyGrief@DrKarenKramer.com.

Stillbirth: White Feathers From Heaven

It humbles you and teaches you to love unconditionally each and every day!

In January 2001, I found out I was pregnant. This was very exciting as I had suffered two miscarriages in the past year. I had wanted a sibling for my daughter Madi. Upon hearing this good news, I was elated.

As the pregnancy progressed, I had many tests to check the health of myself and the baby I was so excited to be carrying. This included a high-resolution ultrasound to check for Down Syndrome as I was an older mother. All tests came back negative, and I was good to go! As the months flew by, everything was moving along as expected as I started feeling movement which then went to kicks and jabs. I do remember at about month six that this baby did not seem to be kicking as much as I remembered Madi kicking. I just shrugged it off as all babies are different.

One weekend, we met friends at the lake. As the day progressed, I was not feeling any movement. What I knew to do was drink a cold glass of water and within 15 minutes, I could feel the hiccups she was experiencing. Of course, I was very relieved!

As the summer and my pregnancy progressed, I went to the doctor for my monthly visits, and everything was going according to plan while I awaited my second daughter's arrival.

On the day of my last maternity visit before delivery, I went to see my doctor. I took my daughter Madi with me as she had stayed home from school that day. My name was called, and I went into the room and waited for the nurse to examine me.

When she came in, she asked a few questions as to how everything was going and then she then took her stethoscope out to listen for the baby's heartbeat.

As I watched, I thought I saw a look of uncertainty on her face. She then told me she would be right back.

After a few moments she came back in and told me she needed to do an ultrasound. At this point I suspected that there might be an issue. As she started the ultrasound, I noticed her face looked concerned. She looked up at me and simply said "There is no heartbeat." It was as if everything in my world stopped. I can tell you it takes several moments for that statement to sink in.

After that I don't remember the exact conversation, but she explained how I would have to deliver the baby and they would check with the hospital and set up a date for me to check in.

Since I had my daughter with me, I didn't want to break down as it would scare her. We drove home and I called my husband and asked him to please come home as the baby had died. When he arrived, we sat down with Madi and explained how the baby had passed away while in mommy's tummy. It was a devastating experience as this conversation made it all too real. There is truly nothing harder than knowing you have lost your child.

I had to wait several days before being able to be admitted into a hospital so I could deliver, and that was excruciating for me. I kept thinking I could feel her moving inside of me, but it was nothing more than her floating around in my amniotic fluid.

After three days had gone by, I finally received a call from the hospital and was informed that they had a room available for my delivery. An immense fear came over me and I was having a very hard time deciding if I wanted to see the baby. I had been warned that since she had died several days prior her body might already be starting to decay. I still can't believe how callously they delivered that news to me. My heart just sank.

Once I arrived at the hospital, I was given Pitocin to start labor. I had been in active labor for several hours when a nurse came in to check my progress and told me that I had dilated to five and had several more hours to go. That was at 7:30 pm. The nurse left the room, and my husband left the room to make some phone calls. At 7:45 I sneezed, and I watched my bed sheets move. I had an epidural and had no feeling, but I knew I had just delivered my baby.

I notified the nurse's station and informed them, but it took about 10 minutes as they told me they had just checked me, and I was not ready yet. When the nurse finally came in to check she lifted the covers. I saw a little head with lots of black hair. That's when the bedlam started. Everyone was scurrying around not sure exactly what to do. I was given a shot that made me really dizzy and they took the baby away and cleaned me and the bed up. And just like that it was over.

When you lose a baby, they put a picture of a white rose on your door, so everyone knows. It is really a hollow feeling to not have a baby to hold and marvel over. I felt so lost!

I gave birth on September 6, and my daughter's birthday was the next day, September 7. I informed the staff that I would like to check out by noon as I had promised her that I would take her to get a shaved ice for her big day.

When I left the next morning, I took the white rose picture off my door, and my husband and I headed to the car with no baby to carry out.

As promised, I picked Madi up and took her to get her shaved ice.

The next day was her birthday party with all her friends and their parents. What a shock it was when not one person mentioned what happened or asked me how I was. I now realize they had no idea what to say and I understand.

On the Monday after my Thursday delivery, I decided I did want to see my baby. I called the doctor's office and informed them of my decision. I was told they would check into that for me. The next day, I was told I should not see her as they had done an autopsy on her and had not sutured her up.

At this point I really felt like my world was standing still. It was almost too much to process. The heaviness in my chest was unbearable and tears were flowing almost all day long.

I was informed that a nurse had taken photos of her, and I could come pick them up anytime. I made an appointment to go get them and met with a very kind nurse that looked at the pictures with me. We were both very emotional and as we were viewing the pictures, a white feather fell from the ceiling and landed by my hand. We both looked at each other in amazement and she told me there were no feathers in that room. We sat in awe for a few moments and then we hugged each other, and I left.

As the days went by, I felt so very lost. Things go back to normal but losing a baby created a new normal for me. I cried, I grieved, and I asked God why?

One thing that did not stop was the small white feathers that seemed to find me wherever I was. They were always floating down from what I believe to be heaven. About two weeks had passed after my loss and we received a call from the coroner's office. Had my baby lived, she would have had Down Syndrome. I was shocked as I'd had tests for that. The information caused more tears and grief as it was explained to me that often babies with Down Syndrome have bad hearts and can pass away unexpectedly.

During this time while I was trying to heal, one of the modalities I had been using was meditation. One night while I was deep in meditation, I heard a voice tell me my daughter decided to return home as she would not have been able to accomplish what she came here for with the body she would have had. I really felt like that was the voice of God.

Losing a child is not something I would wish on anyone. It's losing a part of yourself and knowing you can never replace it. That knowledge created a painful reality for me.

My greatest surprise came three months later when I found out I was pregnant again. My third little girl was born one year after I lost my middle child. During a dream I was told she would be much lighter than my first daughter and would have curly hair. And indeed, she does. All my babies were born in September, and all are celebrated with joy and love every birthday! I honor my child's choice to return home, and know I will meet her when I make my journey back home.

I now know what an important and sacred journey it is to grieve. There are no rights or wrongs when you are walking this path. It is about letting go with forgiveness and love and understanding that you will never know the why of your loss. It is choosing to surrender to a higher power and to have faith in the unseen. It humbles you and teaches you to love unconditionally each and every day!

Nicole Harvick
Surfside, SC

The Story in Review

Perinatal deaths represent a form of disenfranchised grief, a type of grief that is not traditionally recognized but has a profound impact on mothers-to-be, as illustrated in Nicole's narrative. In her case, she had developed a deep bond with her unborn child.

Perinatal deaths encompass a range of losses, including fetal deaths occurring as early as 20 completed weeks of pregnancy and live births with only brief survival, up to 28 days after birth (although some sources report this period as 28 weeks gestation and seven days after birth). These losses are grouped together under the assumption that similar factors are associated with them. Perinatal death is not typically reported as an event in itself but is used for statistical purposes. Regardless of the specific gestational period involved, any form of perinatal death leads to grief. Nicole's experience, in particular, falls under the category of *stillbirth*, which is further defined as the death or loss of a baby before or during delivery. (Note: It's important to distinguish *miscarriage*, which refers to the unintended ending of a pregnancy before 20 completed weeks of gestation and is the most common type of perinatal loss.)

Toxic Positivity: In this case, the day after her procedure, Nicole attended her daughter's birthday party with all her friends and their parents. She was taken aback when no one mentioned what had happened or asked her how she was feeling. It seemed that people found it easier to avoid the conversation than to figure out how to engage with someone who had experienced loss. However, Nicole was in need of support.

Body: Apart from the physical loss, no other physical aspects of this story were mentioned.

Gather: The most significant shifts in her story included the moment she found out there was no heartbeat and the day she gave birth.

Relate: Nicole's emotional and mental journey included feelings of shock, a sense that her world had come to a standstill, profound loss, "sunken heart," tears, and fear.

 Involve: Various actions were taken to move herself forward in her grief journey. These actions included telling her daughter about the baby's passing, keeping promises such as taking her daughter for shaved ice, hosting a birthday party for her daughter the day after the procedure, and practicing meditation.

 Ease: Resources that offered Nicole comfort included access to a nurse who allowed Nicole to view pictures of her baby with emotional aid and her husband's unwavering support.

 Focus: Nicole's "new normal" encompasses letting go, forgiveness, love, and an understanding that she may never fully comprehend why she experienced this loss. She embraces surrendering to a higher power, having faith in the unseen, and approaching each day with unconditional love.

It was not intentional to have two maternity stories related to Down Syndrome. However, together, they paint a stirring picture of "what if?" What if Nicole's genetic testing had indicated a likelihood that her baby might not survive? Would she have chosen to terminate her pregnancy? For Karen (in our previous story), would she have grieved "easier" with a stillbirth due to unknown genetic conditions as opposed to being faced with the decision to terminate her pregnancy? (Note: I am not comparing this to live births of healthy Down Syndrome children; I am only highlighting, given these two stories and the known facts, the complexities and difficult decisions that can arise in unfortunate circumstances.)

On a positive note, both Nicole and Karen each welcomed a healthy child after their tragic losses.

Empty Nester: In This Room

I cried to a chapter that has closed and thankful for the new chapter that is starting.

The following is a poem I created when my last child moved out of the house. It captures the hopes, dreams, and sorrows of losing my little boy to becoming an independent adult of his own.

In this room, so many memories are held dear.

In this room, I stuck clouds on the ceiling when I was six months pregnant.

In this room, I laid my baby to rest during the day and cuddled him in my own bed at night.

In this room, I transformed the child's bed into a full bed for my growing toddler.

In this room, my toddler learned how to play quietly next to the bed while his exhausted mom napped in the middle of the day.

In this room, the Belly Mouse and Tickle-Kissy Monster brought laughter and giggles.

In this room, I answered questions like "Why doesn't hair bleed when you cut it?" and "Why are they called 'windows' when wind doesn't blow through it and it's not made of dough?"

In this room, I knew I was raising a future UN Negotiator... or Lawyer!

In this room, I told him he was going to have four older siblings and a new dad.

In this room, we made a bunk bed for him and his new brother.

In this room, I tip-toed through landmines of Legos to kiss my boys good-night before bed.

In this room, my son read stories to ME before bed... then I would sneak off and read a couple chapters ahead because I got sucked into the Harry Potter series. :)

In this room, I comforted a child who couldn't sleep by rubbing their back.

In this room, the door was slammed by a child... or a parent.

In this room, I told my son his grandpa had passed. I never imagined three months later, I'd be telling him his dad passed away too.

In this room, I held my son, cried with my son, got frustrated with my son, and did my best to hold it together when my son's health declined.

In this room, my son thrived after breaking through to heal himself utilizing the same techniques I use with my clients!

In this room, he put on his cap and gown with pride to graduate with his peers after completing his high school senior year in seven weeks!

In this room, he applied for jobs and college.

In this room, I watched him pack for that day.

Out of this room walked a man.

For that man... moved into a house.

That house was built by my grandparents in the 1940s.

That house has supported numerous generations of family members over the years... including myself when I was building my own house.

That house... is the place where a new chapter will begin.

If I only had a crystal ball to foretell the future it would hold.

For now, I remember all the room has held, the house has supported, and wish all the best for the man who is carrying on a new chapter of his own.

In this room, I sat... on the empty floor... recalling all the memories this room has held for the last 22 years since it was built... and I cried to a chapter that has closed and thankful for the new chapter that is starting for that young man.

Dr. Karen Kramer
San Diego, CA

The Story in Review

As I aimed to wrap up this maternity chapter with a touch of light-heartedness, I couldn't resist delving into the curious world of being an empty nester beyond my own experience. So, here's what I uncovered...

I stumbled upon a *BetterHealth* article that rather fittingly dubs it "Empty Nest Syndrome," defining it as the grief that many parents feel when their kids finally fly the coop.[70] This condition seems to hit women more often, especially those who've held the fort as the primary caregiver. Well, that sort of matches my story, but it's the first time I've heard it called a "syndrome." Naturally, I couldn't help but dig deeper.

According to *BetterHealth*, mothers might find themselves feeling a tad worthless, disoriented, and downright clueless about what the future holds. And then, there's the *Healthline* article titled "Moving from an Empty Nest to Post-Parental Growth," which suggests that parents could be plagued by loneliness, depression, or a sense of purposelessness, all of which might mess with their emotional well-being and daily routines.[71] *PsychCentral* chimes in with its piece "The Bittersweet 'Empty Nest,'" adding feelings of sadness and anxiety to the mix, as well as a general loss of purpose.[72]

But don't fret! A *Science of People* article called "Empty Nest Syndrome: How to Cope as a Parent Feeling Lost" proposes that there are just three stages to this empty nest thing: grief, relief, and joy. *That's it?!* Now, to answer my burning question – "How long should this take?" – *BetterHealth* comes to the rescue with, "Most mothers adapt in time. Psychologists suggest that it may take between 18 months and two years to make the successful transition from 'mum' to independent woman." *Two years?!*

And so, I found myself pondering: Is empty nest syndrome even a real thing?

According to WebMD, "Empty nest syndrome isn't a clinical diagnosis, but it's a term used to describe these feelings."[73] Phew, a collective sigh of relief from every parent (including yours truly) not looking for another "syndrome" to add to the collection. Or am I the only one feeling this way? The article goes on to explain that these bittersweet emotions can be bewildering, often clashing with the pride parents feel about their child's accomplishments. I might add (as Jan's retirement story suggested in the chapter "Retirement"), that it can also mix with a dash of "Woohoo! You're child-free now! Time for the parents to party!"

Okay, thanks for indulging my research quest, and I hope it brought some laughs or nods of recognition to those of you facing the symptoms of "empty nest syndrome."

Now, let's get back to our regularly scheduled program and dive into my poem with the knowledge that it doesn't cover every facet of the stories we've previously explored.

 Gather: The poem itself chronicles two decades of the rollercoaster ride known as parenting, from the ups to the downs. The biggest shift occurred the day my youngest son spread his wings and moved out.

 Relate: I must admit, I shed a tear or... 20 (but who was counting) on that departure day, even though he'd only relocated a stone's throw away, just a five-minute stroll. Typically, the last child leaving the nest stirs up a cocktail of emotions (as my research confirmed). I savored my newfound freedom to do as I pleased, only to find myself pondering over my son because he wasn't there anymore. I missed our shared moments and activities. Naturally, my feelings post-departure were heavily influenced by our close-knit relationship.

 Involve: Suddenly, I was not only an empty nester but also the sole inhabitant of the house (unless you count the cat and two dogs). To ease into this new phase, I took up hobbies like reading and binging on Netflix series, and I even expanded my business (which conveniently included my son's old bedroom).

 Ease: I sought support by reconnecting with old friends. I also set up "Mom and Son" date nights for the initial weeks, complete with dinner and Netflix, to help ease the transition – for *him*, of course.

 Focus: The "new normal" entails living my life as my son lives his, without the daily check-ins or constant reminders for him to call his mama. Okay, I'm still working on this one!

In Summary

"You can learn many things from children.
How much patience you have, for instance."
~ Franklin P. Jones

What's your story? Have you, or someone you know, experienced the heart-wrenching loss of a child before, during, or soon after childbirth? How did you react, or how did they react? Perhaps you've faced the bittersweet experience of becoming an empty nester. How did you handle it, or how did your loved ones cope with this new chapter in life?

Through the heart-wrenching stories of **pregnancy termination** and **stillbirth** (and, yes, being an **empty nester**), we were exposed to other forms of *disenfranchised grief*. Upon further review, these narratives also introduced us to the concepts of *advanced maternal age*, *perinatal deaths*, and *"empty nest syndrome."*

Our reactions in these challenging moments are deeply intertwined with our **cultural** influences and the beliefs, values, and attitudes that shape our worldview, ultimately impacting our thoughts, feelings, actions, and reactions of our **mind**. While these stories primarily focus on the emotional aspects of grief, I chose not to explore the scientific intricacies on the body surrounding maternity defects and diagnoses.

As we navigate these narratives through the lens of the **Healthy GRIEF Framework**, it becomes evident that the journey is a highly personal one for each individual. Setting aside the story of empty nesting and concentrating solely on the two maternity stories, here's a concise summary:

Gather: The most pivotal moments in these stories revolve around receiving the initial diagnosis or medical news and the emotionally charged moments of termination or childbirth.

 Relate: Within these stories, a wide array of thoughts and emotions surfaced, including a profound sense of overwhelm, shocking revelations, deep despair, a feeling of being utterly lost, the tenacious grasp of hope, moments of denial, a longing for miracles, an overwhelming sense of brokenness, the burden of self-blame, the bitter taste of resentment, the fiery sting of anger, and the ever-present fear of the unknown.

 Involve: To navigate their grief, each took various actions including seeking distraction through activities (particularly with their other children), granting themselves the space to grieve (including canceling commitments), exploring holistic health practices (like meditation, breathwork, and participation in spiritual boot camps), and turning to writing as a therapeutic outlet.

 Ease: One found comfort and support in spiritual counseling, meditation groups, breathwork sessions, somatic practices, or spiritual communities. Both engaged in conversations with empathetic individuals who didn't shy away from discussing loss such as a compassionate nurse and a supportive partner.

 Focus: The recurring themes in their "new normal" included the profound act of surrendering and letting go, the transformative power of forgiveness (towards oneself and others), finding comfort and faith in surrendering to a higher power and the unseen, and a commitment to love unconditionally each and every day.

Discover within these stories echoes of your own journey. May they serve as a source of reflection and inspiration as you navigate your unique path through grief, or that of someone you know.

Healthfully grieving your physical abilities that are no longer.

HEALTH

"You can't always choose what happens to you, but you can always choose how you feel about it."

- Danielle Laporte

Who are we without our health? Whether from the moment of birth, an unexpected accident, a life-altering diagnosis, or facing the inevitable end-of-life, we navigate an array of health-related transitions throughout our lifetime. In this chapter, we delve into narratives that encapsulate various journeys through health-related grief.

The inaugural tale is my own, recounting the aftermath of a car accident that left me encased in a "halo" brace. This journey explores how, as a teenager, I struggled with the sense of losing "everything."

Next, we embark on Jarie Lyn's remarkable voyage through the realm of health diagnoses. Her unwavering willpower, determination, and an unshakable positive spirit served as armor, shielding her during even the darkest days.

Finally, we encounter Suzie's story, who courageously confronted seven years of life marked by a debilitating disease. This narrative intertwines her personal journey with my own, as a family united in offering unwavering support – both throughout her life and as she embarked on her final transition.

In contemplating these stories, we realize that health is the foundation upon which we build our lives, our dreams, and our very identities. Through these narratives, we glimpse the essence of who we are in the face of health-related grief, and we find unity in our shared experiences and emotions.

As you immerse yourself in these narratives, take heed of what resonates with your own experiences and feelings. It is through understanding and empathy that we can begin to heal, offering solace and support to one another on this profound journey.

Car Accident:
Beauty, Brains, and a
Fist-Sized Knot of Hair

My mission was to have others see me through the halo, beyond its confines.

T he year was 1987, and the fall semester at San Diego State University was underway. It was a crisp Saturday, just on the cusp of Thanksgiving, and the prospect of a Disneyland adventure beckoned. Accompanied by three friends, we embarked on a two-hour drive from San Diego, ready for a day of excitement. The mode of transportation was the topic of deliberation – between Mike's truck and my Honda, the truck emerged as the choice due to its additional space for our quartet.

Mike's truck featured what was referred to as a "carpet kit." In essence, it comprised a board that matched the truck bed's dimensions, concealing a treasure trove of DJ equipment beneath. The cab compartment elevated this truck's potential. On that morning destined for Disneyland, Mike took the wheel, Meesh occupied the passenger seat, while Steve and I lay sprawled in the back. The constraints of the cab's height left us no option but to recline. With no seatbelts securing us, the scenario was far from ideal.

As the checkpoint loomed ahead, an unexpected maneuver by another vehicle resulted in Mike rear-ending them. In the ensuing collision, I collided with the cab's window frame. Though specific details remain hazy, I do recall Meesh's face smeared with blood, an outcome of her fingernail meeting her eyelid. Amidst the chaos, my arm became temporarily paralyzed, a sensation that sent shockwaves of panic through me.

Hospitalized in the aftermath, I attempted to reassure my friends that I might end up donning a neck brace and be wheeled around Disneyland – a lighthearted notion to mitigate the gravity of the situation. X-rays were ordered, interspersed with periods of stillness in the hospital hallway. Friends lingered nearby, their inquiries echoing my own uncertainty. I requested an update from the nurses, only to be met with silence. In a moment of clarity, I turned to them and questioned, "What's the diagnosis?"

The nurse's response left me numb and incredulous. "You broke your neck."

I what?!

I was stunned, coming to grips with the sheer disbelief of her words. It wasn't the response I had anticipated, and the weight of the revelation sank in slowly. In my haze, I still clung to the idea of continuing our Disneyland escapade. I assured myself that I was fine. Reality, however, belied my hopeful façade. I wasn't fine; I couldn't be, with a broken neck.

Eventually, I found myself escorted by ambulance to a hospital closer to home, with Mike by my side. Amidst the chaos, the EMTs misinterpreted his role, assuming he was my boyfriend and playfully jesting about my plight. They suggested that he should keep a wallet-sized X-ray next to my picture in his wallet so he could say, "Hey, here's my girlfriend. And she has brains too." As we navigated the journey, their humor provided a respite from the mounting pain and the impending challenges.

Arriving at Kaiser, my local hospital, my mother awaited me. I could only imagine the whirlwind of thoughts running through her mind, compounded by her earlier apprehensions about my trip. She had queried me about Mike's driving safety, a question I had brushed aside with youthful optimism. (Don't all kids answer "yes" to the safety of their friend's driving abilities when they really want to go somewhere?) In hindsight, her intuitions were eerily accurate.

My quiet hope lay in the prospect that my mother might miraculously mend me with her hands-on healing abilities, sparing me from the impending ordeal. Unfortunately, the doctor shattered that hope with the announcement of a "halo" – a metal brace to immobilize my neck. The description drifted away as I fixated on the concept of screws penetrating my skull. This contraption would be my new companion for the next three months, an unexpected cage of confinement.

My injuries were grave – a fracture in my C5 vertebra, with C6 thrust out of alignment. In layman's terms, I had miraculously survived a situation that often resulted in paralysis or death. A temporary paralysis gripped my left arm, a stark reminder of the fragility of life.

During that fateful weekend, my father was attending a barbershop choir convention. Unbeknownst to him, he was ensnared in the traffic snarl resulting from my accident, stranded alongside his companions in our motorhome. In the pre-mobile phone era, news of my mishap didn't reach him until his return home a day or two after the incident.

The image of my father's face remains etched in my memory – a rare instance where his tears flowed freely. His expression reflected a parent's helplessness, the yearning to trade places with their child, to bear the pain instead. Yet, in the face of adversity, he stood powerless.

Before the accident, my hair cascaded down to my waist, a hallmark of my identity as a Polynesian dancer. Then came the aftermath – my hair knotted, thanks to my mother's careful but hair-raising attempt at washing it over the kitchen sink while avoiding the screw holes on my head. Days of tearful effort ensued, as I sat cross-legged on the bathroom counter, painstakingly untangling my hair strand by strand. Eventually, a fist-sized knot succumbed to the scissors. The loss was shattering; it symbolized my lost identity, a connection severed.

My self-worth was intertwined with my appearance, a sentiment especially potent for teenagers. The simple act of driving was now beyond my reach, reinstating my dependence on my parents. I had lost it all – my independence, my identity, my looks, my first college semester.

Gradually, the clouds of self-pity dissipated, and I rekindled my engagement with life. My friends played a pivotal role, their presence a balm for my wounded spirit. As Christmas break beckoned, the camaraderie of friends who had returned home proved restorative. Crafting ornaments from Christmas balls and ribbons, we decorated my halo and the tree in tandem. It was a lighthearted attempt at restoring normalcy, a testimony to the power of friendship.

Amid this journey, I encountered a man with a physical disability in a store. Our eyes met in a silent understanding – a shared recognition of our differences that united us. It forged an appreciation for those battling physical challenges, revealing a newfound empathy.

Returning to college for the second semester, I resided in the sorority house on campus, eliminating the need to drive. A return to the campus landscape was a unique experience. My halo stirred curiosity, prompting second glances and unspoken questions. To dissipate the discomfort, I assumed the role of an icebreaker, openly sharing details of my situation. I aimed to be seen through the halo, not defined by it.

My renewed confidence found expression in humor. I wove jokes about my predicament, using humor to both lighten the atmosphere and forge connections. Lines like "I need that like I need another hole in my head," "I'm a little screwy," "I'm a little nutty," or "Excuse me, I'm a numb skull," became my arsenal against awkwardness. This wit not only humanized my situation but also helped break down barriers.

My mission was to have others see me through the halo, beyond its confines. It was a declaration that I was not the halo; it was a temporary accessory, not my essence. A little sister pledge event for a local fraternity showcased this newfound confidence as I accompanied one of my sorority sisters. A glance laden with disdain met me, yet it was a gaze I could deflect with newfound self-assurance. The incident stood as a testament to the resilience I had cultivated.

Support, particularly from my sorority sisters, classmates, and teachers, bolstered me throughout this ordeal. I recall my big sister Pauline's gesture of cutting my meat at dinner – a simple act yet deeply touching.

Amid the triumphs, there were setbacks. A bump to my halo misaligned one of the screws, presenting a decision: an agonizing repositioning or a risk-prone acceptance. I had my eyes closed while the technicians were discussing what to do with me. One of them said they could take the screw out and reposition it. I opened up my eyes and I said, "You are not putting another screw in my head!" Opting for caution, I continued my journey with a crooked screw, a choice that challenged me to navigate with care. The final month with the halo held both apprehension and determination.

My halo's removal was a pivotal moment. My return to the sorority dining table that evening was a silent declaration of triumph. Most didn't even notice its absence, and that was victory in itself. Their ability to see beyond the halo to the person beneath, the person I was, spoke volumes.

Emerging from the halo, I embarked on the journey to rebuild my physical endurance, a challenge for someone who had been a dancer since the age of four. The three-month halo stint had extracted a toll on my muscle mass, endurance, and flexibility. As I re-entered an exercise class, the stark reality hit – the breathlessness, the fatigue, the undeniable loss of what I had once possessed. Grieving for the dancer within became a chapter of my healing process.

Dr. Karen Kramer
San Diego, CA

The Story in Review

Let's embark on a journey to uncover why navigating grief in a healthy way was important to me following and even decades after the car accident.

Body: Since the car accident, I tend to carry stress in my shoulders and next. I know when I'm starting to get stressed when I wear my shoulders as my earrings. (See the Story in Review for the chapter "Family Estrangement" for questions regarding shoulders.) Ten years after the accident, while working long hours typing on a work project, I ended up with excruciating nerve pain and temporary paralysis in my left arm again. It was a wake-up call teaching me to listen to my body. Using Jensen's *The Healing Questions Guide*, here are a series of questions related to the neck. Some of the answers may already have made a surprise appearance in my story.

Neck Problems

1. What issues are coming up for me that I do not believe I can handle?
2. What will it take to be willing to loosen up my perspective and see things in a different way?
3. What will it take to release the need to control things and allow life to flow through me with ease?
4. What will it take to be able to safely express all that seems to be coming to the surface?
5. What benefit is there and being so rigid and controlling regarding how I think things need to happen? Is it really serving me? What would be a healthier way to handle life?
6. What will it take to express what I am feeling without the fear of retaliation?
7. What will it take to tune into my emotional needs and attend to the presenting issues?

Broken Neck

1. What do I need to learn regarding the level of control I expect to have over life?

 Gather: The major shifts in my story were the day of the accident, the diagnosis of a broken neck, and installing the "halo."

 Relate: My emotional rollercoaster included feeling numbness (emotionally and physically), denial, overwhelming sadness, and a full-blown pity-party. Anger surfaced followed by the thought that "I was lucky to be alive," and eventually a newfound confidence!

 Involve: My game plan involved escaping the house, hanging out with friends, returning to college, and eventually living back on campus.

 Ease: I owe my sanity to the laughter and jokes shared with friends, sorority sisters, college professors, and classmates. Oh, and let's not forget the unwavering love and support of my dear parents!

 Focus: My "new normal" involved embracing lifelong self-care, because neck arthritis and surgery are not on my to-do list. Regular massages and chiropractic adjustments are a core part of my monthly routine.

The Diagnosis:
A Life Fighter with a Smile

Life is too short, and none of us know when our time is up.

/t was August 2022 while on vacation in Lake Tahoe that I realized something was very wrong with me.

For months, I had been experiencing frequent heartburn and acid reflux that kept getting worse. It was so bad that when I would get heartburn, I could predict that I was going to vomit my food. It had gotten to the point where it was happening more frequently, at least three times per week. So, Lake Tahoe was a turning point for me. My husband and I were walking around looking at the sights and I had to sit down every few feet because I was so weak. I also knew that the dinner I had just eaten, which was a salad, wasn't sitting in the right place. I could feel it as I walked, and I mentioned it to my husband.

Have you ever drunk too much water at one time and when you roll over or change positions, you can feel it sloshing around? Well, that's what it was like with my food, except it was more uncomfortable. When we got back to the room, I vomited about three days' worth of food. I was miserable. I was also disappointed that this was ruining our vacation, our fun time together.

The next day, I felt fine. Even after eating. Then about two days later, I vomited again. The ride home back to Vegas was miserable. I threw up several times and my husband wanted to take me to the hospital right then, but I put him off and said, "If I'm not better tomorrow, then you can take me." So, the next day, which was August 29, after throwing up and experiencing my heart race, we drove to the ER.

I spent the next five days in the hospital, and it took a while before the doctors could figure out what was going on. There was a mass on my stomach that was pushing against the wall where the stomach meets the intestines, and the food could not pass. So, the only way for it to come out was by going up. According to the doctors, they thought the mass was an ulcer. They put a stent in my stomach which allowed it to open so that food could pass.

Once released from the hospital, I finally felt like my old self again. I was eating, the heartburn and acid reflux were gone, and my food was digesting properly. But the stent was only temporary. It was only supposed to remain for a few months, and the theory was that it would help the stomach remain open after the stent removal.

The doctor who placed the stent also specialized in colonoscopies, so I scheduled an appointment to have that done and the results came back as positive for colon cancer. He supposedly removed it but there was still a polyp that he said wasn't cancer.

I got the stent removed in October or November. That was a huge mistake, because I was back to vomiting and feeling weak. I never got sick after day one of eating, it was always on day three or four after the food piled up so much that it needed to come up to escape.

One day in December I wasn't feeling well so I took myself to an urgent care ER and told them I thought I might be dehydrated. After some blood tests confirmed that I was indeed dehydrated, they hooked me up to an IV and then they said my potassium levels were so low that they didn't want to release me. Because they were an urgent care ER, they couldn't keep me overnight, so they had me transferred to Mountain View Hospital by ambulance.

My husband came and got my purse, etc. We thought I was only going to be there overnight. Boy, were we wrong. The first night, after the nurse gave me potassium pills to take, something happened to me. I felt an excruciating pain in my lower right abdominal area. It was so bad that I could hardly breathe or move. I couldn't even walk. I thought my appendix had burst. I frantically pushed the nurse's button and was doing my best to call out, but my voice was so small. When she finally answered the call, she didn't believe me. In fact, I told the story to the doctors over several days and nobody believed me. I begged them to take another CT scan or MRI. That wouldn't happen until the fourth day I was in the hospital.

In the meantime, different surgical teams would come into my room and tell me they've never seen a case like this. They couldn't figure out what to do or what the problem was. One doctor told me I might need to have a feeding tube inserted. Another doctor told me that my entire colon would have to be removed and another doctor talked about rerouting everything surgically. I felt like they were treating me like an experiment.

I thought I was dying. And what made it worse is that one doctor said to me, "Man, I don't know what you did in a past life, but it must have been really bad." For a doctor to say that to me was terrifying.

I think I had three endoscopies during this visit, the third one putting the stent back in and doing a biopsy on the mass. The results came back positive for gastric cancer. And another colorectal surgeon did another colonoscopy and removed the cancer that the first colon doctor said wasn't cancer.

Then, the lead doctor who was assigned to my case finally ordered another CT scan and the results showed I had a perforation which could have been fatal. They explained to me that somehow it had healed on its own, otherwise, I would be deathly ill. They don't know what caused it, but I know it happened after taking those potassium pills my first night at the hospital.

During my five-day hospital stay in December, I wasn't allowed any food or drink for almost the entire time I was there. On the fourth day, they allowed me to have ice chips and then a clear liquid diet. By the time they released me, I was on a G.I. Soft Diet which means very low fiber.

I began Chemotherapy in January and finished my last treatment in March. I always cheered up the nurses because I'm such an optimistic and happy person in general. They loved seeing me and even asked me once to give some words of encouragement to a new person who had just been diagnosed with breast cancer.

The dreaded surgery still loomed around the corner and even though I was diagnosed with cancer, I never thought of myself as a cancer patient. I didn't think about cancer at all. If I had a scheduled treatment, I would acknowledge it then, but I never dwelled on the C word.

During treatment I was tested for a genetic defect because it runs in my family. I tested positive for Lynch Syndrome which makes me more prone to five types of cancers that are very aggressive. Instead of doing surgery with the original doctors that scared the crap out of me, I decided to have a discussion with a surgeon at the City of Hope, a Cancer Research Hospital that specializes in Lynch Syndrome. They did CT scans, MRIs, bloodwork, colonoscopy, endoscopy with ultrasound, biopsies, and another genetic test.

Friends and acquaintances who knew about my diagnoses would often ask me in a very sad and depressed voice how I'm doing. They all wanted to know how I was feeling.

Once I was out of the hospital and had a real plan, I was fine. I'm an action taker and just knowing that I was moving forward with chemo and surgery was all I needed to shift my mindset to be more positive.

Chemo made me tired, but I never got sick. I remained in a positive state of mind and would listen to business podcasts and celebrity podcasts during chemo. It kept me focused on the present moment, something good to feed my mind instead of embracing the negative side effects.

Back to the friends and acquaintances who wanted to know how I was feeling... I can honestly say that I had more energy than they did. It may not have been so in the physical body, but my personality and what I exuded, sure had more energy than what they projected.

I had friends calling me up and crying because they were worried about me. My attitude was this: "I am fine, I feel great, everything is going to be OK. I'm a fighter and this THING isn't going to kick my ass or take me down. So, stop worrying. When I have something to worry about, then you can worry, but that isn't now."

Although I went through chemo treatments and had upcoming surgery scheduled, I didn't dwell on any of it. I got up and went to work every day with a legitimate smile on my face, grateful to be alive.

Going through this, though, did allow me to reassess what is important to me. I realized that stressing over credit card debt and medical bills wasn't doing me any good. I do hate being in debt but I'm not fretting over it like I was. Also, I realized that life is too short and none of us know when our time is up. It could happen without warning, and I decided to start implementing more fun into my life and spending more time with my parents and my siblings. In the big scheme of things, I realized that levity and connection is what is important; nothing else really matters.

I've always been a curious person who likes to explore new things and be adventurous. Now, that curiosity and the need to explore is more prevalent within me now.

It's August 2 today, almost one year since my husband took me to the ER after we arrived home from Lake Tahoe. It's surreal to think that I had my surgery just three weeks ago today during which the doctors removed 40% of my stomach, a portion of my colon, and four types of cancers. It almost seems like a lifetime ago. My recovery has been phenomenal. I'm still in the healing process and I'm sore. Six cuts on my stomach are visible still, and yet, people are amazed at how well I'm doing. Even the doctors.

I'm not surprised at all, though. I have a very strong will and I am naturally optimistic. I got that will power from my dad. And I'm a fighter. I don't dwell on the negative things. I just do what needs to be done to move forward in all areas of my life.

After my surgery, my mom had said to me, "Oh thank God they got all the cancer. You're whole again."

"Mom, I've never not been whole."

That comment from my mom was so surprising to me that, in her mind, I wasn't whole because of the cancer invading my body. I was more alive than most of the people I come across daily.

I know that we all face adversity differently. For me, it was to acknowledge that I was scared I was going to die in the hospital in December. Then I got a second wind and decided I wasn't going to die; I was going to live. And I did.

I am grateful for all of the love, support, good vibes, and prayers that I have received from so many people. More than I ever thought possible. Thank you, thank you, thank you.

Jarie Lyn Robbins
Las Vegas, NV

The Story in Review

Let's dive into why navigating grief in a healthy way was crucial for Jarie Lyn.

 Mind: Jarie Lyn was like a rock, holding onto positivity, determination, and an action-oriented attitude. Her sunny outlook on her diagnosis and her journey toward healing shone brightly. She's the definition of strong-willed, naturally optimistic, and a fighter who doesn't dwell on the negatives. She credits this resilience to her dad, saying, "I just do what needs to be done to move forward in all areas of my life."

 Toxic Positivity: Jarie Lyn is essentially a human rainbow, radiating optimism and happiness. Her story illustrates how this relentless positivity can be perceived by others. When her diagnosis hit, friends and family were reaching out in tears and worry. Her response? "I am fine, I feel great, everything Is going to be OK. I'm a fighter and this THING isn't going to kick my ass or take me down. So, stop worrying. When I have something to worry about, then you can worry, but that isn't now." Jarie Lyn marched into work every day with a genuine smile because she was thankful to be alive. However, some people might have perceived this as fake or forced positivity, especially those who knew about her situation. At times, Jarie Lyn chose not to disclose her health situation to others because she didn't want their worry or concerns to interfere with her healing process. As supporters, we should be conscious of our expectations regarding how others should grieve and respect their unique journey.

 Gather: The major shifts in her story occurred with each diagnosis and significant medical event.

Relate: The emotional rollercoaster included disappointment, fear, anxiety, unyielding determination, optimism, happiness, and positivity.

Involve: Her action steps were remarkable, including her choice to move forward with chemo and surgery while continuing to work every day. To maintain a positive mindset during chemo, she listened to business and celebrity podcasts. She was selective about whom she informed regarding her health journey. In addition to conventional treatments, Jarie Lyn shared with me that she also explored holistic healing methods such as Reiki, meditation, sound therapy, and crystal bowls.

 Ease: Support played a vital role in her journey, including her loving and supportive husband who stood by her side. She also shared with me that she accepted help from her mother-in-law for three months during her recovery. Her parents provided unwavering support, and she received an abundance of love, support, good vibes, and prayers from numerous people in her life. Throughout her journey, she made the decision to say "YES" to all the help and support that came her way.

 Focus: Jarie Lyn's health journey continues, and her "new normal" involves reevaluating life's priorities, including what's worth stressing over, like work and debt. She focuses on infusing more joy into her life, prioritizing quality time with her parents and siblings. She emphasizes the importance of recognizing life's unpredictability, with the understanding that "life is too short, and none of us know when our time is up."

The End of Life:
Living a Life Well-Lived

I felt guilty for wanting her to die!

My brothers were 16 and 21 years older than me; my parents were in their late 40s when I was born. We still chuckle about the wedding photo of my eldest brother, Gene, holding me when I was just eight months old. Gene and his wife, Dale, soon had their own bundle of joy, Suzie, who arrived just before my third birthday. Our closeness in age often led me to describe her as my sister or cousin to others, given our mere three-year gap. Suzie remained an only child until her brother's birth when she turned nine. Meanwhile, I might as well have been an only child, with my second eldest brother already married and out of the house by the time I was six. Suzie and I naturally formed a strong bond.

I vividly remember my senior year in high school when Suzie was a freshman. I adopted the role of protective "big sister," even nearly resorting to punching a boy who had teased her in math class. (For clarity, I'm not one to resort to violence; the "evil eye" was enough to deter him. My mission was accomplished!)

We shared living space for two years during our college days, until she embarked on her journey to veterinary school at the University of California, Davis. I always admired her aspiration to become a veterinarian. Nurturing animals came naturally to her from her upbringing on a farm and actively participating in 4-H and FFA (Future Farmers of America). Her path seemed destined to lead her to a flourishing veterinary practice, inheriting the mantle once she completed her degree.

Suzie graduated with honors in May 2000 and married her longtime college boyfriend in November 2001. (Incidentally, I followed suit by marrying my first husband a month later.) However, her anticipated honeymoon was not meant to be. Having fallen ill with "bronchitis" on her wedding day, she weathered her Renaissance-style fairy tale ceremony through sheer determination and the assistance of modern medicine.

Her condition took a darker turn, as further tests confirmed micro-aviary complex disease, also known as the "bird flu," just two months after she was married. Suzie waged a fierce battle against this debilitating, life-threatening ailment for the next seven years. Her illness cast a shadow over the splendid life she was poised to lead with her husband and a promising veterinary career.

To manage her condition, she navigated a maze of medications, reaching nearly 30 at one point. Amid the mix, she even had to take birth control pills to prevent pregnancy due to the complex drug interactions. A term of endearment I coined for her during this period was the "walking medicine cabinet."

Suzie's journey was a roller coaster of good days and bad, a norm for someone in her early thirties wrestling with an all-consuming diagnosis. Despite the challenges, she embraced life to the fullest. She ventured into new territory by playing golf and even embarked on a Harley ride, oxygen tanks stowed away in saddle bags. Her dog, Bertha, was one of her favorite companions throughout her journey. She continued working until her condition no longer allowed.

Lung transplant wasn't an option due to the likelihood that her disease would also afflict the transplanted lung. She was labeled terminal. Several close calls prompted her to wear a medical alert device around her neck, which she could activate to summon the fire department during an attack when she couldn't breathe. Numerous calls were made using this panic button, more than one would care to count. Once, a violent cough resulted in a hole in her lung, necessitating a chemically induced coma for her lungs to heal. I remember feeling angry after one of these hospital stays – an emotion whose target I couldn't quite pin down. The unsettling thought "I wish she'd died!" flashed through my mind, quickly replaced by guilt for even thinking such a thing.

Of course, I never wanted Suzie to die. She was my cherished sister. I'd still defend her, just as I was prepared to do back in high school. My sentiment was less about wanting her to die and more about wishing for her peace. It was difficult personally to witness the continuous hospital rushes, uncertain whether they marked her final moments.

Living nearby, every sound of a fire truck siren would send my heart racing as I strained to determine its direction. If it sounded nearby, I would sprint down the hill in panic toward her house. I wished for an end to her suffering, for her pain to cease. I wished for her peace. Simultaneously, I wished the same for myself. As her family, we suffered with her, each episode leaving us wondering if it might be her last.

I distinctly remember the day I took her to the hospital, a rare occasion without the accompaniment of a medical transport. The details escape me now, but I recall it might have been for extended tests. Like a soon-to-be mother preparing for a hospital stay, Suzie had an overnight bag ready, complete with a checklist. Yes, she had a travel list for hospitals, a testament to her numerous stays. The most extensive section of the list comprised her medications – 29 in total on that particular day.

Days later, I was there to pick her up. I clearly remember the scene as we sat together on the edge of her hospital bed. She turned to me and shared that she had opted for hospice care, choosing to forego life-saving measures and medications. The world seemed to stand still. I felt her searching my eyes for a response. Although shocked, I understood that her choice was deeply personal, something she truly desired.

"Is this what you want?" I asked.

She nodded.

"How can I support you then?" I queried as I fought back the tightness in my throat and the tears welling up in my eyes.

I became the first person to hear her decision, a precursor to her informing her husband, parents, brother, grandparents, and anyone else who needed to know. Over the next two weeks, her health declined as she surrendered control to her ailment. She made the conscious choice to let her disease take its course. She was tired. I watched as her condition deteriorated.

Propped up on her living room couch, she existed in a comatose-like state. Her body was gradually shutting down. In her final hours, I sat by her side on the arm of the couch. I sang softly to her, brushing her hair, and offering reassurance that it was okay to let go. I watched as my nephew arrived next door, only to leave after a few minutes in tears. Witnessing the passing of a young loved one is heart-wrenching, particularly one who had so much ahead of her.

Her husband found a comforting distraction in the garage, warmly joking that he hadn't been issued a return receipt upon marrying Suzie. I commend him for steadfastly standing by her side throughout those trying times.

The remaining moments are somewhat blurred, save for the presence of the compassionate hospice nurse who ensured I had the space and time to be alone with Suzie, stepping in as needed. I dampened her lips with a tender touch of a water-dampened sponge. Scheduled as advised by the hospice nurse, I administered drops of morphine onto her tongue, ensuring her comfort. I still vividly remember the rasping sound and the subtle shift in her breathing, signaling her gradual transition into her final breath.

And then, she was no more.

I lost my sister.

She was just 36.

The profound question arose: *How do you arrange a funeral for a life taken so prematurely?*

The answer lay in our conscious decision not to. The concept of "Celebrations of Life" had reached my ears, though I had never witnessed one. Following thorough research, we settled on this approach. The dress code was vibrant, everyone donning bright colors, specifically those reminiscent of flowers – an ode to Suzie's fondness for roses. The event was crafted to be a collection of anecdotes representing the most cherished and joyful moments of her life.

We curated a slideshow that recounted her journey, capturing her essence. Additionally, I read aloud Linda Ellis' poignant poem, "The Dash Poem," underscoring the importance of celebrating the life she had lived rather than solely commemorating her birth and passing.

From that moment onward, a resolute determination emerged within me. I vowed that future end-of-life commemorations, including my own, would be characterized by celebration rather than the somber and mournful events traditionally associated with loss.

Suzie's legacy persisted, even in her absence. She gifted her body to science, contributing to the pursuit of understanding the ailment that had afflicted her, and potentially saving lives in the process. Her lustrous, cascading hair was donated to Locks of Love, a gesture that held the potential to bring comfort and courage to cancer survivors. Even beyond her earthly existence, Suzie continued to bestow her spirit of giving upon others.

For in the grand existence, lives are meant to be celebrated!

In memory of Suzie, may you live your "dash" ~ see poem on next page.

Dr. Karen Kramer
In Memory of Suzanne Marie Peterson
1972-2008

The Dash
by Linda Ellis

I read of a man who stood to speak
At the funeral of a friend
He referred to the dates on the tombstone
From the beginning... to the end

He noted that first came the date of birth
And spoke the following date with tears,
But he said what mattered most of all
Was the dash between those years

For that dash represents all the time
That they spent alive on earth.
And now only those who loved them
Know what that little line is worth

For it matters not, how much we own,
The cars... the house... the cash.
What matters is how we live and love
And how we spend our dash.

So, think about this long and hard.
Are there things you'd like to change?
For you never know how much time is left
That can still be rearranged.

If we could just slow down enough
To consider what's true and real
And always try to understand
The way other people feel.

And be less quick to anger
And show appreciation more
And love the people in our lives
Like we've never loved before.

If we treat each other with respect
And more often wear a smile,
Remembering this special dash
Might only last a little while

So, when your eulogy is being read
With your life's actions to rehash...
Would you be proud of the things they say
About how you spent YOUR dash?

The Story in Review

Let's dig into why gracefully navigating grief was so vital, considering **culture**, **toxic positivity**, the **mind**, and the **body**. In this context, I'm intertwining them all. Someone once remarked to me that we often treat animals with more compassion at the end of their lives than we do humans. I fully grasped this analogy when I had to make the difficult decision to euthanize my two oldest cats, solely for their own well-being.

As an 11-year-old, I witnessed my mother agonize over the slow decline of my grandfather. He had become frail, lost his mental faculties, and his body was deteriorating. She faced the heart-wrenching choice to let nature take its course aided by slowly weaning him off food (thanks to the loving advice from a doctor who understood). Both my parents made it explicit in their will and trust that when their time came, they wanted to pass without extreme life-saving measures as well. Although I will not go into the details here, there is now medical support to aid those whose body is failing them and request an easy passage from this life.

Suzie had numerous close calls with death. Fortunately, she had the agency to decide when her journey would end.

I have a client who's determined to choose medically assisted death by the age of 85, which is about 10 years away. She's faced opposition from therapists, life coaches, friends, and family, but I empathize with her decision.

Culturally, there's a stigma around someone wanting to end their life at a predetermined time. It's often labeled as "suicide." Conversely, families sometimes hold onto hope for their loved ones to recover, only to see them live a fraction of their former quality of life. Who should make these life-and-death decisions? These are the questions I pose, and what matters most is what this means to you.

On a lighter note, during a recent update of my will and trust with my attorney, I was asked to decide whether I should be kept alive until the birth of a potential baby and designate its guardian if, for any reason, I were pregnant and on life support. Now, considering I'm in my mid-50s, I found this inquiry quite amusing.

With that aside, let's proceed with the review...

Body: Using Jensen's *The Healing Questions Guide*, here are a series of questions related to that I might otherwise explore with a client in Suzie's situation.

Lung Problems:

1. What is causing me to give my love away in relationships with those who do not have the love to return what I need?
2. What do I need to believe about myself so I am no longer being exploited by others?
3. What will it take for me to receive real love?
4. What is holding me back from living life fully?
5. What will it take for me to override the patterns of disapproval that caused me to feel like I do not belong?
6. What will it take to fully include myself in the gift of life?
7. What secrets, restrictions, inhibitions and passions, desires and emotions do I keep shoving down? what will it take for me to be free to express these things?

Right Lung:

1. What abuse, real or imagined, am I still feeling guilty or angry about?

Left Lung:

1. What will it take to let go of being ashamed that I require energy and resources?

Gather: Suzie's most significant shifts in her story were her terminal illness diagnosis, the day she opted for hospice care, and the day of her passing.

Relate: Suzie displayed remarkable strength throughout her ordeal. While I know she experienced a range of emotions, she mostly shared with me her sadness and fear. To this day, I'm awed by how positively she confronted her reality. Some of it might have been a form of masking (toxic positivity) to shield her family (including me) from worry, but I witnessed a newfound confidence in her approach to life that contrasted starkly with the Suzie I knew in our childhood. As for me, my emotions ran the gamut from fear, anxiety, sadness, and anger to guilt and survivor's guilt (*Why not me?! Why Suzie?!*).

Involve: Suzie's various actions included living her life to the fullest for as long as she could, continuing to work (as she adored animals), exploring new hobbies, and engaging in experiences she had never tried before.

 Ease: Suzie's support network during her recovery included medical professionals such as doctors, specialists, local firefighters, and EMTs. She used a medical response device for added safety. Her husband, family, friends, and coworkers provided crucial emotional and practical support, and her loyal dog, Bertha, was a comforting presence throughout her journey.

 Focus: The "new normal" for Suzie (before she passed) meant accepting and savoring every moment of her life until she was ready to let go of the fight. For me, it involved respecting Suzie's choice to enter hospice care, guiding her through her end of life, celebrating the colorful life she lived, and preserving her memory.

In Summary

"Pain is only bearable if we know it will end, not if we deny it existence."
– Viktor Frankl

What's your story? What does "living healthfully" mean to you? How has your health changed throughout your life, and who in your life is currently navigating their own health journey?

These narratives guided us through the harrowing encounter of a near-death car accident, an unpredictable and tumultuous hospital experience leading to a diagnosis, and the heroic perspective of someone bravely approaching the end of her life.

Culturally, we ponder how individuals facing terminal diagnoses choose to navigate their life paths.

From the perspective of the **mind**, Jarie Lyn's story serves as a testament to the transformative power of maintaining a positive, determined, and action-oriented attitude. Jarie Lyn's narrative also exemplifies how an emphasis on **positivity** might be perceived negatively by others. This raises important questions about how we support grievers, avoid projecting our emotions onto them, and refrain from dismissing their genuine positivity as inauthentic.

Although we consciously refrained from delving into the meanings of various physical (the **body**) ailments, an exception was made in my own story concerning a broken neck, aiming to ensure the focus remains on the overarching message of these narratives.

In terms of the **Healthy GRIEF Framework**, each individual's journey is unique, as reflected in the following summary:

Gather: Major health events, diagnoses, and crucial decisions regarding treatment or hospice care marked significant transitions in these stories.

 Relate: Emotions ranging from numbness, denial, sadness, and fear to determination, optimism, and gratitude fill the hearts and minds of those navigating their health journeys.

 Involve: Actions such as returning to routines, making critical health decisions, embracing distractions, and seeking healing modalities became integral parts of their journeys.

 Ease: A robust support system, encompassing the love and care of family, friends, and medical professionals, played a pivotal role in easing the journey.

 Focus: The "new normal" materialized as they learned to communicate their situations effectively, prioritize what truly matters, infuse more joy into their lives, and ultimately accept and embrace the best life possible.

I hope you leave this section with invaluable takeaways for you or a loved one.

Healthfully grieving a series
of events when what once
was is no longer.

TRILOGY

"My life has not been about fixing what is broken. It has been about engaging in a loving and tender archaeological dig back to my true self."

– Jewel, *Never Broken: Songs Are Only Half the Story*

 Experiencing a single event in life that leads to grief can be profound, but what if one must contend with three or more such events in close succession? In this section, we delve into chapters that unveil the journeys of individuals burdened by *compound* (or *cumulative*) *grief* stemming from multiple losses.

Please take special note of how each narrative underscores the profound impact of these losses on both the mind and body. First and foremost, it's crucial to recognize how our early experiences of grief can shape the limiting beliefs we hold about ourselves and the world. These beliefs play a significant role in determining our ability to navigate the grieving process in a healthy manner. As discussed in the chapter "Mind," such beliefs often take root during childhood, typically before the age of ten.

Secondly, it's essential to understand that the concept of grieving "healthfully" is not just about the emotional aspect but also about safeguarding your body's neurological well-being. Doing so can help prevent the development of minor to potentially life-threatening health issues in the future. Fields of study like *psychosomatics* and *psychoneuroimmunology*, which we explored further in the chapter "Body," are increasingly shedding light on the intricate connection between our emotions and their impact on our physical health.

The key takeaway here is that the body is profoundly affected by the experience of grief. By recognizing this connection, we can proactively identify and release emotional burdens before they potentially lead to irreversible damage to our body. With that, let's see what stories we have in this chapter …

Our first story centers on Chris, whose narrative revolves around the conflict within his career, a turmoil that profoundly affected his self-esteem and, ultimately, his identity. Simultaneously, he struggled with the loss of someone close to him.

Next, we journey alongside Susanna, whose narrative begins with the trauma of her early childhood. She later confronts the loss of her mother and older sister, which eventually leads her to confront and accept the toll it was taking on her body.

Third, we explore my own narrative, entwined with my son Tyler's experiences. It encompasses the death of his father, my divorce from his step-father, and the profound ways in which he internalized his grief and the key to his recovery! This narrative concludes with one of the transformative stories that significantly inspired the creation of this book.

Stephanie's journey comprises the fourth story, serving as the final impetus for me to write this book. She invites us into her world, marked by childhood trauma, and takes us through the depths of her grief following the loss of her husband. A shocking health diagnosis becomes her awakening to life.

In the fifth story, we journey alongside Erica, whose adventures take us from her first marathon at the tender age of three to that New Years Day that truly marked the "New Year, New You." Her story is a heartwarming narrative of triumph over life's major obstacles to summiting the heights of what most "able bodied" people ever do in a lifetime.

Our section concludes with my personal story, marked by the loss of my brother and mother within a span of two weeks, followed by distressing news that left me feeling as though I were losing another family member as well. These stories intertwine with earlier narratives shared throughout the book.

I trust that you will discover facets of these stories that resonate with your own experiences in some profound way.

Career, Identity, and Death: A Man's Story of Grief

Sometimes the devil you know is better than the devil you don't.

$\mathcal{S}$everal years ago, I went through a "grief trifecta." In just one year, I lost my career, my identity, and my mother. It felt like I had lost everything.

As a man, it's not always easy, or encouraged, to share our deepest fears and emotions. Heck, we barely talk. Perhaps it's our caveman brain telling us to be quiet, lest the saber-tooth tiger might hear us and run away before we bag dinner, which means the family goes hungry.

Once I went to Southeast Asia for five weeks and came back and a buddy said, "How was your trip?" "Good," I said. "Cool," he replied. And that was it... Dudespeak at its finest! Nevermind the famous secluded beach from that movie we found, or my near arrest for trespassing at a world-famous hotel, or the naughty monkey that attacked me and ensured I'd be spending my next four weeks visiting rabies clinics for shots.

As men, we have often been taught that oversharing and vulnerability are negatives, and that expressed emotions can and will be used against us. We often feel that we need to stay positive and protect those around us.

My story of how I lost myself and descended into grief started in the workplace and largely centered in that area. Up to that point, I had been on a steady career progression in business and in sales. I felt good, I looked good, and I took pride in myself and what I brought to the table. I knew my worth.

Many years ago, I accepted a sales position at a closely held family business that touted their Christian ideals. My first clue that it was a unique workplace should have been that my interview didn't start till 7 pm and ended at almost midnight. Despite that, I took the job and immediately immersed myself in learning their products and solutions. Integrity is one of my highest values, so I wanted to represent the brand well.

After a few months, I was at my first trade show. That night, after a 12-hour work day, we were at a networking dinner. The alcohol was flowing and everybody was having a great time. At around midnight, I was talking to a buyer and realized I had drunk way too much. I started to feel woozy and tactfully excused myself to go to the bathroom, but instead made a beeline to our hotel room. I never made it. My boss eventually found me passed out in front of the wrong door and got me inside. Not only that... I had also gotten sick and he had to clean it up. We were both former fraternity guys, so overdoing fun and taking care of each other is part of the territory. Still, not my finest hour.

I committed two cardinal sins of sales... I drank too much at a work event, and I couldn't answer the opening bell for meetings the next morning. I missed half a day and my boss covered for me. I probably should have been fired on the spot. Which brings up another of my key values, loyalty. After my boss covered for me, even when he probably shouldn't have, I immediately felt indebted to him and the company. My loyalty clouded my judgment from then on and I started to forget who I was, what my worth was, and what my boundaries were.

Months later we're at another tradeshow... a very large, very fun trade show in Las Vegas. Imagine anything that's sold in any retail store being exhibited... energy drinks, magazines, hats, sunglasses, cigars, you name it. And lots of free swag that no exhibitor wants to drag home after the show, so they were gladly handing it all out. Everyone loves freebies, so we grabbed a lot of stuff!

On the last day of the show we checked out of our hotel room at 6 AM, which seemed strange since we still had a full day in front of us. I'm new, so who am I to question the decision? 12 hours later the tradeshow ended, and we incorrectly assumed we'd call it a day and get another hotel. Nope... the bosses tell us we need to take down the booth and load the trailer, which we did. Now it is 10 pm and we're

16 hours in... we're exhausted and certainly going to get hotel rooms now, right? Nope. The bosses decide we're going to drive home now to save money on hotel rooms. Keep in mind that we're in Las Vegas, a direct 6-7 hour drive to San Diego with a truck and trailer in tow, plus we had to drop off one of our co-workers in Orange County! All to save a few bucks.

We take off and finally get to my house around 5 AM, 24 hours after our day had started. I'm exhausted and say goodnight to my boss, who has been downing Mountain Dew and Red Bull like a chain smoker the entire drive home. He's still in the truck, but totally jacked up on caffeine and says he wants to come inside my house and go through the stuff I got from the trade show. I tell him absolutely not, that it's been a 24 hour day, and I'm exhausted. Undeterred, he follows me in and sits down on my living room floor, grabs a bag, and hands it to me and tells me to open it. He is adamant, so I do, and he made me go through every one of my bags, including my clothes, until he was satisfied. Satisfied of what, I still don't know. Clearly, they don't understand boundaries and limits... and I was losing my judgment on what mine were.

By now I realized that I was now part of a hugely dysfunctional, toxic workplace, but I felt powerless to leave..., I owed my boss. The only saving grace was that I worked remotely and was somewhat insulated from the craziness for the most part.

Another trade show comes. We offered a 5% show special to incentivize folks to write orders at the show. I write an order and start to deduct the 5% discount. The owner sees what I'm doing and stops me, then asks me if the customer specifically asked for the 5% discount. I say, "No, they didn't... but it was on the flyer and banner as I took their order." She says to remove the discount and see if they call us on it later. All to save $25... ridiculous! And yet, they were paying me, so I did as I was told, all the while I was dying inside. After all, I was violating most of my own values.

Around this time, I brought in my first large National account. It was a 600,000 unit order of a product that we had in stock, and we had six months' notice to deliver it. Despite the lead time, we were late on 12 of the 14 deliveries across the country. This large retailer vowed not to do business with us again. Once you screw up with an account, they rarely forget it. Another promise of mine made to a customer that went unkept.

Losing one's identity can be a slippery slope. Here's the issue... I was being given information by people I'm supposed to trust. I pass that information on to my accounts. More often than not, the info turns out to not be true, and I am the one who pays the price for the disparity between our words and actions. Can I ever trust what others tell me? Can I trust what I tell others anymore? Who am I becoming, that I would continue to sacrifice who I am and what I stand for to serve people like this? By this point, I just don't know who I am anymore.

The stories are endless, but I'm sure you're getting the idea. There are dozens more. For instance, the newly hired VP of sales had major anger issues and would yell at us and call us idiots. Or the grown adults crying and yelling in sales meetings. Or the product I was told was enroute to our warehouse, which I passed on to my customer, only to later find out we didn't have the money to pay for the order and it was still in China, waiting to be paid for and put on a slow boat to the US. Or the time I came into the office dressed up, tan, and in good shape and my boss said with a straight face, "You look good... clearly you haven't been working enough." Or, on the other hand, the one time I came in after working all night on a multi-million dollar proposal and looked like I had been on a three-day bender... I hadn't slept and was sweating, shaking, and looked horrible. The boss smiles and excitedly says, "Nice job! I can tell you're putting in a lot of effort!" Or the fact that we moved manufacturing onsite, and the workers making minimum wage in the warehouse were inhaling activated carbon, essentially black dust, all day long often without filtration or proper safety equipment. I truly felt like each time I walked out to the warehouse I was seeing people I cared about being slowly poisoned. I couldn't do anything for them and it was killing me.

The worse we looked and felt, the happier they were. I learned that if I wanted to please the work gods, I must let myself go, physically and mentally. I dropped my standards for myself. I was now deeply entrenched in a victim mentality, feeling I was powerless to change the situation.

I was no longer engaging fully with my family, friends, or my aging mother. About the time I started working at this company, my mom had a health scare, breast cancer, but they caught it early. They said that after a mastectomy was done, old age would likely take her out, not cancer. Still, work concerns kept me from really maximizing my time with Mom, even after that wake-up call. I was there, but not fully present.

Around this time, I bought a used BMW convertible for $11K, not a ton of money. However, I knew the reaction I'd get from my bosses and coworkers for having something nice, so I parked a couple of blocks away on the street for three months and walked in to work whenever I had to go into the office. When the boss finally found out he said, "Clearly we're paying you too much money." To survive, I started conditioning myself to play life small. Fit in and don't ruffle feathers. Do OK, but not good enough to stand out.

The final straw was me closing a potential $4-$8M a year account two years in a row, and each year we couldn't fully supply, or chose not to supply for various reasons. I wondered if the company was self-sabotaging our own success. Once again, I had promised a customer something that we weren't able to deliver on, despite all assurances from management that we could. That account would likely never do business with us again.

I no longer trusted my own word... why should anyone else trust me? My words and actions were incongruent, and congruence is another key value of mine. Another value violated.

As these experiences piled up, I was at the low point of my life. I'm a pretty upbeat guy, and that was no longer the case. I was hiding my true feelings from friends and family because, well, men often don't feel comfortable being vulnerable to others.

Our office did not have direct deposit, so on payday we had to go ask the boss for our check. One day late in my time at this company, I walked into the owner's office and asked her if I could grab my paycheck. Her reply was the same one that others and I heard over and over for 10 years. "No, you can't pick up your paycheck, you didn't earn it." She would then always smile an evil grin and hand it over to me. The proverbial straw that broke the camel's back.

For years I took that abuse, but this time I had reached my limit. I walked to my car and as I shut the door I began to cry uncontrollably, something I never do.

I then looked in the mirror and screamed at myself, "You're a fucking prostitute!" After all, I was taking money from people I didn't respect, and doing things not in alignment with who I am.

After 10 years of this my soul felt lost. I was a hollow shell of who I used to be. I started to question whether life was worth living. I faced the daily struggle of wanting to give up, versus not wanting to let my former employers have the satisfaction of beating me into submission.

As you would expect, my body started showing the effects of all the negativity associated with my decision to forget my self-worth and stay at this company for so long, and it was letting me know that something had to change now. One morning I woke up with heart palpitations... I went to the urgent care clinic and my resting heart rate was over 170 bpm. I called in sick and that was my last day working before a year-long battle that took its toll on myself and my family, mentally and physically.

By this time, my mom was in her late 80s. Her mind was sharp, but her body was failing her. When asked how she was doing, she would often say, "Today is a rough one, but tomorrow will be much better." This was no ordinary woman... at 89 years young she was still teaching at the Community College level. However, the stress of watching her son be miserable was wearing on her. Being a mother, she tried to protect me and had been urging me to leave that company for years, so that she could see me happy again. I could see the toll my unhappiness was taking on her, but I wasn't able to distance myself from the company at that time. After all, sometimes the devil you know is better than the devil you don't. I chose to stay in a toxic workplace because it's what I knew.

Mom's health rapidly declined, and she was admitted to the hospital. Over the next few weeks, I spent as much time as possible with her while we got things ready for her to come home. Mom got totally tuned up in the hospital! She said she felt better than she did in her 20s, and was the happiest I had ever seen her. She was excited about getting back to teaching her class, so that she could say she taught into her 90s! However, a chest X-ray for a pesky cough overlapped part of her abdomen. They found that mom's breast cancer had spread into the bones and metastasized. At that point hospice was called in and right then she made a decision that she was done. She made it home and was able to spend some quality time with family and friends, we even had a hairdresser come to the house to get Mom all ready for Happy Hour with friends and family. She put on her makeup and looked amazing as we sipped wine and told stories with her! After a couple of nights, she passed quietly and peacefully in her own bed, in her own house, with full dignity, as she wished.

I was gutted. I lamented all the years she had been healthy, but I was too concerned about work to be fully present with her. That person who was always there to pick me up if I fell was no longer there. I further isolated myself. My only saving grace was the numbness I felt while being distracted by food, drink, TV, or travel.

Over the course of one year, I dealt with the loss of a career, the loss of my personal identity, the decline in Mom's health, mom passing, the sale of my house and having to purge a significant amount of my belongings, the sale of Mom's house and having to move or toss 50+ years of memories in a short amount of time. I was overwhelmed and couldn't bring myself to go through my parent's possessions. I only took one thing out of Mom's house... her cherished Keurig coffee machine, which I still use today.

That's a lot to unpack... I apologize for all the background stories, but I felt it was important to weave a tapestry that shows how a decline into depression and grief is not always linear.

What did I do after all of this? Well, initially I shut down. I retreated. I isolated myself. I was lost and on my own and any concepts I had of home and security were now gone. Thankfully I had put myself in a financial position to shut down, but it still wasn't healthy. I spent entirely too much time engaged in distractions. I went into full self-protection mode. I looked for jobs, but it's hard to put your best foot forward when you've been beaten down and don't believe in yourself anymore. I had no purpose.

That said, there is the other side, once you move on. When a man loses his purpose, and forgets who he is at his core, it is a dangerous thing. The sooner you can recognize the negative spiral, and the quicker you can reverse it, the quicker you can get on to getting on. Be an observer of yourself and proactively course correct.

So, what did I learn on this journey that may help you on your journey? A few things... first, accept responsibility for your part in the situation – avoid the temptation to play the victim card. Second, have a strong support network and use it. Third, let go of how you thought things should be and accept how it really is. Remember that bitter resentment is like drinking poison and expecting the other person to die. It serves no purpose.

And here are a few things that helped me move forward. First, focus on others, not yourself. It's virtually impossible to be depressed when you're serving others. Second, stay engaged... with family, friends, hobbies, etc. Third, nourish your body, mind, and soul. Take time to do the things you love. What do you love that you haven't done in some time? Perhaps it's taking a road trip, catching sunset at the beach, walking around the lake, or going fishing. Whatever fuels you, do it, and make yourself a priority!

As a man, it's critical to rediscover your purpose and get laser focused on what you want. Get a hobby, learn martial arts, workout... do whatever it takes to engage that masculine part of you which drives you to kick ass and take numbers! Think back to those times where you overcame against all odds... you've already done this! Remember how it felt to conquer obstacles, and think about the things you did then which brought you success. Do those things that worked!

What else? Be OK with being vulnerable. Share your true feelings with friends and family. Forgive. After several years, I finally reached out to my former employers, not for their sake, but for mine. Know who you are, know your worth, and know what you will and won't tolerate. Move on.

Now it's time to retake control of your life, redefine your purpose, and set out to be the man you were destined to be... happy, content, and with grief in the rear-view mirror, only as a reminder of how far you've come. Realize that your loved ones, ancestors, spirit, guiding force, Creator, whoever and whatever is important to you, want you to push on and lead a happy, successful, fulfilling life. Do it now!

Good luck! You've got this!

Chris P.,
Client

The Story in Review

Let's dive into Chris' *cumulative grief*.

Mind: Chris's story serves as a vivid illustration of how his beliefs, values, and attitudes began to deteriorate in a toxic work environment. The once-confident, self-assured, and high-integrity person slowly withered under the weight of crumbling self-beliefs:

- "I felt powerless to leave."
- "I owed my boss."
- "I'm violating most of my own values."
- "I just don't know who I am anymore."
- "To survive, I started conditioning myself to play life small."
- "I no longer trusted my own word."
- "I didn't believe in myself anymore."
- "I had no purpose."
- "It was killing me."
- "I started to question whether life was worth living."

Culture and **Toxic Positivity**: Chris' narrative intricately weaves culture and toxic positivity from a male perspective. As he puts it, "As men, we have often been taught that oversharing and vulnerability are negatives, and that expressed emotions can and will be used against us. We often feel that we need to stay positive and protect those around us." He further elaborates, "I'm a pretty upbeat guy, and that was no longer the case. I was hiding my true feelings from friends and family because, well, men often don't feel comfortable being vulnerable to others."

Body: The toll this all took on Chris' body manifested in heart palpitations and high blood pressure. Let's explore this through Jensen's *The Healing Questions Guide* with questions I might have asked a client facing similar physical symptoms at the time.

Blood Pressure - High:

1. What benefit is there and believing I am always in danger or something disastrous is about to happen? What would be a healthier, more realistic outlook?

2. What will it take to bring my mind and my thoughts to dwell on safety and peace?

3. What resentment of the past is calling to be forgiven?

4. What will it take to truly believe I have the power to reverse the unwanted direction my life seems to be taking?

5. What internal anger needs to be addressed? What will allow me to productively process this anger without hurting my loved ones?

6. What benefit is there in believing I cannot count on anyone or anything? Is it really true? What would be a healthier and more realistic outlook?

7. What relationship needs to be resolved? What will it take to resolve it once and for all?

8. What will it take for me to accept and receive higher levels of real love?

9. What will it take for me to learn how to nurture and parent myself as an adult to fill the gaps in my childhood?

10. What would my life be different if I knew, at the deepest part of my soul, that I am acceptable, enough and sufficient, and there is nothing I need to prove my worth?

11. What am I trying to prove by needing to control and dominate everything? What would it take to approach life differently?

12. What will it take for me to come into balance with money, sex and time so my health could improve?

13. What will it take to approach life more gently and peacefully, knowing that all I have come to do and learn will be accomplished whether I stress over it or not?

Gather: The most significant shifts in his story involved losing his career, moments of realization regarding the loss of his identity, and his mother's declining health and eventual passing.

 Relate: In his emotional journey, he experienced numbness, powerlessness, fear, exhaustion, depression, anger, and isolation, along with physical symptoms like sleeplessness, sweating, shaking, and a deteriorated appearance. He distanced himself from family, friends, and his aging mother, concealed his true feelings, engaged in incongruent actions, doubted himself, lost trust in his word, felt out of alignment with his values, conditioned himself to shrink, and lost trust in himself. Yet, there were also moments of happiness and contentment amidst these struggles.

 Involve: Chris's advice and actions involve maintaining close connections with family and friends, pursuing hobbies like martial arts and exercise, and rekindling his love for activities such as road trips, beach sunsets, lake walks, and fishing. This has allowed him to rediscover his sense of purpose and set clear goals for his life.

 Ease: His support network comprised friends and family. As my client, I also know he re-engaged with NLP and participated in Tony Robbins' Date With Destiny events.

 Focus: Chris' "new normal" involves becoming more self-aware and engaged in life. He focuses on nurturing his physical, mental, and emotional well-being, prioritizing self-care, and setting clear goals. Chris also embraces vulnerability by openly sharing his feelings with loved ones, practicing forgiveness, and reestablishing a strong sense of self-worth and boundaries. This journey allowed him to move forward with life with a renewed perspective and purpose.

Childhood Trauma, Death, and Health: A Trilogy of Life Changing Events

I woke up the next morning a different person. A woman ready for the world!

Life Changing Health

In the spring of 2016, I was experiencing familiar abdominal pain that would normally last three to four hours off and on for approximately four years. The pain was always extreme, but after a few hours of pain, the symptoms would subside until this one day.

In the spring, the pain went on and on... It became more and more painful so I had no choice but to go to the emergency room. I was diagnosed with an infected gallbladder and stones. This surgeon stated that these surgeries were very common and that I will be discharged the next day with minimal pain.

When I was undergoing a routine gallbladder removal, the doctor noticed something very rare! My body had formed a "film" of tissue around my gallbladder that, over the years (due to the infection), had evolved into what he later explained "petrified wood" – a stone-like material that protected my body from being septic. As he broke the barrier to get to my gallbladder, the substance quickly streamed through my body and my heart, lungs, and kidneys – all major organs started to fail. This routine gallbladder surgery suddenly became a life threatening procedure.

What seemed like minutes passing was actually more than 24 hours. As I awoke, I was surrounded by the main director and doctor of the hospital, a cardiologist, a nephrologist, a social worker, and the hospital priest. It seems as though I was lucky to be alive. I noticed I was hooked up to oxygen, heart, and lung monitors and heard the nephrologist stating that I was a very sick patient. I felt fine, just a bit sore.

I was put in ICU for monitoring. My heart and lungs were going back to normal. However, my kidneys took too much stress and were only working at 14%. I was discharged 10 days later, on a Friday, with kidney failure. I was told to follow up Monday to discuss my kidney disease.

I ignored the follow up recommendation and continued my life in denial for over a year. My thoughts were "I feel fine, I feel normal. I still urinate normally. I was misdiagnosed." Denial, denial, denial! I told NOBODY! I was just in the hospital for gallbladder removal. The fact that I lost a lot of blood and needed blood transfusions to live, and that I was in ICU for 10 days was because that's what doctors do. Help people.

One year later, when my doctor needed to refill my prescription, he insisted I come in for my routine annual exam. He asked how my follow ups were going with the cardiologist, nephrologist, and internal medicine. When I told him that I never followed up, he scolded me so harshly that I felt like a five year old little girl being put in the corner for punishment. I was so embarrassed, ashamed that a grown woman was being "told off" by her doctor!

He said, "We go out of our way to save your life. We wake up in the middle of the night hoping and praying that you survive and you don't even care about yourself!" He continued "Why?! Give me one good reason why you took this long to follow up?!!" My response: "I was scared, and in denial."

On the drive home from my office visit, I thought about my answer to the doctor's question. I had finally admitted out loud to someone that I was scared and in denial. I got home, I looked at myself long and hard in the mirror, and said "You have kidney failure!" The lady in the mirror was so strong and serious she told me: "You will follow up. You will learn all you need to learn about your disease. You will see all the specialists, counselors, and group therapists that you need. You are the most important person in the world right now. There's nothing to deny. Kidney disease runs in the family. You got this. You got to fight."

I woke up the next morning a different person. A woman ready for the world!

My Family's Story

I was born to Mexican immigrants. Both parents were about 18 to 19 years old when they came illegally to the United States through Tijuana. They migrated to San Diego and had six children so we were all born United States citizens.

My parents were not educated, raised on a ranch, born to single mothers, and raised poor. My father was a very violent man, drank a lot, used drugs, and was always high, as far as I remember. He had a mean streak and loved to beat his wife to a very submissive state.

Throughout our lives, there were "favorites" (the kids). The oldest sister, Liz, the oldest brother, Jr., and the youngest daughter, "Li'l Mommy." The second born was diagnosed with mental retardation and uncontrollable seizure disorder. Myself and my twin sister were never, or hardly ever, noticed. It was always special treatment for the favorites and no-to-little treatment for the others. That would go on until adulthood.

Father worked and barely took care of his family. He was always in a drunken or drugged state almost every night, beating our mother and sometimes us.

One early morning, we were awakened to police squads breaking into our home at gunpoint. There were at least 30 to 40 armed officers! They ransacked our poor and humbled home. Our father was nowhere to be found. The police informed my mother that there was a murderer and my father was a suspect.

My father shot and killed a young father and husband. They worked together and had arguments which resulted in murder. Our family lived in terror. There were threats. There were so many horrible things we had to endure from society, neighbors, and family.

That was the beginning of my stressful life. I was eight years old. My father was "America's Most Wanted." Dead or alive. I always told myself someone killed my dad in denial of facing the truth about him going to prison, a denial which continued for many years thereafter.

After almost a year and a half at-large, my father was captured and booked in a state penitentiary for 15 years. He was released and he lived eight or nine years longer, then passed away due to drugs and alcohol abuse.

Years later, I grew up, worked full time, and continued life. At 77-years-old, my mother had normal aches and pains as we do as we age. She took care of my special needs older sister who had a lot of health issues herself. One day Mom didn't have the strength to get up. Too weak, we took her to the ER. After hours of different tests and X-rays, we learned that she had stage four pancreatic cancer. She was given two weeks to live. Less than two weeks later, she passed. All her children were at her side – her "favorite ones" and the "others." I was left parentless and very sad.

One year later, my oldest sister passed away from an overdose of fentanyl. We buried them together. For how could we not – she was the favorite. After everything that happened – lost Mom, Dad, sister, and my kidney function – I pushed all those feelings aside and pretended everything was fine.

But now, my whole family went their separate ways. My business was strained. My living brother and sisters were nowhere to be found. They we all became non-family – no contact no nothing.

My Story

I continued my life as if nothing happened, refusing to cry and mourn after all. Everything was fine and going normally.

I started to be vigilant with my medical history. I saw all the doctors that I needed to see. I ran all the testing and X-rays. I became very aware of my body. My mind, it just focused on work and kids. I always hide my illness. Only my good friends and some family knew that I kept myself alive.

I chose to treat myself at home instead of going to the clinic for treatments. I have completed all tests required to be placed on the kidney transplant list. It is a 10 year wait.

I sometimes wonder if my family will reunite. My brother is reaching out and checking in on me. My youngest sister hardly keeps in touch and my twin refuses to speak to any of us. She took charge of our sister with special needs but refuses to allow us to see her or contact her. I have come to terms that everyone grieves in their own way. All I can do is reach out to my siblings and let them know that they are loved and thought of every day.

Susanna V.
San Diego, CA

The Story in Review

Let's delve into Susanna's journey through grief...

Culture: Susanna endured the stress of being raised by a father with substance abuse issues and had to face the stigma associated with his illegal actions and eventual incarceration. She recalls, "There were so many horrible things we had to endure from society, neighbors, and family."

Toxic Positivity: Susanna has always been a positive person throughout the many decades I've known her. Numerous studies indicate that positivity can be beneficial in recovering from major illnesses, such as kidney disease. In Susanna's case, her positivity both helped and hindered her, as it led to her denial of the severity of the disease.

Mind: Susanna's attitudes, beliefs, and values strongly influenced her initial stubborn denial, as she kept saying, "I got this. I'm fine. I feel fine," until her doctor scolded her. These same factors influenced her decision to carry on with life as if nothing had happened, refusing to cry or mourn following the passings of her mother and older sister.

Body: Holding onto grief likely added further strain to Susanna's health diagnosis. Using Jensen's *The Healing Questions Guide*, here are a series of questions I might ask a version of Susanna about *Kidney Problems*:

1. What will it take to finally stop hyper-vigently seeking what is wrong in my life and focus on the beauty all around me and within me?
2. What will it take to purge all of my negative experiences and transform them into lessons of hope?
3. What will allow me to express my emotions in a productive, healthy way?
4. What will it take to seize the self judgment and criticism of others?

5. What will it take to see every setback as a stepping stone rather than a failure?

6. What is required to be free of my struggling lack of abundance?

7. What does it feel like to completely trust that I will be supported in my attempts to create meaningful experiences?

8. What will it take to completely accept myself on all levels regardless of all my weaknesses and imperfections?

9. What will it take to infuse my life with selfless service and a compassionate attitude towards others?

 Gather: The most significant shifts in her story occurred when her father shot someone, the passings of family members, and her major medical events, such as gallbladder surgery and the diagnosis of kidney disease.

 Relate: The spectrum of emotions and thoughts included denial, fear, sadness, embarrassment, shame, and stress.

 Involve: Various action steps Susanna took included being vigilant with her medical history, diligently following prescribed medical processes, completing all tests required to be placed on the kidney transplant list, and focusing her mind on work and her children.

 Ease: Resources that supported her included doctors, a cardiologist, nephrologist, specialists, a social worker, and a hospital priest. She also benefited from counselors and group therapists, as well as the love and support of her family and close friends.

 Focus: Susanna's "new normals" included following medical protocols to maintain her health while awaiting her kidney transplant, being acutely aware of her body, directing her mind towards her work and children, and coming to terms with the fact that everyone grieves in their own unique way. She expressed, "All I can do is reach out to my siblings and let them know that they are loved and thought of every day."

Death, Divorce, and Illness: Internalized Grief to a Miraculous Recovery

May the narrative of Tyler's growth and healing stand as a testament to the potency of addressing emotions holistically.

Kevin and I parted ways in divorce when Tyler was a mere five months old, a pivotal moment elaborated upon in the chapter "My Divorce." Owing to California law, it seemed every two years became a rhythm of courtroom discussions to navigate child custody and support. The year 2012 fell right into that pattern, a notable chapter in our story.

Early October 2012 arrived just three months after my father's passing, an event detailed in the chapter "A Father's Passing." Having recently returned from a lavish week-long retreat at a destination spa, I was ready to embrace my responsibilities. With it being Tyler's dad's designated weekend, I eagerly collected him that Sunday evening.

The ensuing Tuesday brought an unexpected call from the school, a message that left my heart heavy. Tyler, my son, was in the office in tears, as his dad had not arrived for pick-up after school. While Kevin had his moments of tardiness, this occurrence was unusual during the midweek rotation.

Rapidly, I made my way to the school to console Tyler. My attempts to contact Kevin yielded no response, and even a visit to his apartment proved fruitless – his truck remained parked outside, undisturbed. As evening wore on and silence persisted, my concern deepened. By 10 pm, my growing unease compelled me to contact the police for a wellness check. The visit revealed no signs of distress, prompting further confusion.

On the following day, I was determined to confront Kevin about his conspicuous absence and his neglect in addressing my texts and Tyler's waiting at school. However, Kevin was absent once more. Anxiety gnawed at me, so I encouraged Tyler to reach out to his grandparents in Oregon, seeking any insight. Learning that they too had no contact with Kevin, I took it upon myself to communicate my growing apprehension.

An hour later, a sheriff contacted me for more information, as Kevin's parents had also voiced their concerns. Anxiety-stricken, I shared all I knew, my imagination spiraling into worst-case scenarios. By late afternoon on that Wednesday, the gravity of the situation became painfully evident as law enforcement entered Kevin's apartment. A coroner's report later revealed that his demise had occurred late on a Monday night, attributed to a pulmonary embolism – a result of complications stemming from skin grafts after a work-related accident ten months prior.

Racing to the apartment, my current husband and I experienced an altered sense of reality. Time seemed to stretch and twist, the shock immobilizing our senses. The sensation was surreal, and we were met with an overwhelming numbness.

Next came the formidable task of informing Tyler of his father's passing. At nearly ten years old, Tyler's experience of his father had been impacted by his father's work-related travels and our divorce. Despite these dynamics, Tyler's affection for his dad was undeniable, reciprocated in kind. As Tyler's stepfather, Roger, my current husband and I assumed the primary parental roles. Thus, Roger and I convened in our bedroom, surrounding Tyler with love and support as he laid between us on our bed, and attempted to convey the news. The specifics of the conversation blur, but the memory of Tyler's reaction, seemingly "taking the news well," persists.

Hindsight sheds light on Tyler's following behavior, a series of stages reflecting grief. Initially, shock claimed his emotions. This process was further complicated by Tyler's introverted nature, his habit of concealing his feelings – except, of course, when he sought a new toy or evaded household chores. Unfortunately, Tyler internalized his sorrow, leading to physical symptoms like stomach aches, a manifestation of the grief he struggled to vocalize.

Kevin's passing came a mere three months after the loss of my father, and just two months following the departure of my cherished 18-year-old cat. It was a period of profound upheaval, but within those moments, I sensed a shift within me. Initially, I believed it marked a step forward in my journey through grief, though time has shown that this perception was only partially accurate.

Amidst the emotional whirlwind, another responsibility was placed upon me – my in-laws requested that I take on the role of Kevin's Probate Administrator. Given that I resided in the city while they did not, and already found myself overseeing my parents' affairs following my father's passing, I found myself once again facing the task of managing intricate matters.

There's a saying that suggests, "If you don't care for someone, appoint them as your Probate Administrator." In Kevin's case, his probate journey was anything but ordinary. Thankfully, I was fortunate to have the support of a skilled probate attorney who adeptly guided me through the labyrinthine process.

My mother had a profound fondness for cruises. The last time our family embarked on a cruise was five years prior to my father's passing. In those final years, my father's struggle with sciatic pain and numbness in his feet hindered his ability to maintain balance. Tenderly, following my father's passing, my mother joyfully declared, "Let's plan a family cruise!"

Given that I was married and had a total of five children (including my four stepchildren), I wrestled with the idea of allowing my mother to cover the expenses for such a sizable group to join the cruise. Furthermore, arranging for my husband to take time off work and coordinating all the children's absence from school for a 14-day Hawaiian cruise posed considerable challenges. Eventually, we decided not to attend the cruise with the rest of the family.

Then, two weeks before the departure date, my mother phoned me. "Pack your bags! You and Tyler are going on a cruise!" My brother Ed and his wife faced an unforeseen business commitment that prevented them from attending. My mother was extending an invitation for us to take their place. I told her I needed some time to consider it. I confided in my husband about the situation. His response was laced with humor, "Your ex-husband passes away, and you get a free trip to Hawaii! What's the issue here?!" He had an uncanny knack for injecting levity into any situation.

Tyler and I chose to go on the cruise in November 2012, a decision I'm immensely grateful for. During the initial week, I sensed I was still caught up in "go mode," with the remnants of stress pulling at me like taut rubber bands. It wasn't until the second week that I finally managed to unwind and find my equilibrium. It was a welcome relief, allowing those internal rubber bands of tension to fully slacken – a feeling that had eluded me for almost a year, commencing with my father's health deteriorating in the early months of that year.

In hindsight, the probate process afforded me the opportunity to revert to what I excelled at – tackling logistics. By that point, I had worked through a significant portion of my grief stemming from both my father's and my ex-husband's passings. This journey also encompassed the crucial step of granting forgiveness to my ex-husband for the strain that marked our marriage and the child custody conflicts that took place.

Roger and I first crossed paths as high school sweethearts, our story beginning during the summer prior to my high school initiation at the age of 14. At that point, Roger, a grade above me, entered my life. Despite the hiccup when we briefly parted ways just before his Senior Prom, a decision fueled by his desire to ask another girl out, our relationship was fundamentally solid. Our bond even weathered that storm as he eventually returned to me. In this dynamic, my parents embraced him as an extended family member, and likewise, his parents were woven into my life.

Our chapter drew to a close after three years, culminating during the summer following Roger's high school graduation. His relocation, a three-hour drive from our locale, prompted our parting. Throughout the years, he remained a cherished memory – the one who introduced me to love. Our connection epitomized the kind of partnership I envisioned for my future offspring, a template of affection I longed for them to experience someday. Never did I fathom that Roger would reappear on the canvas of my life.

"You'll never guess who's here?" my mom's voice brimmed with excitement, setting the stage for a surprise encounter. At the tender age of three, Tyler was witness to the reappearance of Roger, who graced my parents' doorstep. Seated on the couch, Roger and I engaged in an uninterrupted conversation that stretched over two hours. Meanwhile, Tyler, in his own little world, swiftly forged a friendship with Roger's youngest, Jake (then seven-years-old). An accidental brush of our hands while sharing photos of Roger's eldest child ignited a spark, evoking memories of high school emotions. It felt akin to slipping into a beloved pair of old jeans that hugged all the right places.

Amidst the chatter of conversation, my inner landscape was painted with vivid memories of my initial adoration and affection for Roger during our youth. Yet, I consciously pushed these feelings aside, cognizant of Roger's ongoing divorce proceedings. Eager to dive back into the dating realm after being divorced for two and a half years, I ventured into the realm of Match.com, a deliberate effort to embrace a new chapter of my life. Despite the lingering sentiments I held for Roger, I committed to redirecting my energies toward dating others.

Two weeks later, Roger took the bold step of asking me out, a move that unequivocally affirmed our mutual connection. It was a realization that resonated deeply within both of us – we were destined to be together.

18 months onward, we stood before our loved ones, vowing our forever commitment in marriage. With Tyler now at the age of four, he not only acquired a stepfather but also gained four older step-siblings. This marriage united our lives into a blended family dynamic, bridging an astonishing 17-year age gap among our offspring. We stood at the intersection of parenting children in preschool, elementary school, middle school, high school, and even college – a multi-faceted journey that we embraced wholeheartedly.

Our marriage blossomed into an enchanting mosaic woven from adventuresome road trips to far-flung destinations and exotic travels. Beyond the captivating landscapes we explored, our union also thrived on family cruises, lively birthday celebrations, and heartwarming gatherings with extended family members during festive holidays.

Around the eighth year of marriage, the seams of our relationship began to fray. The atmosphere grew tense, arguments became more frequent, and disagreements were a constant backdrop. In a bid to salvage what was slipping away, I initiated a course of marriage counseling. Although we engaged in this therapeutic process for a span of two or three sessions, the improvements didn't last long.

I vividly recall soothing one of our children after a particularly intense argument, assuring them that their dad and I would find a way to mend our differences. It was a promise, a reassurance that I clung to amidst the turmoil.

The blueprint of my parents' marriage developed over an impressive span of 68 years, culminating in my father's passing at the age of 90. Their journey bore witness to its share of disagreements and heated debates, yet they consistently navigated their way back to harmony. Conversely, Roger's parents faced their own trials and tribulations, their bond enduring until the passing of his father the year preceding our marriage. These examples served as testaments to the resilience of enduring partnerships.

The memory of that poignant Valentine's Day week in February 2018 remains etched in my mind. Upon returning from a dance rehearsal, I entered an emotionally charged atmosphere that felt akin to an unexpected ambush. Fuelled by the hint of alcohol, Roger's discontentment with me and our marriage spilled forth.

Our history was marked by a pattern: when disagreements erupted, a silent stand-off often ensued, usually lasting a trifecta of days before either of us made the initial attempt at reconciliation. Within these days of silence, the bouquet of a dozen long-stemmed red roses, thoughtfully gifted to me for Valentine's Day the day prior to our argument, found itself unceremoniously discarded in the late hours, while the heartfelt Valentine's card I had left by his bathroom sink was nudged back in my direction, unopened. And so, I maintained my vigil, counting down the hours until the third day emerged.

On the morning of that third day, I sat in the living room absorbed in a book, the weight of uncertainty casting its shadow. Roger entered through the front door, a large box in his possession. Averting my gaze, he embarked on a trajectory toward our bedroom, his purpose evident as he began to pack his belongings. Struck by shock, I scrambled to engage him in conversation. My efforts fell on deaf ears, his resolve steadfast. He recited a well-rehearsed litany of reasons underpinning his decision to sever our union, his words bearing an air of finality, devoid of the space for dialogue.

In a disheartening instant, the love of my life walked out of the narrative we had painstakingly woven together. Unbeknownst to me, his emotional departure from our marriage had occurred long before that fateful day. Blinded by my own veil of denial, I failed to discern the fractures that had stealthily crept into the foundation of our bond.

Over the following weeks, a flood of emotions inundated my being. Treading through the terrain of another divorce, I found myself veering toward silence, a reluctance to divulge my circumstances to many. I continued to navigate life, sporting a half-hearted smile that concealed my turmoil. Hurt and sorrow intertwined, stemming from the abandonment I felt. Self-blame entangled itself around my mind, amplifying the weight of his departing words, intensifying my emotional pain and guilt. In time, anger erupted, directed at him for his actions and inactions, for forsaking our shared life, for leaving me with the shattered fragments of a once-whole existence.

Fear, anxiety, and apprehension for the uncertain future gripped me. Having stepped away from the corporate realm nine years prior, I had leaned on him financially while nurturing our family. The complexities of financial independence and the implications for Tyler's and my future weighed heavily on my mind. The burden of the impact on our children exacerbated my sense of responsibility, and I struggled with guilt over their emotional turmoil.

Several months into our separation, an encounter at a McDonald's marked a low point in our strained interactions. In the heat of the moment, anger erupted, words flung like daggers, both of us exiting with the bitter residue of that explosive exchange. It wasn't the finest moment for either of us.

Yet, six months into our separation, a pivotal point emerged. A dear friend posed a question that reverberated within me: "If he were to return, after all that has happened, would you truly welcome him back?" That query forced me to confront the turbulence that had marked the final three years of our marriage.

Despite attempts to mend the fractures through counseling and earnest efforts, the weight of my own work eclipsed any semblance of shared endeavor. It dawned on me that perhaps he felt the same. It was a turning point that propelled me toward clarity.

For the second time in my life, I initiated the process of divorce, motivated by a desire to shield my children from further uproar. This decision marked a reclamation of my power, relinquished in the preceding months while I awaited the verdict on our relationship's fate. It was a move toward liberation from the turmoil that had enveloped us. (Note: This narrative doesn't aim to assign blame to my high school sweetheart and former partner. He is a remarkable individual. In the end, we simply found ourselves veering apart.)

Tyler stood on the precipice of adolescence, a 15-year-old whose world was upended the day his stepfather departed. Roger, who had assumed a paternal role since Tyler was merely three-years-old, had become more than just a figurehead in his life. With the loss of his biological father, Kevin, a mere six years prior, the void was now compounded as he faced yet another rupture in his parental foundation.

In retrospect, the lens of hindsight casts a spotlight on how my own emotional turbulence inadvertently cast shadows over Tyler's well-being. In those tumultuous times, he too found himself entangled in a web of negative sentiments towards Roger. This once-beloved father figure now bore the brunt of Tyler's resentment for walking away. Moreover, Tyler carried an unexpected burden – a sense of responsibility for the disintegration of yet another parental relationship.

Unbeknownst to me at the time, the echoes of Tyler's struggle reverberated within him. Roger's and my final argument etched itself into Tyler's memory. He overheard Roger's comments about Tyler's health struggles, particularly his recurrent stomach issues as Roger did not believe them to be of severity. The gravity of Tyler's internalization became apparent in that moment. The emotional cocktail he consumed included hurt from Roger's lack of belief and support, anger at his departure, and a crippling guilt that he somehow bore the weight of our shattered marriage. My heart ached for my son, his innocence overshadowed by the emotional storm swirling around him.

Amid my own battles to navigate life's currents and navigate my feelings, I failed to realize that Tyler was being consumed by his own emotional whirlpool. As my struggles took center stage, his silent struggle emerged in the shadows, his pain and turmoil accumulating with each passing day.

Tyler's struggle with stomach aches began to manifest around a year after the loss of his biological father, when he was in the fifth grade. Despite his intelligence and dedication, his attendance at school gradually declined. The situation escalated when he entered middle school. Shockingly, I received a letter from the school warning that a police officer would be dispatched if Tyler's attendance didn't improve, given that he was nearing the state's legal limit for middle school absences. The weight of this revelation left me horrified.

Tyler's physical pain, which often immobilized him for days or even weeks, was accompanied by academic strain. I consulted doctors, dietitians, and even an alternative herbalist in search of answers. Though Tyler resisted, we eventually tried therapy as well.

A diagnosis of Irritable Bowels Syndrome (IBS) provided some clarity, defining Tyler's condition as irritated bowels without an identifiable underlying cause. This diagnosis led to a 504 Plan at school, affording Tyler accommodations such as bathroom access and extended homework deadlines. The plan was reviewed annually to reflect his evolving health status.

When his step-father and I separated, Tyler's foundation crumbled even further. Adrift in a sea of emotions, I found myself swaying back and forth between frustration at dealing with Tyler's recurrent episodes, medical appointments, school absences, and academic setbacks. We were both floundering in our own suffering.

Heartbreakingly, Tyler's downward spiral became more pronounced as he entered high school. A child who had excelled academically in elementary school now found himself struggling to simply pass his high school courses due to frequent absences. A once star water polo player, now removed from the team for failing grades. A promising Boy Scout on the cusp of becoming an Eagle Scout, Tyler's extracurricular aspirations disintegrated in the face of his health challenges.

Despite his wonderful group of friends, the cloak of his silent and internal ailment isolated him.

The marital separation during his freshman year in high school was a devastating blow. Academic struggles that were already underway intensified, resulting in failed classes and barely passing grades. By his sophomore year, Tyler had missed all but two days of the initial six weeks of school. While his drive to stay in school remained strong, his physical capabilities were compromised. Faced with this dilemma, we decided to transition him to homeschooling.

Despite my attempts to suppress it, twinges of jealousy arose when I saw the accomplishments of Tyler's friends posted by their parents – water polo victories, Boy Scout advancements, academic achievements. Lost in the quagmire of despair, I felt powerless to rescue my son from the abyss. Witnessing his once-promising future slip through our fingers, I mourned the loss of the brilliance that once shone so brightly in Tyler's path.

Several pivotal experiences reshaped our lives, each leaving an indelible mark.

One significant turning point occurred when Tyler and I sought the expertise of a holistic chiropractor who astutely identified lingering guilt within Tyler's body. This revelation catalyzed a profound conversation between Tyler and me, centered on the night of my last argument with Roger. It's a common phenomenon for children to internalize responsibility for their parents' divorce. Yet, it wasn't until our exchange that I truly grasped the depth of Tyler's emotions.

This newfound understanding led Tyler to embrace the idea of therapy. Given the recent separation, Roger and I embarked on therapy for Tyler's sake. Though the duration was brief, it proved beneficial for all of us, offering Tyler the attention and support he had been yearning for.

Simultaneously, I recognized that my own lingering resentment over the divorce had repercussions on Tyler's well-being. Taking action, I engaged in personal growth through modalities like NLP, Time Line Therapy, and Hypnotherapy. A comprehensive NLP Breakthrough session enabled me to effortlessly release pent-up negative emotions and limiting beliefs, fostering self-forgiveness and forgiving

Roger. This transformation allowed me to actively nurture Tyler's relationship with his stepfather, granting him the warmth and backing of his blended family.

Around this time, Tyler faced a medical crossroads, with his health continuing to decline. The doctor suggested heart medication, but I firmly rejected the idea.

In tandem, my pursuit of a master practitioner's certification in NLP brought me a deeper understanding of psychosomatic connections between mind and body. I was struck by an intuitive realization: Tyler's ongoing stomach issues were a physical manifestation of his struggle to process the changes around him. These symptoms emerged shortly after his biological father's passing and exacerbated after his stepfather left.

Because of the nature of working with close acquaintances in the realm of subconscious mind exploration, I sought the intervention of my mentors for Tyler. His own curiosity about my work, coupled with his developing rapport with my mentors, paved the way for his collaboration.

The transformative process emerged over the initial weekend of January 2020. I vividly remember the sight of Tyler returning after his second day of intensive self-discovery, his face radiating with newfound determination. "Mom, I want to return to [my previous high school]!" he declared. Despite my deep belief in the efficacy of this process, a hint of fear still gripped me. "But what if you encounter health issues again? What if you struggle or feel stressed?" I asked.

This marked the middle of what would have been Tyler's junior year in high school. Up to this point, his academic journey had been a struggle, even during homeschooling, leaving him nearly two years behind in school credits. Yet Tyler's resolute determination and the transformative work he undertook began yielding remarkable results. His motivation surged, and, remarkably, he ceased experiencing the debilitating episodes of IBS that had plagued him for weeks on end.

Bolstered by unwavering support from his extraordinary counselor, vice principal, principal, teachers, and the flexibility offered by online learning amidst the COVID-19 pandemic, Tyler achieved the seemingly impossible. He managed to make up for lost time including completing a senior year's worth of coursework in a mere seven weeks to graduate alongside his peers. As a mother, I'm incredibly proud, yet my emotions transcend mere pride; words fail to encapsulate the depth of what I feel.

16 years ago, I'd uttered the words "I do." Five years ago, the echo of "I don't" resounded from my then-husband. As of this moment in my narrative, the final stamp of divorce has been affixed to a journey that spanned 16 years of marriage, the last five and a half marked by the laborious process of separation.

Approaching this chapter in my life's story, I find it essential to pay tribute to the manifold blessings that accompanied my resounding "I do" back in 2007. The union blessed my son with four incredible older siblings, granting him a larger family to thrive within. I, in turn, was blessed with the role of "Bonus Mom," a privilege that imparted profound life lessons through the unique lens of each child. Together, Roger and I ventured to idyllic tropical destinations that had long inhabited our bucket lists. Among these, the cherished memory of the little sanctuary known as Kia Ora Sauvage off Rangiroa in the French Polynesia stands out. We embarked on countless road trips, curiosity propelling us to explore the roads and dusty paths that beckoned with the question, "What lies beyond?" The arc of our narrative intertwined with the fabric of life's cycles – we stood shoulder to shoulder in grief, supporting one another through the loss of our respective parents. We celebrated milestones – our children's high school and college graduations, their achievements in Boy Scouts, water polo, and tennis, even our children's marriages. The birth of our first grandchild bloomed like a radiant blossom of joy in the garden of our lives. We embraced existence in its entirety, hand in hand, bound by love, and eagerly sought to unravel the mysteries woven into the fabric of life. I fondly cherish this chapter in my life even if it came to a close.

Tyler, now a thriving young adult, is on the cusp of turning 21. The journey he navigated through life's twists and turns has imparted valuable wisdom about the significance of listening to his body and effectively managing stress. Through this process, he discovered a means to liberate himself from the grip of grief, achieving a rapid, gentle, and enduring release that required no reliance on medications, medical procedures, or the grim taste of herbal concoctions.

On my own path, these experiences illuminated a profound lesson – the ability to swiftly and gracefully untangle my emotions, preventing their adverse ripple effect on others. Equally significant, it underscored the necessity of releasing emotions from the physical realm, preventing them from manifesting as physical ailments. Tyler's story, alongside the transformative tales of my clients, has inspired the creation of this book – a culmination of insights and discoveries meant to be shared.

May the narrative of Tyler's growth and healing stand as a testament to the potency of addressing emotions holistically. As readers navigate each chapter of their lives, may they find comfort in the reminder that the end of one chapter should never overshadow the richness of experiences and lessons it holds. Here's to embracing every twist and turn that lies ahead, to welcoming the boundless adventures that new chapters offer, and to celebrating the beauty of life's ever-evolving story.

Dr. Karen Kramer
San Diego, CA

The Story in Review

Let's dive into Tyler's journey, with a focus on his health...

 Culture: Tyler faced the influence of cultural and societal beliefs about thriving children and the expectations placed on them. Additionally, he wrestled with the stigma surrounding a "dis-ease" in his body, which some might perceive as "all in the head," as indicated by the Canadian Digestive Health Foundation in an article titled "Mental Health, IBS, and Removing the Stigma."[74] This article highlighted that IBS, while physically debilitating, can also significantly impact a person's mental health due to the unpredictable and embarrassing symptoms associated with the condition. This often leads to increased depression and anxiety among individuals with IBS.

 Toxic Positivity: One significant aspect of Tyler's experience was his decision to not share what was happening with others and to continue with life while wearing a half-smile. This coping mechanism resembled the way I handled my separation, where both of us chose not to express our pent-up emotions only later to explode, usually at each other.

 Mind: Tyler had developed various limiting beliefs about himself and the world around him. One of the most notable beliefs was that he was responsible for the end of my marriage, which is not an uncommon belief for young children experiencing their parents' divorce.

 Body: Tyler's health issues were the driving force behind my decision to purchase Jensen's The Healing Questions Guide. After reading the questions related to various stomach issues, you'll easily understand why I turned to this resource for guidance.

Stomach Ache

1. What will it take for me to release all ideas of competition and the need to be the best?

2. What will it take for me to feel the love all around me?

3. What will it take for me to feel secure from within?

4. What would my life look like if I was no longer fearful of negative consequences?

5. What will it take for me to feel one with those around me rather than focus on our separateness?

Stomach Aches in Children

1. What would it take for me to stop feeling that it is my responsibility to make everything better?

2. What will it take for me to know that there is nothing I need to do to earn love, I am lovable for who I am?

3. What will it take to attract people in my life who will show me how to care for my emotional needs and help me feel more secure?

Stomach Problems

1. What will it take to recognize and release unnecessary burdens?

2. What will it take for me to digest new ideas, suggestions and criticisms with ease?

3. What is blocking me from knowing I am capable?

4. What will it take for me to see beyond the worry?

5. What will it take for me to allow new ideas to flow through me effortlessly?

6. What will it take for me to see myself and others as equal?

7. What will it take for me to allow things to happen easily?

8. What value is there in making things so hard?

9. When will I finally accept that it does not all depend on me? What will it take to understand what part is mine and what is not?

Gastritis

1. What will it take for me to move forward with what I want to do in my life and the absence of all the perceived blocks and excuses?

2. What would I do differently if I no longer feared rejection or abandonment?

3. What will it take for me to express my true feelings?

4. What pending disaster do I keep entertaining in my mind? What will it take to release it?

5. What will it take to predict a positive outcome?

 Gather: The significant shifts from Tyler's point of view were the passing of his father, his step-dad leaving, and receiving his official diagnosis.

 Relate: Both Tyler and I went through waves of emotions and thoughts, from denial, shock, and numbness to worry, panic, stress, fear, and embarrassment. We dealt with deep sadness, hurt, abandonment, and feelings of being lost, as well as moments of hopelessness. Guilt and a sense of responsibility weighed heavily on us, and anger found its outlet through cussing, screaming, irritation, and resentment.

 Involve: In response to our situations, we both engaged in various activities like family outings and sports, including water polo and regular workouts. Additionally, he became more involved in social organizations, including Boy Scouts.

 Ease: We sought support from various resources, including a marriage counselor, therapist, medical professionals like doctors, dietitians, and a Chinese herbalist, as well as school counselors, vice principals, principals, and teachers. The biggest and longest-landing support for both Tyler and I was an NLP Breakthrough – a quick and effective method for releasing emotional trauma, triggers, and limiting beliefs.

 Focus: Tyler's "new normal" involves thriving as a young adult who pays attention to his body and effectively manages stress. He also possesses an understanding of the effects of negative emotions on the body and has the tools to release them swiftly and easily.

Childhood Trauma, Death, and Diagnosis: The Deep Dark Forest

I landed and hit the ground running... I flourished and I started laughing and the smile that I lost came back.

*T*ime. The thought of time without my husband scared me the most. I wanted to fast forward ten years to avoid the inevitable pain I knew I was about to endure. I learned quickly that the grief would devastate me and that the only way to emerge from it was to go through what I called the deep dark forest.

That day haunted me, and, five years later, I still do not have the ability to speak about it openly. I can't form the words and speak them out loud, for now they will remain in my heart.

I was 19 when I met Ronald. He was only 17. He was my entire world. He saved me. As a survivor of childhood trauma and sexual abuse, he walked into my life and the moment he held me in his arms, the world faded away and I felt safe. Losing him sent me into a spiral. I walked into the house that fateful day and desperately tried to save him, to breathe life back into his lungs. I held him in my arms knowing that he was gone. Next thing I knew, I laid in the middle of the street, unable to stand, wailing in the arms of a police officer and firefighter. Then my world went dark.

Grief is not an emotion that can accurately be described in words. I remember one night thinking I had to call everyone I know that lost their spouses and apologize. Apologize for not understanding the magnitude of the silence that fills your mind when you are alone. For thinking when they smiled or went back to work, that surely they are hurting but seem to be doing well. I was wrong, so wrong and now I had to navigate through my own grief and somehow manage to do the same for my four children. How did that go? I failed miserably. I did not want to live, the husband who saved me when we were teenagers was gone and in my mind at the time, I failed to save him. I held his lifeless body in my arms, and I did not save him. The burden was deep, and I was willing to endure the pain as a sort of punishment for my failure, for the rest of my life.

It was months before I was able to pick myself up off the ground and find my feet to stand on again. I wanted to lay in bed all day, losing track of the days. My kids lost their father and were now seeing their mother die slowly every day. I fought so hard to live when I just wanted to die, to make the pain stop. I think that when we are in pain, our first reaction is to just make it stop. Unfortunately, life never seems to be that easy.

My children guarded me around the clock, taking shifts to sit with me. I avoided running into people, so I didn't have to talk about it. In my mind, I pretended that Ronald was just gone temporarily, visiting family and would walk through the door soon. That day never came. The sun continued to rise every morning, people running around living their lives while I laid down curled up in a ball crying myself to sleep every night. I was surrounded by family and friends that never wavered in their support for me, but I felt so alone.

If I could describe my grief in one word at that time, it felt like I was drowning. Someone pushed me off Niagara Falls and I was getting hammered in the water trying to come up for air. Fighting to come to the surface in a wave of emotions. It was so real. I leaned on my faith, it kept me alive. But, I was angry that life as I knew it was taken from me. Why do other people get to have their happily ever after and I don't? It's not fair, I already survived so many difficult times. Why me? It made me question everything I knew. But God was with me and even though my faith was ugly, I knew he could handle all my emotions and still never leave my side. It was raw and it was real.

I hated hearing the obligatory, but well meaning, comments from people. "My condolences," "I am so sorry for your loss," "Be strong for the kids," or "You are still young," "You'll find love again" – were all trigger phrases for me. Ironically, a few years before, I said all the same things to people suffering from the loss of a loved one. I often thought to myself, "Be strong?" What does that mean? I am trying to live, doesn't that count? Every time I saw another widow, I would grab them and beg them to tell me how they did it, how they survived and were standing before me. Their presence and advice gave me the most comfort because without saying a word, we knew we shared the same pain.

My strength emerged from down deep in an effort to live for my kids. I call it "mom mode." I now pray to let me live for as long as possible for my children. This is not their story, their truth... I need to get up despite the pain and grief. I'll take it from here and from now on, whatever my heart feels I am going to make an effort to smile for my kids. I told myself I am glad I am the one who has to live through the pain, because I would never want Ronald to feel what I was feeling, I would make the sacrifice for us, for our family.

It was a slow process, I did not sleep in my room for over a year. I did not change one thing in my room, his clothes, shoes, and toothbrush remained where he left them. I now felt comfort knowing that it seemed familiar. The first night I slept in our bed, I cried and cried until I passed out from exhaustion. Grief is a solo journey, there is not one book or piece of advice that gives you the answer you seek to heal. I was only focused on surviving the next hour and praying for the day to end so I could cross that day off. That was my game plan going into year two. I fell, I failed, but I persevered. I always considered myself a very strong person, but I was honest with my kids, they were going to see me collapse and struggle, but I promised them I would find my way again.

I became intentional with my time. Planning out ways to drown out that silence, to get out from the waves pummeling me in the water. Three things happened in succession that I credit with the push I needed to breathe again. I had a conversation with someone, who I never met in person, and shared my story about finding Ronald that day. If you ask me today, why I opened up to this person I didn't know, I can't answer that, but it gave me a sense of relief. Someone knew my deep dark secret, my pain. God sent for sure. There was exactly one person that knew and it was empowering for me. In my mind, I will probably never share that story ever again. It is a special bond that gave me purpose. So, what did I do with that? I jumped out of a plane and went skydiving.

On the way up, I was surprised that I had absolutely no fear, not even a little. That is not normal, right? I figured that I survived the greatest pain I know, this is nothing. I jumped out of that plane, with absolutely no control, tethered to someone. What shocked me is that I just jumped out of a plane at 13,000 feet and actually never felt MORE IN CONTROL of my life than in that single moment. I saw a glimmer of light, silently hearing Ronald's voice as I floated to the ground. His presence was permeable, a glimmer in the clouds while the tears fell. I landed and hit the ground running.

I found part of myself in that moment. I started to hike and I discovered that nature had the power to heal me. I walked many steps in the third to fifth years of my grief journey. I climbed mountain summits that culminated in a summit of Mount Whitney, in California, where I spread some of my husband's ashes. It was symbolic of my grief journey. One foot in front of the other until I reached the top. I left a piece of both of us on that mountain.

I was a different person, the Stephanie I had been, no longer existed. I looked in the mirror and did not recognize the person looking back at me, but I was living, I was surviving. People rallied behind me. I found comfort hiking with other women and discovering we were all surviving our own pain and grief because it comes in many forms. I thank God every day for the people he brought into my life. I did not feel so alone. It filled the void, the silence even though I would still find myself crying on the way home after a wonderful day. I always allowed myself to break down when I was alone and it surprised me how the emotions always seemed to creep to the surface.

Meanwhile, I desperately tried to hold on to Ronald and his memory. I hated when people said you need to move forward. "Screw you" I thought to myself... "Don't tell me what to do!" If I want to lay here in my sorrow or if I want to get up and smile, that is my decision. Trigger words were always hard for me even though I knew people meant well. I was learning how much power words have in your life.

I did it. I got up. I was strong, I told myself that every day. "Steph, you can handle this, you are strong..." I beat it into my brain and heart. I flourished and I started laughing and the smile that I'd lost came back. Surely, I was going to be okay. It was a rollercoaster of emotions, highs and lows came in waves, but I was determined.

Then the diagnosis came five years after Ronald left – "It's cancer." I sat still and motionless on the phone, pulled over in a grocery parking lot to take the call. I never felt more alone than in that single moment. I needed my husband to hold me tightly in his big strong embrace, to tell me, "It's going to be okay babe," and make the world disappear. That never came and I was left with the realization that I was alone. I won't burden my children anymore, they suffered enough. For the first time, I felt sorry for myself, truly felt sorry for myself. Why me? It's not fair! I already suffered so much... but no tears fell.

As I told my family members, the sorrow in their faces struck me. I knew I was loved as I watched their expressions of sadness and shock, it was so hard for me to see that. During a conversation with the doctor who discovered the tumor, he said it was slow growing and had probably been there for quite some time. Really, I thought to myself? "Do you know how long?" His answer still resonates in my mind, about five years. I almost dropped my phone, I replied "Well that makes sense." It was exactly five years ago that I lost my husband. I explained how I fell apart and my body followed my sorrow. When I lost Ronald, I was so depressed and sick that I was hospitalized and little did I know a tumor started growing inside of me. I believe now that in my story... MY OWN GRIEF JOURNEY and the sorrow that broke down my body, causing it to be susceptible to illness and ultimately a cancer diagnosis.

True story... this was my wake up call! Five years into my grief journey, I thought I was doing good, but my body and mind knew the deep feelings I shoved so deep down in my soul and it was time to address it. I needed to do something drastic. I finally reached out to Dr. Karen Kramer and said "It's time to talk and truly heal. This time, from the inside out. My life depended on it." She was waiting for this exact moment after knowing me for so many years, she said she could help me. After one long five-hour session with her, I discovered that my pain stemmed from early childhood trauma. It was a shock to me because I truly thought I put my past to rest.

I found that little girl again, the girl I often said is "no longer me." I discovered that she is every bit a part of me and always will be. I kneeled down and hugged that little girl so tightly, and I watched her walk away from me. She finally found true peace. A few days later, I walked by a mirror and stared at myself – really looked at myself for the first time since I lost Ronald... and I realized I did not hate the person looking back at me. I felt a burden lifted for the first time that only came, ironically, because of a cancer diagnosis. Funny how life works. I stopped questioning the why and came to the realization that I won't have the answers I seek on this side of heaven and I was okay with that. I was ready to live and to live with intention. I am stronger now than I have ever been before. I am addressing the root causes of why I received this diagnosis, and I am working on every aspect of my journey. Healing my mind and soul so that my body will follow. I am confident and have the unwavering faith that God will heal me or bring me home to heaven. It really is that simple. Life is fragile, that is the greatest lesson I learned in the fifth year. I no longer look far into the future; I try to only live for today with the best intentions for me and my children.

I never thought that was possible, that forest I was in was so dark. The waterfall pummeling me at Niagara Falls was drowning me. Five years later, I can look back and reflect on my journey. God placed rocks in the form of people and a pathway for me in that dark forest so I could find my way. I can see it clearly now. He gave me a boat to swim to, so I could climb in and lay back to look up at the blue sky. My eyes are wide open now and I am on a journey to live and learn to love myself again. I know that it is inevitable, I still have deep valleys to walk into and mountains to climb because that is the nature of life, but now I am prepared with tools to help me cope that I never had before. The plan is still the same, the lessons from the last five years are clear, I am going to take it one step at a time.

Stephanie MacGilfrey, Client
San Diego, CA

Stephanie MacGilfrey updated her profile picture.
July 12 · 🌐

When I was a kid, I played on the swing for hours... now I'm just a grown up trying to embrace that little girl that was lost inside me.

I'm pretty sure, I found her 🖤

#learningtolovemyself #cancerfighter #journeytoheal

 Karen Peterson Kramer
She's been waiting to be found for decades! She was there all along. Embrace her innocence & PLAY! 🖤🖤🖤

Like Reply 9w

 Stephanie MacGilfrey
Karen Peterson Kramer Thank you KP for helping me to find her and discover how much of her still exists within me. You truly changed my life and set me on a different course of self discovery. I am finally on a path to heal and finally love the person looking back at me in the mirror. 🖤 ☺

Love Reply 9w

 Karen Peterson Kramer
Stephanie, I'm so fricken proud of you! 🥹 That person looking back at you in the mirror has waited a long time too to be seen, heard, felt, & understood. 🖤🖤🖤

Like Reply 9w

The Story in Review

Stephanie's story is rich with the highs and lows, the "waves of emotion" as she felt "plummeted" with the depths of her proverbial Niagara Falls and the "no fear" control over life as she jumped out of a plane in the freefall of her existence. As a client, I will add to the summary of Stephanie's story. Let's review ...

Toxic Positivity: Stephanie perfectly described a key form of toxic positivity when she stated that she was good at putting on a happy, smiling face when she was "dying inside." Little did she know that that would end up being the case with a later health diagnosis.

As described in the chapter "Toxic Positivity," here are some of the well-intended yet poorly delivered phrases Stephanie received that invoked a less-than-positive response:

- ✧ "Be strong for the kids"
- ✧ "You are still young, you'll find love again"
- ✧ "You need to move on!"

As Stephanie so eloquently put it, "If I want to lay here in my sorrow or if I want to get up and smile, that is my decision." This is when Supporters may just want to help by "fixing" the grief to make it go away for their own sake. To truly help someone in grief, a Supporter's silent presence, full attention, and listening ear can speak volumes over any word spoken. For more on how best to respond and support a Griever, refer back to the chapters "Gather" and "Ease."

Mind: When faced with the sudden, tragic loss of a loved one, the mind can go to a very dark place based on one's values, beliefs, and attitudes. One, common in this situation, is survivor's guilt defined by the Oxford Dictionary as "a condition of persistent mental and emotional stress experienced by someone who has survived an incident in which others died." As such, Stephanie adopted beliefs such as "It's my duty to carry that grief," and "I don't get to be happy." These were not logical beliefs; they were locked tight in the recesses of her subconscious mind leading her to think, feel, act, and react to the world around her with these beliefs as her core drivers.

Body: Working with Stephanie was one of the final catalysts for me writing this book. More people (like YOU) need to hear and understand both how grief can settle in the body as well as how it can be released. The goal is to identify and release it before it creates irreversible damage.

Be mindful of the words we speak and the thoughts we think for our body and subconscious mind are always listening. Here are some phrase Stephanie used within the five years after Ronald's passing:

- ✦ "I internalize everything."
- ✦ "My sorrow is at the pit of my stomach."
- ✦ "I'm dying a slow death."

In the field of *psychosomatics* and *psychoneuroimmunology*, Stephanie's dis-ease in her body developed into a tumor that was then diagnosed as "Stage 2 Colon Cancer." Let's explore these further in two ways.

First, there is research that indicates that one may develop (or be diagnosed with) cancer within five years after a traumatic incident. *Does this not grab your attention as to grief being a silent killer?!* I saw this happen with both my brother and sister-in-law who were diagnosed with prostate and breast cancer respectively within the same month, five years after their daughter (my niece Suzie) passed away. Stephanie was diagnosed five years after Ronald passed away. To quote Stephanie's doctor, "You may have been diagnosed now, but this has been growing in your body for five years."

Second, let's explore Stephanie's experience through Jensen's *The Healing Questions Guide* for tumor, cancer, and colon.

Tumor:

1. What harmful thought patterns and attitudes am I holding onto that I can no longer ignore? What will it take for me to start thinking differently?
2. What will it take to see the higher learning in life rather than continue believing I am being punished?
3. What am I allowing to block my ability to grow?
4. What would my life look like if I believed there were others who cared about me?
5. What changes are required in me to attract others who care about me?

6. What resentment of the past am I harboring in this tumor? What will it take to allow the power of forgiveness to dissolve this resentment?

7. What will it take for me to give up the idea that I am any better than anybody else?

Cancer:

1. What is my soul yearning for but I am denying it?

2. What do I need in order to feel emotionally and spiritually complete?

3. What one thing in my life, if completely changed, would allow me to experience true inner peace and hope?

4. What do I need to rearrange my thinking so I can align with the divine abundant source?

5. What in my life am I refusing to acknowledge?

6. What will it take for me to deal with my deep inner feelings so I can create a simple and more empowered life?

7. What will it take to distinguish between serving without forethought and serving with wisdom?

8. What do I need to rearrange my life so I can take care of my needs and the needs of those I love and care for?

9. What will it take to stop making others' needs the reason I am not tending to my own life and purpose?

10. What will it take to acknowledge when I make good choices and when I have made good choices in the past so I can learn to trust myself?

11. What will it take to find a way to express my internal anger in a productive way that is healthy and does not damage others or myself?

12. What will it take to release the belief that I have been blocked or will be blocked from progressing?

13. What long-held pains or resentments do I need to forgive?

14. What will it take to let more love in?

15. What will it take to start using my imagination to envision a happy, productive life?

16. What will it take for me to disassociate with my suffering or the need for others to suffer?

Colon Problems:

1. What will it take to convince me I can handle my personal issues?

2. What distortions in my thinking are ready to be purged and realigned to create a healthier body?

3. What needs to be removed in my psyche so I can effectively channel my energies, resources, and intentions?

4. What will it take to cease communicating to myself with disregarding and abusive language?

5. What injustices and abuses of the past am I refusing to let go of? What will it take to finally be free of them?

6. What will it take for me to believe in myself?

7. What will it take to effectively process my deeper toxic emotions so my body can heal?

8. What unexpressed, suppressed grief is still haunting me from my past?

9. What will it take for me to feel accepted by God [or whatever version of divine source is] so I can accept myself?

Note: Not all of these questions may resonate with a client like Stephanie. This is not to place any form of blame on the client. This is only to raise awareness to any subconscious programming that may lead to the manifestation of the physical ailment. When it is released at the subconscious level, it allows the body the ability to heal naturally. This is not in ALL cases nor with everyone. The point is to raise the awareness that it IS possible.

 Culture: Medical professionals are trained to cut, radiate, or medicate the "cancer." This has also perpetuated the societal norm that this is the only way to recover from cancer. Luckily, more research is being done to challenge and expand the options. In the meantime, there is still tremendous pressure placed on cancer patients to concede to medical treatment for recovery. Stephanie described being "bullied" into making a decision by well-intended medical professionals, friends, and family members. While friends and family members are typically driven by "wanting only what's best," medical professionals are also driven by their education that tells them "what's best." As emphasized in the chapter "Body," this is not the fault of the medical field; it is how they are trained. It is ingrained in our culture that doctors know best. It is ingrained in the medical field that cancers are things that need to be radiated, chemically attacked, and/or surgically removed. Fortunately, more research is becoming mainstream to help medical professionals and patients alike know about alternative treatments (as noted in the chapter "Body").

 Gather: The two most significant shifts in her story were the day Ronald passed away and the day of her diagnosis.

 Relate: Stephanie went through a tidal wave of emotions and thoughts, ranging from shock, devastation, sadness, and depression to feelings of anger, hate, guilt, and failure. Loneliness and a sense of emptiness also haunted her, but she eventually found safety and relief. Over time, she transitioned from mere existence to regaining control and moments of true laughter and authentic smiles.

 Involve: Stephanie took various action steps, both positive and challenging. Initially, she was in denial and tried to pretend that her loss was temporary. She allowed herself grace and sometimes spent the day in bed but also made an effort to smile. At times, she avoided interactions with people and focused on surviving one hour at a time, moving slowly through life. She became intentional with her time, connected and communicated honestly with her kids, and sought advice and comfort from fellow widows who understood her pain. She engaged in movement, activity, and nature, including skydiving and hiking, as part of her healing journey.

 Ease: She found support from a variety of resources, including her family and friends who stood by her during her difficult times. Her faith and belief in God provided her with strength and comfort. She also formed a supportive hiking group consisting of women who, like her, were dealing with their own forms of pain and grief. Additionally, as my client, she sought guidance through NLP Breakthrough sessions.

 Focus: involve honoring Ronald's memory while fully embracing her own life. She has shifted into "mom mode," dedicating herself to her children and taking each day as it comes, always with their best interests at heart. Her journey includes rediscovering self-love, acquiring new coping mechanisms, and gradually moving forward. Stephanie has also taken charge of her health choices and advocates for herself in that regard.

Defeat, Challenges, and Triumph: This is Not the Life I Ordered!

In life, 10% is what happens to us, and 90% is what we do with it.

*M*y journey into athleticism began unexpectedly on a sunny day in the Bay Area. My mom was running a 10k race, and my dad was supposed to watch over us three kids. As her determined footsteps neared the finish line, a spark ignited within me. At just three years old, I became an eager participant, crossing the finish line beside her, an unforgettable moment.

This marked the start of my unwavering dedication to sports. I was an active and spirited young girl, drawn to the thrill of challenging sports like football, basketball, and softball, often playing with boys. At Lodi Academy, I excelled in various athletic endeavors, participating in flag football, volleyball, basketball, and softball. Small school advantages allowed me to thrive in each sport.

After earning my Bachelor of Science degree in Exercise Science and teaching credentials, I entered a new phase. In my senior year, I was convinced by the cross-country coach to join the team. The first race was daunting, as my sprint background left me unprepared for a 5k's endurance. I struggled to keep up, and, about a mile in, I quit - a decision I'd later regret.

Following my education, I accepted a position at the Hawaiian Mission Academy in Oahu. Over six months, I balanced teaching physical education and health with pursuing triathlons. Inspired by someone special, I embraced triathlon training and the camaraderie it offered, facing the challenges of ocean waves and rigorous running and biking.

Driven by a lofty goal, I aimed to participate in the Hawaii Ironman. Life, however, had other plans. I left Hawaii's paradise, returned to Lodi, and found myself back in my parents' home.

Undeterred, I continued triathlon training, achieving a significant milestone by securing the sixth position in my division in my first official triathlon. Balancing work, training, and massage school. I was about to start my master's degree in Kinesiology at Sacramento State, specializing in Strength and Conditioning. I was excited to take that knowledge with me into my teaching and coaching in the future.

Life was unfolding as planned..

A Fateful Morning

Life took an unexpected turn on December 27, 2005, just after Christmas, when I woke up with a severe backache. Initially attributing it to muscle soreness from a run the previous day, I sought both massage therapy and chiropractic treatment, which proved ineffective. As the pain intensified and tingling sensations emerged, my mother and I rushed to the emergency room on day four, kicking off a perplexing medical journey.

The six-hour ER visit yielded no concrete answers despite X-rays and concerns about a pinched nerve or tumor. I left with muscle spasm pills and painkillers. However, that evening, my left side especially grew increasingly uncooperative, and I found myself crawling in the middle of the night. The next morning (day five), I crumbled out of bed and scooted down the hallway and stairs on my butt not knowing I would never see my upstairs bedroom ever again.

New Year's Eve 2005 marked a pivotal moment as I returned to the emergency room, with limited resources due to the holiday weekend. After various tests, I received a life-altering diagnosis – Transverse Myelitis, an inflammation of the spinal cord. We later found this to be a misdiagnosis. That night, as the calendar flipped to a new year, I was on my way to UC Davis. Transferred with a paramedic at my side, I asked them to turn on the siren for me so when people say "New Year, New You," that was extremely liberal for me.

UC Davis became my home for 24 days, marked by endless MRIs, tests, and blood draws. Despite the challenges of hospital life, I avoided surgical interventions.

During my stay, I underwent a unique procedure involving tubes sticking out of my neck for a couple of weeks, a constant reminder of my battle. It was already hard enough trying to put a shirt on without core muscles, let alone with those three inch tubes!

The cause of this ordeal traced back to a cluster of tangled blood vessels in my back since birth, which we didn't know were there, which weakened over time. A microscopic drop of blood leaked into my spinal cord, causing nine inches of inflammation, known as cavernous hemangioma, a one-in-five-million rarity. My life was forever altered, and I embarked on a whirlwind of medical challenges.

In 2006, I endured three more hospitalizations, totaling 46 days spent in hospitals. Despite the physical and emotional trials, I maintained my spirits. I actually told people from the get-go that I only wanted positive thoughts in my room as we still didn't totally know what was going on.

No matter how hard I tried to maintain a positive outlook when people visited during the day, the nights could be incredibly lonely. Many nights, I found myself shedding tears or quietly saying my prayers before drifting off to sleep. Fear gripped me, as I was in the dark about what was happening to my body. I would lie there, attempting to will my toes into movement, but nothing would respond.

Returning home presented fresh challenges. After a month of near-constant lying down, I had to relearn how to stand supported by my standing frame. Initially, I could only stand for ten seconds before fainting, but gradual progress gave me hope. A month and a half later, I detected movement in a single toe, marking a significant milestone. My dad and I sat there staring at it and laughing. You rejoice in those little things!

As far as feeling goes, I could not feel anything from below the chest down for 11 months! Paralyzed! This is not something you would ever even imagine! Now I can feel and be able to tell exactly where you're touching on my legs. It's not a normal feeling, but I'll take it!

Throughout this challenging journey, my family provided unwavering support. My parents, two brothers, and their families stood by my side. I could not have done this without them and good friends who have stuck it out with me.

In Lodi, I met a fellow wheelchair user who introduced me to handcycling, a sport that became integral to my life. With determination, I embraced this new challenge and earned my first "gold" medal in an 8k race in Sacramento.

Moving to Carlsbad, California, for specialized spinal cord therapy expanded my world. I ventured into triathlons, marathons, and over 40 handcycling races. I have won nearly half of them. I try and stay humble about it, but often times I have beat many men in the process! My first year doing the Silver Strand ½ marathon I beat the previous record by 17 minutes, and 35 of the 40 guys! The satisfaction of setting and achieving goals in adaptive sports was unparalleled. Training with Paralympic teams opened new doors, and I was part of the journey toward equalizing monetary rewards for Paralympians. I was glad to see that for the 2021 Tokyo Paralympics, that pay has finally been equalized between Paralympains and Olympians, something that has been a long time coming!

An encounter with Melanie, a woman with profound physical challenges, who swam in an ocean race, redefined my beliefs about limitations. Melanie had lost all four limbs above the knees and above the elbows due to spinal meningitis. Guess what! Melanie did the 1.2 mile ocean swim in a triathlon! I had no reason to make excuses! Oh and I did learn how to swim after that. I realized that sometimes, we needlessly impose boundaries on ourselves.

Sometimes, what initially appears to be a limitation can transform into an unexpected advantage and asset. Did you ever dream of competing in the Olympics? I certainly did! However, due to my injury, I now have a much better chance at excelling in the Paralympics than I ever would have in the Olympics. I've had the incredible opportunity to train multiple times at both Olympic Training Centers in Colorado and California working with the Paracycling team, the Paratriathlon team for several years, and later, the Paracanoe team. My injury hasn't dimmed my ambitions; I still hold the same goals and dreams I had before my injury. The next big goal is the Los Angeles 2028 Paralympics.

As Jesse Owens wisely said, "We all have dreams. But in order to make dreams come into reality, it takes an awful lot of determination, dedication, self-discipline and effort." This statement resonates deeply with my journey. During my time in San Diego, I embraced a wide range of activities, including cycling, swimming, rock climbing, surfing, tennis, softball, basketball, paddleboarding, kayaking, team outrigger canoeing, monoskiing, sailing, inner-tubing, wakeboarding, sled hockey, curling, golfing, dancing, prone paddling, triathlons, race chair, and wave skiing. I even made history as the first female para-athlete to race in personal watercraft jet skiing in the ocean.

In 2012, I achieved a significant milestone by becoming the USA National Champion for my division. This accomplishment opened doors for me to represent the United States at the World Championships in New Zealand and London. My journey continued to evolve as I ventured into kayaking in 2015, leading me to compete at the World Championships in 2016. I participated in Paralympic trials in Hungary representing the US to determine what 10 athletes would be going onto the Tokyo Paralympics in 2021. I missed qualifying by just ONE spot out of the world!

I have an unwavering belief that where there's a will, there's a way. The key is to persist and never give up until you find a way forward! My injury wasn't just a disruption; it was a significant turning point. At the crossroads of adversity, I faced a crucial choice, one that has shaped my journey. As you can "witness," I made the choice to rise from the couch and take action. I chose to embrace an active and positive mindset. I chose to tirelessly pursue my dreams.

Nido Qubein said, "When a goal matters enough to a person, that person will find a way to accomplish what at first seemed impossible." This sentiment reflects my unwavering determination.

There's a book title I hold dear, "I Can, I Will, I Believe." However, I've added a word to it: "I can, I will, BECAUSE I believe." It all begins with self-belief, deep within us. Regardless of the habit or dream you seek to cultivate, that inner belief is the foundation upon which everything else is built.

In life, 10% is what happens to us, and 90% is what we do with it. So, what will you do with your life going forward? What do you envision for your future? Never give up, pursue your goals with unwavering self-belief!

Climbing to New Heights

In October 2009, I received an intriguing call from the Challenged Athletes Foundation. The question was simple: Would I be interested in climbing Mt. Kilimanjaro? My answer? A resounding YES!

After I hung up the phone, I realized I needed to locate Kilimanjaro on the map – Tanzania, Africa. It was a remarkable opportunity, and if I could accomplish it, I would become the first female paraplegic to summit this majestic peak. However, the clock was ticking, and I had only three months to prepare.

The preparation was grueling. I focused on core strengthening and getting my arms in peak hiking condition, a shift from my usual cycling workouts. I even challenged myself by pushing my everyday wheelchair up steep streets and taking my custom climbing chair out on demanding trails.

The journey was undoubtedly challenging, yet incredibly exhilarating. We found ourselves hiking for 7 to 11 hours each day, moving from one camp to another. Altitude sickness symptoms hit us at various points during the trip, leaving us exhausted and sore with stomach aches and headaches. It wasn't just a physical challenge; it tested us mentally and emotionally. Spiritually, I knew God was at my side.

Despite these daunting obstacles, I was determined not to give up. This monumental mountain climb became the greatest achievement of my life, one that I am immensely proud of. We confronted and overcame various challenges as a team, and together, we reached the summit.

I hope my story serves as an inspiration to you. You've only heard a glimpse of the setbacks and formidable challenges I've faced, but I've always maintained the perseverance to pursue what I believe in. On the next page I'd like to share a heartfelt poem written by a dear friend, even before we met in person.

During the first year and a half after my injury, my mom cried every day. But she once heard me say on stage that if I had the chance to go back and live my life as if my injury had never happened, I would choose the life I have now, even with the wheelchair and the extra challenges. I never would have had the opportunities I've had, the people I've met, and the places I've been able to go.

Maybe you are not paralyzed, or maybe you are. Maybe you're not in a wheelchair, or maybe you are. You might have just gone through a complete life-altering injury or setback. Everything that I did proves that you can still have a great life.

This is Not What I Ordered!
by Steve Dahl

This is not what I ordered,
Please send my life back!
There's been a mistake!
And my life is off track!

This is not what I ordered,
I have plans to unfold,
I see climbing and biking,
And competing for gold!

But life changed in an instant,
When my legs wouldn't go,
My heart screamed "Get going!"
But my body said "No!"

This is not what I ordered!
This is not what I planned,
But this IS what I'm given,
I've been dealt a new hand.

But there's no time for sorrow,
For the life I've been handed,
Now my Spirit says "Go!"
Begin where you've landed.

There are mountains to climb,
There are races to win,
I can still reach my goals,
As I reach deep within.

You can climb any mountain,
When your vision gets clear,
You can win any race,
When you let go of fear.

This is not what I ordered,
So I choose a new track,
I am living my dream,
And I'm not looking back!

My journey as an athlete, advocate, and speaker has been a remarkable adventure of highs and lows, triumphs and challenges, and it's far from over. I'm committed to advocating for inclusivity and excited about the growing presence of individuals with disabilities in sports, media, and business.

Despite obstacles, resilience, determination, and support have been my allies. I've learned that with the right mindset and focus, we can conquer even the greatest challenges.

As I move forward, I'm reminded of Helen Keller's wisdom: "Optimism is the faith that leads to achievement." With hope, confidence, and belief in human potential, I embrace the next chapter and thank you for being part of this journey. May your own journeys be filled with resilience and the joy of discovering your limitless potential. I'm here in support!

Erica Davis
Carlsbad, CA

The Story in Review

The statistics are staggering for those with spinal cord injuries according to the National Spinal Cord Injury Statistical Center, Traumatic Spinal Cord Injury Facts and Figures at a Glance 2023, 2021 Annual Statistical Report.[75] See the figure on next page for statistics. This does not include spinal cord injuries due to disease as in Erica's case.

Let's explore Erica's powerful story ...

 Culture: Thankful, there are organizations that support, encourage, and adapt to those with physical disabilities. Image the resources and opportunities that may not have been present for Erica had this been 25, 50, or even 100 years ago.

 Toxic Positivity: Erica did her best to maintain a positive outlook when people visited during the day, yet was incredibly lonely at night. It can be tricky to find the balance between remaining positive while also being able to be real and authentic with at least key people about her true emotions.

 Mind: Erica overcame a number of mindset obstacles to step back into athletics. One of the mindset shifts was in meeting Melanie, who had lost all four limbs above the knees and above the elbows, and did the 1.2 mile ocean swim in a triathlon! This motivated her to learn to swim. She realized then that "Sometimes, we impose boundaries on ourselves needlessly."

 Body: When exploring physical manifestations in the body due to a "hereditary disorder," the answers may lay in past generations. Various techniques (including hypnotherapy) can help to answer and release it from the body. Utilizing Jensen's *The Healing Questions Guide*, here are questions that I might ask a client in Erica's situation. (*Note: These questions are generalized and not specific to Erica.*)

Paralysis:
1. What will it take to trust my surroundings?
2. What will it take to bring more clarity and ability to cope into my world?

Spinal Cord Injuries in the US

2023 Facts and Statistics

New Injuries Per Year

Approximately 18,000 new spinal cord injuries occur each year in the United States (54 incidents per 1 million). This does not include those who die from their injury at the scene.

~18,000 New spinal cord injuries each year

Total Injured Population

It's estimated that there are 302,000 people with SCI living in the United States. Estimates range between 255,000-383,000.

~302,000 People with spinal cord injuries in the US

Who's Getting Injured?

79% of people with SCI are male. The average age at time of injury is 43 years old. **Nearly half (47%) of injuries occur between ages 16 and 30.** The most frequent age at the time of injury is 19.

79% Male   **21%** Female

 16   **47% Between Ages 16-30**   30

Average Hospital Stay

When admitted, **patients stay in ICU/acute care for 11 days on average.** Afterwards, the average length in rehabilitation is 31 days.

11 Days ICU/Acute Care   **31 Days** Rehabilitation

Find More Resources at

SpinalCord .com

(877) 336-7192
Support@SpinalCord.com

Sources
National Spinal Cord Injury Statistical Center. Traumatic Spinal Cord Injury Facts and Figures at a Glance 2023, 2021 Annual Statistical Report.

3. What unwanted task, experience or person am I trying to escape from? What will it take to face it with courage and wisdom?

4. What will it take to trade in the stubborn parts of me for a more flexible and open outlook?

5. What will it take for me to learn to be more trusting and hopeful of the future?

Spinal Cord Problems:

1. What will it take for me to believe that I can meet the requirements of life?

2. What will it take for me to move beyond the negative voices in my head and in my life and rise to fulfill my full potential regardless of what others may think or do?

Spinal Fluid Problems:

1. What will it take for me to release the negative feelings I have stored because I do not feel supported in my younger years?

2. What will it take for me to believe that I will be, or can be, supported now?

3. What will it take for me to attract supportive relationships?

4. What can I do to support others?

5. If I do not have to do everything myself, what would I create?

6. What will it take for me to completely revise the way I view things?

7. What will it take for me to move away from my narrow rigid thinking and invite new possibilities into my life?

8. What will it take for me to heal my relationships with God and reconsider what I think God's expectations are of me?

9. What will it take to really know God and stop relating all my misfortunes as being His will?

10. What if God's greatest desire was for me to be abundantly blessed and happy?

Note: References to the Universe or God are intended to be replaced with whatever form of one's word or phrase for their higher power.

Gather: The major shifts in her story include a decline in her health and eventual diagnosis.

 Relate: Erica's emotional rollercoaster was quite intense. In the beginning, loneliness and sadness weighed heavily on my heart. Fear of the unknown cast its shadow yet was met with a deep determination to persevere. She found herself facing physical, mental, and emotional challenges that tested her resolve. The gradual progress she made infused hope, finding laughter and rejoicing in life's little things. Above all, there was immense satisfaction in setting and, against all odds, achieving her goals.

 Involve: Her action steps were astounding for even many able-bodied people! She engaged in a wide range of activities including marathons, triathlons, handcycling, swimming, rock climbing, surfing, tennis, softball, and basketball, paddleboarding, kayaking, team outrigger canoeing, monoskiing, sailing, inner-tubing, wakeboarding, sled hockey, and jet skiing. This took her to become National Champion and even all the way up Mount Kilamonjaro! The various steps she had to take to engage in those activities are more than I can expand upon here.

 Ease: Support played a vital role in her journey, including her parents, two brothers, and their families who stood by her side. Teams of medical doctors and specialized spinal cord therapists supported her physical body. Coaches and other para-athletes were part of her physical, mental, and emotional endurance team to obtain her athletic wins and help her climb to new heights.

 Focus: With hope, confidence, and belief in human potential, Erica embraces the next chapter of her life. Her "new normal" incorporates a number of learnings for anyone facing challenges, the biggest learning was around mindset. As she noted, "My injury wasn't just a disruption; it was a significant turning point. ... I chose to embrace an active and positive mindset. I chose to tirelessly pursue my dreams." She also states, "'I can, I will, BECAUSE I believe.' It all begins with self-belief, deep within us. Regardless of the habit or dream you seek to cultivate, that inner belief is the foundation upon which everything else is built."

Double-Death and Dementia: Never Taking One's Precious Time for Granted

I could choose to linger on the void left by what once was... Alternatively, I can pay homage to their memory by embracing the life I have.

Losing My Oldest Brother

Gene, my older brother, entered my life when I was born, marrying shortly after and becoming a father to Suzie before my third birthday. Despite the significant age gap, the bond we shared was unwavering. While our relationship didn't follow the typical brother-sister dynamic, I knew I could always count on him. The decline of and eventual passing of his daughter Suzie (as recounted in the chapter "The End of Life") took a toll on Gene and his wife, Dale, lasting seven painful years.

In 2013, five years after Suzie's departure, the unimaginable struck our family once more. Both Gene and Dale were diagnosed with cancer – breast cancer for her, prostate cancer for him. Through treatments, both found reprieve in remission. However, the journey of survival was far from over.

By July 2019, Gene confided in our mother that his cancer had returned, and he was pursuing aggressive measures. Despite his usual sunny disposition, he kept quiet about his condition. He continued to aid me in caring for our aging mother, even attempting grocery shopping for her despite his declining health. It wasn't until an email from my sister-in-law that I realized the extent of his struggle.

Calls from my sister-in-law urged me to reach out to Gene. Unlike the detachment I experienced with my father (described in the chapter "My Father's Passing"), I tried my best to be fully present. I aimed to strike a balance between instilling hope and being realistic about his condition. Dale confided, "He won't tell me things." In his reticence, he turned to my mom's caregiver for support, who urged him to open up to us.

During Thanksgiving in 2021, my brother's ailing appearance was evident. Despite my growing concern, denial clung to me. A few weeks later, a text from my nephew revealed that Gene had taken a fall and was deteriorating. My heartache was familiar, as my family had navigated this journey before.

With prior experiences as my guide, I sprang into action. Gene's weakened state required assistance from firefighters to return him to bed. Hospital assistance was elusive until I intervened, using key phrases to expedite the process. It was clear that my brother needed more help than my nephew and sister-in-law could provide, prompting me to enlist my mom's caregiver service.

Christmas plans changed. Our anticipated family gathering was replaced by a small celebration at Gene's house. Amidst the somberness, my great-nephew, Gene's only grandson, injected joy into the room. At three-and-a-half-years-old, his presence lit up the space. Over the previous four years, I had built up Gene with hope, witnessing his fierce determination to persevere despite the odds. Even a month prior, he recounted his quest for a doctor willing to administer more chemotherapy when his current doctors denied his request. The unwavering spark in his eyes mirrored the big brother I had always known. He was battling to grasp onto hope, to resist surrendering to his illness. Fear became his constant companion.

Unlike my father and Suzie, Gene wasn't prepared for the end. He fought with the looming finality, a sentiment he voiced in his eyes. My typical words of hope faltered; all that remained were the simple yet profound words, "I love you." As three of us helped him back into bed, my mother and I held his hand – a gesture we hadn't shared since my childhood. His hand dwarfed mine, a stark reminder of the passage of time. Memories of my father's final moments resurfaced, yet Gene was only 74.

In those farewell moments, my mother and I sensed that we were saying our goodbyes for the last time. A brief encounter followed, a supply drop-off that offered a fleeting glimpse of my brother. My sister-in-law urged me to visit again, but something held me back. The impending finality of a long farewell was more than I could bear.

On January 5, 2022, Gene peacefully departed this Earth while in the comfort of his home. In the haze of denial, his condition had eluded me. He kept it from his wife, and I, preoccupied with caring for my mother, failed to see the signs. His diminished mobility, forgetfulness, reliance on a cane, and breathlessness were all indicative. Yet it was his pallor during Thanksgiving, just three weeks before his rapid decline, that served as the undeniable wake-up call.

As reality set in, the painful truth emerged – I had been in denial about my big brother's health. Amidst his reluctance to discuss his condition, and the focus on my mother's well-being, the signs were present. I refused to believe that I was about to lose my beloved sibling, my big brother.

Mom's Decline

Following Dad's passing in 2012 (as detailed in the chapter "My Father's Passing"), Mom found herself alone at home. She navigated Dad's passing with resilience, recognizing that his quality of life had declined, and his passing was relatively swift. Mom possessed an intuitive ability to connect with people even after they had passed away, a gift that allowed her to maintain a spiritual bond with loved ones.

An example of this connection took place when my niece Suzie reached out to Mom a week after her own passing (described in the chapter "The End of Life"). Suzie's message, channeled through Mom, conveyed her awareness of my actions during her final moments – singing to her and brushing her hair during her comatose state. These actions were unknown to Mom, yet it served as undeniable proof of her unique connection.

Born to a clairvoyant mother and an engineering-minded father, I consider myself a harmonious fusion of their traits. In the wake of Dad's passing, Mom remained linked to him spiritually. If you're interested in delving further, you can explore my mother's clairvoyant experiences in her own book, *Whispers in the Wind.*[76]

In the months following Dad's passing, my godmother moved in to offer companionship to Mom. Despite being five years older than my godmother, Mom was no ordinary 88-year-old. Constantly engaged in creative pursuits at her art studio, nurturing her garden, and tending to her chickens, she exuded vitality. However, my godmother's increased care needs necessitated her transition to a retirement home community.

Worry gnawed at me whenever I couldn't reach Mom on the phone, invoking irrational anxieties I had dubbed "Little Miss Karen" (as previously discussed in the chapter "My Father's Passing"). One evening, unable to contact her, I dispatched my nephew (who lived next door) to check on her in an S.O.S. mission. The emotional toll was exhausting, and I gradually adopted the notion that I might one day discover Mom peacefully gone in her garden while engaged in her favorite activities.

Thanksgiving morning in 2016 altered this projection. A text from my husband brought news of Mom's hospitalization, albeit with reassurance that she was stable.

Our two younger boys, Jake and Tyler, switched off taking the "chicken bucket" down to Grandma's. (The "chicken bucket" was a large red Folgers' coffee container we used to put scraps of food for the chickens instead of the trash.) On this day, it was Jake's turn.

Jake discovered that Mom hadn't released the chickens from their coop, as she usually did by 7:30 am. Alarmed, he approached the house, finding the back door locked. Concern mounting, he broke through the kitchen window and entered, discovering Mom on her bedroom floor – alive, but cold and disoriented. An ambulance rushed her to the hospital, where it was determined that she had suffered a stroke during the night or early morning. Jake's action saved Mom's life, and her resilience shone through as she regained her footing with the help of in-home caregivers. Her home was equipped with a camera that captured activities in the living room, helping us monitor her well-being.

In January 2018, Mom's strength was tested again. After a routine chicken feeding with her caregiver's assistance, she tripped and fell, resulting in a fractured neck and forehead gash. Despite her injuries, she recovered with 15 stitches and a neck brace.

Around this time, I wrestled with persistent nosebleeds. The physical discomfort was accompanied by emotional turmoil – feelings of fear, helplessness, anger, and despair. I likened my experience to the story of the Little Dutch Boy plugging a leaky dam – trying to hold back the overwhelming pressure of my responsibilities, including Mom's care, estate management, and my son's health (as described in the chapter "Death, Divorce, and Illness"). Unbeknownst to me, these stressors were affecting my well-being and my marriage. Soon after, my husband left (as detailed in the chapter "Death, Divorce, and Illness"), intensifying the feeling of drowning in the challenges of life.

Change was imperative. In early 2019, I embarked on a journey of transformation, becoming certified in NLP, Time Line Therapy, Hypnotherapy, and NLP Coaching. This process included my own NLP Breakthrough, enabling me to identify and release past traumas, negative emotions, and limiting beliefs that held me captive in the past. This breakthrough marked a shift, allowing me to be present, hold space for others, and confront challenges with clarity.

A visit to Mom during this time brought an epiphany. Amidst my divorce struggles and managing my son's health care (as discussed in the chapter "Death, Divorce, and Illness"), the caregiver's well-intentioned logistical concerns triggered an emotional outpouring from me. In that moment, I recognized the magnitude of my mother's sacrifices during her own caregiving days. The memory of her balancing her responsibilities for my grandparents while attending to me as a child was humbling. I longed to be simply her daughter, not a manager of her affairs. This realization sparked a shift in our interactions, transforming our visits into meaningful bonding experiences.

Bonding often involved reminiscing about Mom's past, connecting fragments of memory to weave a fuller narrative. We shared moments of singing and movie watching, and dined at her favorite Mexican restaurant. My physical presence wasn't constant due to travel, but our regular phone conversations kept us connected. Her precious time on Earth was never taken for granted.

In July 2019, in the midst of my 16-day NLP master practitioner training, a call arrived from Mom's caregiver – she had fallen and broken her hip. Luckily, she gave me the backstory before I saw the aftermath on the recording.

We had a camera in my mom's living room which captured who entered or left the front door, if mom was up watching TV, and which caregiver was on rotation. Recordings were available for up to 24-hours.

My older brother Gene had taken my mother out for lunch without her caregiver that day. He wanted to have a private conversation with Mom to tell her about the return of his prostate cancer. Upon leaving the restaurant, my mom's walker hooked on the sidewalk causing her to fall on her hip. Being close to the car, my brother was able to get my mom back into his vehicle.

The camera picked up what happened next. Gene wheeled my mom into the house and told the caregiver, Alyx, what had occurred. Alyx exclaimed that it looked like my mom broke her hip given my mom's foot rotation, and the paramedics were called.

What caught my attention most in that video was my brother. Despite my concern for my mom's care, I watched my brother deflate. As the situation continued with the paramedics onsite, my brother's head dropped more and more, he moved further and further back from the scene. I could sense his guilt and shame.

It was another four hours, midnight by this time, when I was finally able to talk to both Gene and Alyx. After a sentence or two to know Mom was under good care at the hospital, I said "Gene, how are YOU?"

What took place in that conversation shifted for the better, for both him and me. That conversation could have gone so differently had I been in my heightened emotional states concerned for Mom's broken hip and care. It could have easily turned to blaming my brother for putting mom in harm's way further feeding the shame and guilt my brother was already feeling. In fact he even feared calling to tell me, which is why Alyx did so instead. He called my ex-husband for advice and avoided calling me.

My role in that moment was to comfort my brother. My role was to use all the NLP skills I had learned to help my brother release and let go of his guilt and shame. Those feelings did not serve him in the moment and I sure wasn't going to rub salt in his wounds. He was already in pain, and I (his little sister who loved him dearly) wanted him to know I was there for him too.

Mom was scheduled for risky surgery two days after. Next came the decision to drive the four-hours home and leave the middle of an NLP certification program that was also important to me and my healing journey. I chose to stay knowing that I would just be waiting by a phone or a hospital waiting room.

Luckily, Mom made it through the risky surgery as I had anticipated. This was followed by another call that required my intervention – the doctor suggested hospice care after Mom aspirated. I had the phone on speaker as my roommate,

Christina, and I were getting ready for our NLP program that day. She leaned over, placed the call on hold, and told me that her grandmother had been in hospice for five years. "Don't give up," she said. I am so thankful for Christina's words that day! Deciding to let Mom decide her fate, I called her and she seemed to be very chipper! Even the nurse was surprised at her recovery. (Did I mention my mom was the Energizer Bunny?) Mom did make a recovery and was home soon after. She was 94.

Mom continued to surprise us with her strength and energy, yet I know it was also hard. A few times, the caregivers shared her sorrow over missing Dad. I also know her quality of life had significantly changed since her stroke at 92, and more so after each of her events (broken neck and hip surgery). She could get around only with a walker and assistance by the time of her 97th birthday (in July 2021). In the previous five years, she had been mostly confined to the house and watching TV which was distinctly different from the spry and active lifestyle she had prior in her art studio, with her chickens, and in the garden. I'm sure she was also grieving her quality of life as well as the loss of my father nine years before.

In February 2021, I got a call from my mom's caregiver. "Your mom has a message for you." Not knowing what to expect, my mom was adamant that I contact her estranged brother, my uncle Joe, five years her junior. Being intuitive, I knew she sensed something was going to happen. "We need to make amends before something happens to one of us." Although he lived on the property, we had set clear boundaries with my uncle and even (energetically) removed him from the family after some behaviors that legally, physically, and emotionally placed a number of our family members in harm. The estrangement had started 15 years prior, and my mom needed to mend and come to peace with my uncle including forgiving his behaviors.

During a period of COVID-19 restrictions, my aunt and I facilitated a heartwarming FaceTime conversation between Mom and her estranged brother. My uncle, despite mild dementia, engaged in a lighthearted chat. This five-minute connection we video recorded became a cherished memory when my uncle passed away six-weeks later.

Amidst challenges and triumphs, Mom's journey through these years was a testament to her strength, resilience, and enduring connection to loved ones – a legacy I continue to honor.

Saying Good-Bye to Mom

My brother, Gene, passed away on January 5, 2022. The day after, while visiting my mom, she candidly remarked, "I never expected to live this long. I'm curious about what it's like to pass over." Instantly, I was transported back to the day Suzie confided in me about placing herself on hospice (as discussed in the chapter "The End of Life"). Like Suzie, my mom was seeking acceptance in my eyes.

Anticipating this moment, I had thought I would be the one initiating the conversation with Mom, encouraging her to hold on for our sake. In response, I assured her, "If that's your wish, I understand. You don't have to stay alive just for me. I'll be okay."

Though it brings tears to my eyes as I write this, I felt an unusual calmness at the time. In that moment, I knew that I loved my mother deeply, and I was grateful for the life she had given me. Her impending passing presented an opportunity for me to honor her journey.

Two days later, my mom's demeanor shifted. Alarmed, the caregiver alerted me and the paramedics. As I had done for my father a decade earlier, I was prepared with a notebook containing necessary details, including the DNR (Do Not Resuscitate) agreement and my POA (Power of Attorney) status for medical decisions. Composedly, I informed the paramedics of my brother's recent passing and my mother's readiness to follow suit, focused on her comfort.

Following the ambulance to the hospital, I arrived at the waiting room at 8:30 pm. Two calls from the doctor had already given me updates on her condition. I relayed the news of my brother's passing and my mother's similar choice, much like a news reporter delivering a factual account. In that moment, I felt a numbness that stemmed from the cumulative experiences I had had with death, dying, and grief.

The second call from the doctor, shortly before midnight, informed me that I couldn't visit Mom due to tightened COVID-19 restrictions triggered by the Omicron variant. At 7:30 the next morning, the doctor called again, revealing that my mother had tested positive for COVID-19 Omicron. Panic surged within me.

Acting quickly, I texted my ex-husband, Roger, who worked at the hospital. It was early Sunday morning. I informed him of my mom's hospitalization and her

COVID-positive status, emphasizing my inability to be by her side. Roger's immediate response was heartening, "I'll get dressed and I'll be there in an hour."

Despite our recent divorce and strained relationship, I knew I could rely on him in moments of need. Within the hour, he had arranged a FaceTime (video chat) call, allowing me to see Mom virtually. The encounter provided a semblance of connection, which I was unprepared to forfeit. Fresh in my grief over my brother's passing just three days earlier, I wasn't ready to face my mother's departure in this manner.

Roger's presence became invaluable over the following days. He facilitated Mom's cardiology exam, offering critical insights that eased my concerns about a potential second stroke. He continued to connect me with Mom through FaceTime calls, including bringing her a McDonald's vanilla milkshake, which was met with her radiant smile.

As the week progressed, Mom recuperated from COVID-19, although her lungs bore the brunt, necessitating extensive oxygen support. Aligned with her DNR and POA directives, there came a point when it was evident that she wasn't recovering. I faced a pivotal decision, one guided by the provisions laid out in her will. Accepting her wishes, I opted to place her under hospice care and cease life-saving measures, focusing solely on her comfort.

My thoughts drifted back to the past when I was 11 years old, watching my mom care for her ailing father as she followed his wishes to let him pass naturally by slowly weaning him off food. Thankfully, medical practices have evolved, sparing me the weight of a similar decision. This choice also permitted family visits. Clad in hospital gowns, gloves, double masks, and plastic face shields, my 19-year-old son, Tyler, and I visited Mom.

I can vividly recall the moment – her eyes sparkled, creases deepening as her smile widened upon receiving her first dose of morphine. She remained alert, unaffected by the drowsiness of medication. We chatted and held hands, a profound connection despite the barriers.

At Tyler's urging, I removed my mask, allowing my mom to see my face fully. Her smile broadened further. Then Tyler suggested I take off my gloves. We weren't afraid of COVID-19; we were embracing the precious moments. In that instance, I understood that if it meant risking COVID-19 again to have this special connection, I would gladly accept that risk. The tactile touch held immense significance. I traced my fingers along her hands, hands that had cradled me as a newborn, held me during my first day of kindergarten, offered comfort during moments of distress, and celebrated milestones. In that moment, those hands spoke volumes.

We remained by her side for an hour or two before bidding our uncertain farewell. The following days blurred together as I navigated meetings with palliative care and discussed plans to fulfill my parents' wishes – bringing Mom home to pass away surrounded by family. We arranged special equipment, but the transition posed challenges. By the third day, it became evident that her condition wouldn't permit her to return home as planned. So, I spent that third day with her, lingering in her presence, and we both found ourselves dozing off for naps.

I also took the opportunity to connect with family members through FaceTime. My brother Ed, her grandson Gary, Grandson Tyler, and caregiver Alyx – all the people who held significance in that moment – were given a chance to say their last goodbyes. It was a spontaneous yet crucial act, ensuring that those close to her had a chance to share their final moments with her.

Throughout that third day, the effect of the morphine was evident. Speaking became more challenging for her, yet her alertness shone through her eyes. Through subtle gestures and raised eyebrows, I could discern her responses to simple yes or no questions.

Our conversations spanned topics from family matters to cherished memories of her art studio, her beloved chickens, and the enchanting garden she cultivated. It felt as though we embarked on daydreaming journeys together, revisiting places, events, and people from the past.

An odd sensation enveloped me as I sat by her side, half-watching, half-waiting for the inevitable. My desire to be present at the moment of her passing, much like I had been for my father and niece, was profound. After spending several hours together, I reluctantly departed, promising to return the next day. I distinctly remember the parting gesture – a simple turn of her head and a lifted hand to wave goodbye. This image etched itself vividly into my memory, for it marked the last time I saw my mom.

As morning approached, I awoke just shy of 7 AM, a sense of knowing weighing on my mind. Instinctively, I positioned my phone by my pillow, anticipating the inevitable call. Nearly 20 minutes later, the confirmation arrived: she had passed away that very morning, coinciding with the moment I stirred awake.

January 19, 2022, marked the passing of my mother, exactly two weeks after my brother Gene's departure. The preparations I had undertaken seemed to culminate in this profound moment. Reflecting back, it became clear that my parents had been preparing me for this time throughout my life. Their presence had extended into their late 90s, a blessing granted to me due to having me late in their cycle of parenthood. Yet, they couldn't foresee the day when their time would end, leaving me to navigate this world without them.

During those two weeks bracketed by Gene's and my mother's passings, my colleagues gifted me a reprieve through a VR (virtual reality) headset. The experience offered an escape from reality, a way to release stress hormones that had accumulated. I'm certain that this saved my sanity.

Just a week later, I stepped into the heart of a 16-day NLP Master Practitioner's training as a Head Coach. I ensured I was in the right emotional state to guide and empower the staff, team leads, and students – my primary role in the training. This immersion turned into a profound healing process. Although it didn't indicate the conclusion of my grief journey, it marked my healthy progression through the process. I harnessed the techniques I shared with my one-on-one clients and in the classroom to help others navigate their own encounters with grief.

Throughout this period, I also shared my personal journey on social media, chronicling the final stages of my brother's and mother's lives. This was my initial attempt at destigmatizing and normalizing conversations around grief. Recognizing that I wasn't alone in experiencing the complexities of death and dying, many began to follow my journey. This period of my life laid the foundation for the birth of the book you are now reading. The realization dawned that more individuals needed to comprehend that they weren't alone in their grief journey. Connecting and sharing with others who could empathize with their pain, I understood, held tremendous healing and educational potential.

The celebration of life for both Gene and Mom took place in my backyard, a heartfelt gathering just one day before my 53rd birthday. Amid the preparations and reflections, I stumbled upon a realization – I had unintentionally overlooked celebrating myself in the process. A dear friend, Christina, bestowed upon me a delightful surprise gathering, an act that underscored the importance of acknowledging and honoring oneself during the process of grief.

Yet, a monumental task remains at hand, looming large even as I put pen to paper. This involves managing the intricate process of cleaning up, clearing out, and ultimately orchestrating the final sale of the 3.25-acre family land, a legacy dating back to my grandparents' acquisition in the early 1940s. This cherished piece of land holds within it my mother's 3,000-square-foot art studio, a space she inaugurated in 1952 – a repository of seven decades of ceramics, pottery, and other artistic creations.

When news of my mother's passing reaches others, a common response is to offer condolences, followed by an uncertain pause. To streamline these interactions, I've often found myself responding with a smile, saying, "My mom pleasantly passed at 97-years-young in January 2022. She lived a good life and was ready to go." I, too, wish a full life and a passing of my choosing at a ripe age of awe and wonder. I have decades ahead of me ...

Starting to Loose My Brother Ed

My middle brother, Ed, was 16 years old when I was born. He married when I was just six. He and his first wife constructed a house on the family property, a place where I would later build my own home adjacent to his. In 2018, he and his second wife made the decision to move out of state, marking the first instance in five generations where a part of the family land was sold.

Throughout the decline in Gene's and my mom's health, I made a concerted effort to keep Ed engaged and informed. My experience working with numerous clients has underscored the importance of resolving issues before passing, as the aftermath can be quite complex.

There had been tensions between Ed and the rest of the family (as recounted in the chapter "Family Estrangement"), most of which had thankfully been resolved. However, a month after Gene and Mom's passing, during an email exchange, Ed disclosed something that struck me deeply – he mentioned that he had been diagnosed with early onset dementia. The impact of that revelation was profound, and it felt like I had lost my remaining brother in that moment.

As the months went by, subtle incidents began cropping up here and there. Ed would forget that I had sent him important trust documents, prompting me to remind him repeatedly. Facts that he once knew well started slipping from his grasp, and tasks that his capable mind would have easily handled became insurmountable challenges. The signs were unmistakable.

Approaching his 71st birthday as of this writing, Ed is in relatively good health despite his faltering memory. I hold out hope that he will live well into his 90s, following in the footsteps of our parents (or possibly beyond). Nonetheless, the reality is becoming clear – I am now the matriarch of the family.

It's an unusual sensation to realize that you're the sole repository of the names attached to faces in old photographs, with no one else particularly inclined to remember. This thought struck me as I gazed at a picture of my grandparents, leaving me to wonder if future generations might experience a similar indifference when glancing at a photo of me.

However, rather than dwelling on this notion, I found myself immersed in fond memories of the vibrant times I shared with my grandparents while they were alive. This sentiment extended to each family member who has now departed – my parents, my niece, my brother. It's the span between their birth and their passing that holds the most significance, a concept beautifully captured by Linda Ellis in her poem aptly titled "The Dash." (also in the chapter "The End of Life").

I could choose to linger on the void left by what once was – the absence of my mother, my elder brother, and my middle brother's fading memory. Alternatively, I can pay homage to their memory by embracing the life I have, appreciating the role they played in it. The power to make this decision rests with me, and I wholeheartedly opt for a life well-lived!

Dr. Karen Kramer
San Diego, CA

The Story in Review

Let's explore ...

Culture: As already expressed in the chapter "End of Life," cultural and societal beliefs about death and end-of-life decisions can significantly influence our choices. Unlike the challenging situation my mother faced with my grandfather's end-of-life care, my parents were able to express their end-of-life wishes in their will and trust, allowing my mother to communicate her readiness to pass when the time came. This decision reflected a sense of agency over her own life and wishes as well as gave me a sense of ease as the one acting on her wishes.

Toxic Positivity: Toxic positivity can manifest in various ways. Some individuals labeled my grief over losing my brother and mother in quick succession as "hard" or "overwhelming," inadvertently downplaying my ability to cope positively with these losses. Additionally, my brother's reluctance to burden others with his health concerns demonstrates how the pressure to maintain positivity can lead to withholding important information, even from loved ones.

Mind: My narrative touches upon two significant aspects related to the mind. First, I mentioned "Little Miss Karen" (also talked about in the chapter "My Father's Passing") and how a limiting belief from my youth influenced my thoughts, feelings, actions, and reactions regarding death and dying. This demonstrates the lasting impact of early beliefs on later experiences. However, by going through my own NLP Breakthrough to release the fears held by "Little Miss Karen," I was no longer triggered and was able to be more emotionally present during the last four years of my brother and mother's lives. Second, addressing unresolved issues with loved ones (like my mother with her brother, and my brother with my mom) before their passing is highlighted as a crucial aspect of the grieving process. Research, like that of Kara Klingspon, supports the idea that unresolved issues with the deceased can lead to prolonged and intense grief reactions.[77]

Body: Exploring my health issues through Jensen's *The Healing Questions Guide*, let's delve into my six-week period of *nosebleeds* with these questions prompts:

1. What new and concerning information am I trying to process that has altered my perspective? What will it take to process it in a healthy way?
2. What will it take to release these feelings of being overlooked or ignored?
3. What can I do to include myself?
4. What benefit is there and believing I am invisible? What would be a healthier way to see myself?

 Gather: The most significant shifts in this story encompassed major health incidents, moments of significant health decline, and the passing of loved ones, including my brother and mother.

 Relate: My journey through grief involved a wide range of emotions and thoughts, such as denial, fear, panic, sadness, guilt, anger, acceptance, gratitude, comfort, and peace. These emotions reflect the complexity of the grieving process (also closely related to SARAH in the chapter "Relate").

 Involve: My actions during this period were varied and adaptive, including altering holiday plans, engaging in exercise, creating routines, setting boundaries, spending quality time with loved ones, seeking education and training in various therapeutic modalities, and using technology like FaceTime to connect and process unresolved issues. Additionally, I honored my loved ones with a celebration of life.

 Ease: I had access to several resources to support me during this challenging time, including a trust attorney, medical professionals, caregiver services, and therapeutic approaches like NLP, Time Line Therapy, Hypnotherapy, and NLP Coaching.

 Focus: My "new normal" revolves around honoring my family members by living my life and sharing my experiences through this book, which aims to inspire and assist others in their own healthy grief journey.

In Summary

"If the only thing people learned was not to be afraid of their experience,
that alone would change the world."
– Sydney Banks

What's your story? What aspects of your life had you not previously described as grief,
and how did that impact you? Have you experienced an ongoing ache, pain, or ailment?
When did it start? What is that part of your body trying to tell you?

*I*n these trilogies of *cumulative* (or *compound*) *grief*, we share the realism that it's not just one grief event in life; sometimes we are faced with many at one time. The various experiences explored in these narratives included **childhood trauma** (such as physical or sexual abuse), **deaths** of loved ones, parental **divorce**, **career** challenges, loss of **identity**, and **health** diagnoses.

I also emphasized two crucial points that are a theme throughout these stories. Firstly, our early childhood experiences of grief and trauma can give rise to beliefs that may constrain our capacity to navigate the grieving process in a healthy manner. Secondly, it's imperative to recognize the profound impact these experiences of grief and trauma have on the physical body, a central theme in this book. In essence, grieving healthfully lies in our ability to minimize and proactively prevent grief from becoming deeply embedded within the neurological, immune system, and physiological aspects of our body, which can manifest as a spectrum of health issues, ranging from minor to potentially life-threatening ailments in the future.

With that, let's briefly explore the themes and the factors that influenced their grief:

Culture: The cultural aspects highlighted in these stories include the reluctance of men to share their vulnerabilities due to societal norms, the stigma surrounding an incarcerated father, the misconception that IBS is purely psychological and its impact on mental health, feeling pressured by medical professionals or well-meaning individuals to make certain health decisions, and respecting a person's end-of-life wishes.

 Toxic Positivity: Various forms of toxic positivity manifested as denying the severity of their health issues, avoiding burdening family members, and concealing their true feelings behind a "happy face" or a forced "half smile," and men feeling the need to maintain a positive facade to protect those around them. Grievers also encountered well-intended yet poorly delivered comments, such as "Be strong (for the kids)," "You'll find love again," or "You need to move on/forward!"

 Mind: In the face of loss, one's mind can plunge into a profound darkness shaped by their values, beliefs, and attitudes. These challenges manifest in various ways such as a strong-willed denial and avoidance of emotional processing, refusal to mourn or express grief, feelings of responsibility, survivor's guilt, and the influence of limiting childhood beliefs.

 Body: This is one of the cornerstones of this section and the book that we explore further with three fundamental concepts. Firstly, it emphasizes the importance of self-talk, encouraging self-awareness in negative phrases like "I internalize everything," "My sorrow is at the pit of my stomach," and "I'm dying a slow death." Secondly, it delves into research that suggests a potential link between experiencing a traumatic incident and the development or diagnosis of cancer within five years, a theme explored in the chapter "Childhood Trauma, Death, and Diagnosis" and previously in the chapter "The End of Life." Lastly, it addresses various physical ailments discussed in these chapters, including nosebleeds, stomach aches, high blood pressure, kidney problems, and cancer.

As we dove into the **Healthy GRIEF Framework**, the journey emerged uniquely for each individual. Here's a concise overview:

 Gather: In the context of experiencing multiple griefs, this phase included navigating the conclusion or loss of a career or job, identity loss, illegal actions or incarceration of a family member, parental separation or divorce, major medical events, significant health diagnosis, critical points of health decline, and the death of a loved one.

 Relate: The range of emotions and reactions encompassed in this phase emphasized the complexity of SARAH – that it is not linear and can double back in flows of emotional experiences. Feelings, thoughts, and experiences that stood out included surrealism, gutted, powerless, drowning, out of control, spiral, "my world went dark," unable to stand, "silence that fills your mind," "existing in this space, not living," "conditioning myself to play life small," and sensing a lack of purpose.

 Involve: The action steps that supported individuals in progressing along their healing journey closely align with the categories of suggestions outlined in the chapter "Involve." These encompassed using denial as a temporary distraction, granting oneself grace, approaching actions mindfully and gradually, fostering connections and open communication, engaging in physical movement and pleasurable activities, showing reverence for oneself and others, pursuing education, and prioritizing one's health.

 Ease: The formal and informal support resources included friends, family, coworkers, faith and God, support groups, attorneys, medical/school professionals, therapists, counselors, education, and seminars. Since some of these are my personal clients, another highly effective tool is utilizing an NLP Breakthrough for quick and effective subconscious release of emotional trauma, triggers, and limiting beliefs.

Focus: There is hope! Here's some of their "new normal" which are great life lessons for all of us:

- ✵ Increasing self-awareness, both in mind and body
- ✵ Maintaining active engagement with family, friends, and hobbies
- ✵ Prioritizing self-care and self-worth
- ✵ Developing a laser-like focus on personal goals
- ✵ Embracing vulnerability and practicing forgiveness
- ✵ Establishing and maintaining healthy boundaries
- ✵ Complying with medical protocols and taking charge of their health
- ✵ Honoring the memory of those who passed while actively living their lives
- ✵ Living in the present moment with the best intentions
- ✵ Embracing a step-by-step approach to life
- ✵ Advocating for their own healthcare choices
- ✵ Sharing their stories to inspire and assist others in their own journeys

May the tools used in these stories (or even the lessons gleaned) become foundations for your own grief and life.

In Conclusion

"Participate joyfully in the sorrows of the world.
We cannot cure the world of sorrows, but we can choose to live in joy."

~ Joseph Campbell

*H*ealing mandates courage and a full embrace of loss and grief. Brené Brown writes, "To have courage is to tell the story of who you are with your whole heart."[78] Thank you to the many who blessed us with their stories. There is hope and healing in their narratives.

These stories are not just isolated accounts but represent threads in the intricate artwork of the human experience. They offer a profound opportunity for connection, empathy, and shared understanding. Remember that you are not alone in your journey; others have walked similar paths and have emerged stronger, wiser, and more resilient.

May you discover several narratives that resonate with your own life journey. As you immerse yourself in these experiences, allow them to serve as vivid mirrors reflecting aspects of your own struggles, triumphs, and moments of growth. Take note of the emotions stirred within you, the wisdom gleaned, and the insights gained from these shared experiences. Let them be guideposts, sources of inspiration, or lessons learned. Allow them to shape your perspective, deepen your empathy, and empower you to navigate your unique challenges with renewed strength and hope. Your story is an ever-evolving masterpiece, and these stories can be the brushstrokes that add depth and color to your own canvas of life.

When grief is part of your story, it needs to be held to be healed. To that, I hold your heart in my hands along with the story that is uniquely yours, and wish you well on your journey to healthfully grieve and heal.

"

In our deepest moments of **sorrow**, we crave the **comfort** of someone who has felt a comparable ache, even if the causes of our grief may vary. **Our longing is for our sadness to be acknowledged and understood**, rather than brushed aside or belittled by individuals who cannot bear witness to our emotions due to their own reluctance or incapacity to confront sorrows of their own.

~ Dr. Karen Kramer

Part IV

Resources:

Striving for the "New Normal" Toolbox

"Logic will get you from A to B. Imagination will take you everywhere."
~ Albert Einstein

In this section, you'll find a treasure trove of valuable resources to guide you through the demanding journey of loss. While everyone's path is unique, accessing the right tools can assist you in navigating your grief more effectively.

If you're a DIY enthusiast searching for practical tools, there are options for mindfulness, meditations, and journals. Integrate the **Healthy GRIEF Framework** into your everyday practice, using the guide to this book. Scan the QR code or access **bit.ly/HG-Resources** to join the Healthy GRIEF email list and receive valuable tips and tools, including meditations, worksheets, eBooks, and alternative therapy resources.

If you're considering individual or group sessions with a professional to support your grief recovery journey, there are various options available to you. From traditional talk therapy and counseling, alternative forms or therapy, and NLP, allow these resources to guide you toward one or more resources of support.

In times of distress and crisis, immediate support is crucial. Consider these three hotline resources at the end of this section as your go-to support in times of need.

Healthy grief is a journey that allows you to honor your emotions, seek support, and gradually heal after a significant loss. Remember, there's no right or wrong way to grieve, and seeking help when needed is entirely acceptable. Utilize the provided resources to support yourself or someone you care about as you navigate the challenging path of grief.

Healing is possible, and you don't have to face it alone.

Quick Resources

Are you the do-it-yourself type looking for some practical tools?

Mindfulness and Meditation:

Practices like mindfulness and meditation can help you manage overwhelming emotions and stay in the present moment. Consider using apps like Headspace[79] and Calm,[80] which offer guided meditation sessions tailored to grief and emotional healing. For an immediate tool to restore balance, look for my downloadable meditation on the link on page 388.

Journal Reflections:

Maintaining a grief journal can be a powerful tool for self-reflection and emotional expression. Write down your thoughts, memories, and feelings as a way to process your loss.

Process your loss using the **Healthy GRIEF Framework** by incorporating this downloadable quick tool (also found via the QR code/link) into your daily journal practice. It includes the below-questions.

Consider these questions to explore the factors shaping your perception and processing of grief:

 How do **cultural** influences intertwine with your grief? What cultural beliefs, values, or societal norms influence the way you navigate loss?

 In what ways do your personal beliefs, thoughts, emotions, and actions play a role in your experience of grief? (**Mind**)

 Do you experience any minor or major physical discomfort, pains, or health issues within your **body**? When you contemplate the physical stressors of grief, where in your body do you carry these sensations?

On a daily basis, utilize the following **Healthy GRIEF Framework** questions to assess your progress, identify necessary shifts, and support your unique path to the "New Normal." These questions do not need to follow a linear order, and you may not have answers to each question every day. The key is to keep asking yourself:

Gather: What information is missing? What do you need to know to make your next decision? What information is crucial for you today?

 Relate: What emotions are you experiencing? Where in your body do you sense these feelings? What beliefs do you hold about the loss, yourself, and others? Are these beliefs accurate? What are three things you're grateful for today?

 Involve: What's your goal for today? What are the three main targets or activities you want to focus on? Detail the actionable steps for each of these targets. How will at least one of these activities contribute to your journey of healthy grief? By the day's end, what single achievement will make today great?

 Ease: What type of support do you require, and from whom can you receive it? Once you have this support, what benefits will it provide for you and others?

 Focus: What outcomes or results are you working toward? What does the "New Normal" look like today, this week, next month, and next year? What single action step can you take today to bring you closer to your "New Normal"?

Incorporate the **Healthy GRIEF Framework** questions into your daily routine, recognizing that they need not follow a fixed sequence, and you may not always have answers for each one. The key is to keep asking them.

**Your Journey:
Reflection and Action**

Imagine yourself 20 years older. Write a letter from your older self to your current self. What advice would your older self give you now?

Free Website Links:

In addition to the audio versions of the stories in this book, the quick meditation tool, and the journal prompts mentioned earlier, join the Healthy GRIEF email list to receive more tips and tools by scanning the QR code below or going to **bit.ly/HG-Resources**. Your free resources will be updated periodically and include:

- ✺ **Healthy GRIEF Framework**: Stay grounded and focus on your grief progress by asking the five-stage framework journal prompts daily with this downloadable sheet.
- ✺ **Mindfulness Meditations**: Manage your life through these quick and easy downloadable techniques.
- ✺ **Ideal Schedule**: Regain a sense of control and direction by adopting a schedule that provides structure and purpose.
- ✺ **Downloadable eBooks**: Further enhance your path through the Healthy GRIEF Framework with additional tools. Various eBooks will be added to support your journey.
- ✺ **Alternative Therapies**: Educate yourself with and explore alternative forms of therapies that I highly recommend and update on a regular basis on this site.

bit.ly/HG-Resources

Professional Resources

Are you considering individual or group sessions with a professional to support your grief recovery journey? There are various options available beyond traditional therapy and counseling, and this chapter will explore some of them.

Traditional Therapy and Counseling:
While psychoanalysis has seen a decline in popularity in recent years, traditional "talk therapy" remains one of the most established and widely practiced approaches to addressing grief. The fundamental idea behind talk therapy is that discussing the loss in detail and processing it through language can aid in releasing it, leaving it behind, and moving forward.

To find therapists, consider the following resources:

- ✻ **Psychology Today**: This website offers a comprehensive directory of mental health professionals, making it easier to find a local therapist, psychiatrist, treatment center, or therapy support group that suits your needs.[81]
- ✻ **Local Religious or Medical Facilities**: Some religious or medical institutions may offer counseling services or can provide recommendations.
- ✻ **Personal Recommendations**: Friends, family, or colleagues may have valuable recommendations based on their own experiences.
- ✻ **Insurance or Company Benefits**: Check with your insurance or employer for a list of covered providers.
- ✻ **Primary Doctor**: Your primary care physician can often provide referrals to mental health professionals.

It's important to note that in some cases, consulting a mental health professional with expertise in grief, PTSD, or trauma may be the most effective starting point for a healthy path to recovery.

Alternative Forms of Therapy

While talking and understanding are essential, traditional talk therapy has its limitations. Research in neuroscience and other fields suggests that few psychological problems stem from a lack of understanding. Therefore, improving your understanding may not lead to sustained relief and improvement.

Many psychological problems (including grief) originate in deeper regions of the subconscious mind, driving our thoughts, feelings, and behaviors. Today, there are numerous alternative forms of therapy that can pave the way for a more hopeful and healthy "new normal."

In his book *The Body Keeps The Score*, psychiatrist and researcher Dr. Bessel van der Kolk outlines three decades of experience studying the impact of trauma on brain development and emotion regulation in childhood. He highlights the effectiveness of approaches like psychosomatic therapies, which are less commonly used but highly effective. These therapies aim to draw out the sensory information blocked and frozen by grief, help patients befriend negative emotions associated with the loss instead of suppressing them, and allow patients to complete the self-preserving physical actions that were halted during the grief event.

Various non-traditional therapies are recommended in Dr. van der Kolk's book, including **yoga, Eye Movement Desensitization and Reprocessing (EMDR), Schwartz's Internal Family Systems, Pesso's PBSP psychomotor therapy, neurofeedback, movement, theater,** and **dance**. Additional forms of alternative therapies I highly recommend are updated and found on my website. See Free Website Resources in the previous section.

Throughout Part III, you'll find stories that mention various forms of "Ease" or professional support that aided in individuals' recovery. If a particular story or method resonated with you, consider researching that form of support. Keep in mind that this resources section is not an exhaustive list of options.

Neuro Linguistics Programming (NLP)

NLP has played a significant role in aiding grief recovery for my clients. This approach has also been used to address mental health issues such as anxiety, depression, fears and phobias, low self-esteem, weight management, substance misuse, stress, and post-traumatic stress disorder (PTSD).

NLP, created in the 1970s by Richard Bandler and John Grinder, draws inspiration from therapists like Milton Erickson, Gregory Bateson, Fritz Perls, and Virginia Satir. ANLP (Association for NLP) defines NLP as follows: "NLP combines theories, models, and techniques from a range of scientific and esoteric fields to create accessible, understandable 'tools' which can be used to improve outcomes, support well-being, and create change in various contexts."[82]

NLP includes various techniques including Hypnotherapy, Time Line Therapy®, and Mental Emotional Release® Therapy (MER). These methods access and utilize the subconscious (or "unconscious") mind to heal emotional traumas and grief, identify and "reprogram" limiting beliefs, and eliminate unwanted thoughts, feelings, and behaviors.

Practitioners of NLP come from various backgrounds, including psychiatry, psychology, marriage and family counseling, social work, life and business coaching, and athletic coaching. Some practitioners may use NLP in conjunction with other methodologies.

When seeking an NLP practitioner, consider asking questions such as:

- ✿ How often have you worked with issues similar to mine?
- ✿ How do you determine if a client is a good candidate for NLP?
- ✿ Can you explain how NLP works and provide insights into the treatment plan?
- ✿ What is the typical course of therapy, and how is progress measured?

As the head coach for an organization that certified practitioners in NLP, NLP Coaching, Time Line Therapy®, and Hypnotherapy, I've had the opportunity to assist over 1,200 individuals between 2019 and 2023 (as of the writing of this book), particularly during the challenging years of the COVID-19 pandemic. This period presented unique grief challenges, including the loss of jobs, identities, relationships, freedom, social connection, and loved ones.

In conclusion, it's essential to find a method of professional support that works for you. Recognize that there are various approaches beyond traditional therapy and counseling, and what works best for one person may not be the ideal choice for another. The key is to find the support that helps you navigate your grief recovery journey effectively.

Hotline Resources

*D*o you need immediate support? In moments of distress and crisis, support is crucial. These resources are here for you (or someone you know) during your lowest moments.

988 Lifeline - 988lifeline.org
The 988 Lifeline offers free and confidential support, crisis prevention resources, and assistance for individuals in distress and crisis, as well as valuable guidance for professionals in the United States. This national network of local crisis centers is available 24/7, providing emotional support to those experiencing thoughts of suicide or emotional distress. If you're in the United States, accessing this service is as simple as texting 988 to request support promptly.

Crisis Text Line - www.crisistextline.org
You can reach out to Crisis Text Line by texting HOME to 741741 from anywhere in the United States at any time. Crisis Text Line offers support for various crises. Trained Crisis Counselors are ready to assist, all from a secure online platform. They'll help you transition from a moment of crisis to a more composed state. Their support extends to issues such as gun violence, anxiety, eating disorders, depression, suicide, and self-harm.

International Association for Suicide Prevention - www.iasp.info
The International Association for Suicide Prevention (IASP) is committed to preventing suicide and mitigating its effects. IASP plays a global leadership role in suicide prevention by actively fostering strong collaborative partnerships and advocating for evidence-based actions aimed at reducing suicide rates and suicidal behavior.

If you're struggling, don't hesitate to share your feelings. To begin, you can use one of these pre-written messages and send it to a trusted contact.[83]

Reach Out - When you get a chance can you contact me? I feel really alone and suicidal, and could use some support.

Contact a Loved One - I don't want to die, but I don't know how to live. Talking with you may help me feel safe. Are you free to talk?

Express Your Feelings - This is really hard for me to say but I'm having painful thoughts and it might help to talk. Are you free?

Check in - I'm struggling right now and just need to talk to someone — can we chat?

Crisis Text Line 741741

It really helps to talk about it, and I guess just figure out how to stop thinking so negatively.

It's understandable to feel that way when it's so hard to see past your depression. Would you be interested in coming up with ways to manage the racing bothersome thoughts?

An example exchange between a texter and a Crisis Counselor.

In Conclusion

*I*n closing, let me emphasize the power of healthy grief as a transformative process. It's a journey of self-discovery, self-compassion, and resilience. As you've delved into the valuable resources provided in this section, you've equipped yourself with tools that can guide you through the challenging terrain of loss.

Remember, grief is a deeply personal experience, and there is no single "right" way to grieve. Your unique journey is a testament to your strength and capacity to heal. Seeking help when needed is a sign of wisdom and self-care, and the resources mentioned here can be your companions on this path.

Whether you choose the DIY approach with mindfulness, meditation, and journaling, or opt for professional guidance through various therapeutic avenues, know that you're not alone. The support you need is within reach, and there are numerous ways to find it.

In times of crisis, the hotline resources provided offer immediate support. It's essential to reach out during those darkest moments and lean on the network of caring professionals and organizations that are dedicated to helping you through the storm.

As you move forward on your journey of healthy grief, embrace the truth that healing is possible. Every step you take, every resource you explore, and every emotion you honor is a stride towards your "New Normal." You don't have to face this journey in solitude – reach out, lean on the resources available to you, and remember, you have the strength to heal and emerge from your grief even stronger.

Your Journey:
Reflection and Action

*What's one **thing** can you implement today?*

Closing

"Grief is just love with no place to go."
~ Jamie Anderson

Grief is an inescapable facet of the human experience, a powerful and intricate emotion that touches us all at some point in our lives. Whether we grapple with the loss of a loved one, the end of a significant relationship, or other life-altering changes, grief is a natural response. Nevertheless, how we navigate this profound emotion can significantly influence our well-being and long-term healing.

As we conclude our journey thro ugh the landscape of grief, remember that it is not a path to be feared or avoided, but rather a testament to the depth of our human capacity to love and connect. In these pages, we've explored the myriad of emotions that accompany loss, and we've embraced the idea that grief is a natural response to a profound impact when what once was is no longer.

But now, as you turn the last page, I want to leave you with a message of hope, resilience, and the transformative power of healthy grief. For within the darkest moments of our lives, there exists a seed of possibility – the potential for growth, healing, and renewal.

In the face of loss, we find strength we never knew we had. We unearth the well of empathy within ourselves, connecting with others who have walked this path. We learn to cherish the memories and honor the legacies of what we have lost, keep the positive memories alive in our hearts, and continue to live our lives.

As you navigate the waves of grief, remember that it is not a linear journey. There will be days when the pain feels unbearable, and others when you glimpse the light of hope. Embrace both with equal compassion, for they are all part of the mosaic of healing.

In time, you'll discover that grief is not an end but a beginning. It is a journey toward a more profound understanding of yourself and the world around you. It's a testament to the enduring power of love.

You are not alone on this path. Utilize the **Healthy GRIEF Framework** to illuminate your unique path to healing, reach out to those who offer their hand in support, and seek professional guidance when needed. Trust that healing is possible, even when it seems elusive. Your capacity to heal and find joy after loss is a testament to the resilience of the human spirit.

So, as you close this book and step back into your own life, know that you are equipped with the wisdom to navigate the ever-changing tides of grief. Embrace the process, honor your journey, and remember that, in time, the scars of grief become the foundation of a life well-lived, rich with empathy, compassion, and love.

May your heart find peace, and may you carry the positive memories of what-once-was with grace and gratitude. Your journey continues, and within it, you will discover the strength to not only survive but to thrive once more.

With love and hope,
Dr. Karen

Endnotes

INTRODUCTION

1   Brown, Brené. *Atlas of the Heart: Mapping Meaningful Connection and the Language of Human Experience*. Random House, 2021. See specifically Chapter 6, "Center for Complicated Grief."

2   https://www.psychiatry.org/patients-families/prolonged-grief-disorder

3   https://georgetownpsychology.com/2021/07/the-distress-of-cumulative-grief/

4   https://www.apa.org/topics/trauma

PART I ~ CULTURE

5   Cain, Susan. *Bittersweet: How Sorrow and Longing Make Us Whole*. Crown Publications, 2023, pp 118-120.

6   https://embassy.science/wiki/Theme:B4f7b2e3-af61-4466-94dc-2504affab5a8#

7   https://www.sciencedirect.com/science/article/abs/pii/S0065260119300152

PART I ~ MIND

8   Brown, Brené. *Atlas of the Heart: Mapping Meaningful Connection and the Language of Human Experience*. Random House, 2021, p. .

9   https://en.wikipedia.org/wiki/Thought

10   https://www.psychologytoday.com/us/blog/the-pleasure-is-all-yours/202202/the-important-difference-between-emotions-and-feelings

PART I ~ BODY

11   https://dictionary.apa.org/physiology

12   https://www.brainfacts.org/thinking-sensing-and-behaving/emotions-stress-and-anxiety/2018/the-neuroscience-of-stress-061918

13   https://www.apa.org/pubs/highlights/spotlight/issue-33

14   https://www.sciencedirect.com/journal/neurobiology-of-stress

15   https://www.physio-pedia.com/Biopsychosocial_Model

16   https://www.sciencedirect.com/science/article/abs/pii/S1934148210005149

17   Van Der Kolk, Bessel. *The Body Keeps the Score: Brain, Mind, and Body in the Healing of Trauma*. Viking, 2014.

18   Maté, Gabor. *The Myth of Normal: Trauma, Illness, and Healing in a Toxic Culture*. Penguin Young Readers, 2022.

19   Canfield, Cheryl. *Profound Healing: The Power of Acceptance on the Path to Wellness*. Healing Arts Press, 2003.

20   Rediger, Jeff. *Cured: The Power of Our Immune System and the Mind-Body Connection*. Penguin Life, 2020.

21   https://www.cdc.gov/mmwr/volumes/72/wr/mm7218a3.htm

22   Jensen, Wendi J. *The Healing Questions Guide: Relevant Questions to Ask the Mind to Activate Healing in the Body.* Createspace Independent Publishing Platform, 2015.

PART II ~ INTRODUCTION

23   Kubler-Ross, Elisabeth. *On Death & Dying: What the Dying Have to Teach Doctors, Nurses, Clergy & Their Own Families.* Scribner Book Company, 2014.

24   https://open.spotify.com/episode/02NfXb67kxDN55vNIURgPV

25   Brown, Brené. *Atlas of the Heart: Mapping Meaningful Connection and the Language of Human Experience.* Random House, 2021. See specifically Chapter 6, "Center for Complicated Grief."

PART II ~ FOUNDATION

26   The graphs on page 53 are amended from Kubler-Ross' model. https://speakinggrief.org/get-better-at-grief/understanding-grief/no-step-by-step-process

27   Bridges, William. *Managing Transitions: Making the Most of Change.* Da Capo Press, 1991.

PART II ~ GATHER

28   https://www.urmc.rochester.edu/encyclopedia/content.aspx?contenttypeid=90&contentid=p03043

29   https://www.verywellmind.com/what-is-toxic-positivity-5093958

30   https://whatsyourgrief.com/what-should-i-say-to-someone-grieving/

31   Brown, Brené. *Atlas of the Heart: Mapping Meaningful Connection and the Language of Human Experience.* Random House, 2021.

32   https://www.linkedin.com/posts/susanadavidphd_learning-to-label-emotions-with-a-more-nuanced-activity-6977325615397937152-WC8u/

PART II ~ RELATE

33   Brown, Brené. *Atlas of the Heart: Mapping Meaningful Connection and the Language of Human Experience.* Random House, 2021.

34   https://study.com/academy/lesson/accommodation-in-psychology-definition-lesson-quiz.html

35   Eggerichs, Emerson. *Love and Respect Workbook: The Love She Most Desires; The Respect He Desperately Needs.* Thomas Nelson, 2005.

36   https://study.com/academy/lesson/accommodation-in-psychology-definition-lesson-quiz.html

37   https://www.ted.com/talks/susan_david_the_gift_and_power_of_emotional_courage?language=en

PART II ~ INVOLVE

38   Brown, Brené. *Atlas of the Heart: Mapping Meaningful Connection and the Language of Human Experience.* Random House, 2021. See specifically Chapter 6, "Center for Complicated Grief.")

PART II ~ EASE

39   Cortez, Alise. *Coloring Life: How Loss Invites Us to Live More Vibrant Lives.* Something or Other Publishing, 2023.

PART II ~ FOCUS

40   https://jamanetwork.com/journals/jamapsychiatry/article-abstract/2648691

41   https://journals.lww.com/psychosomaticmedicine/Abstract/2016/02000/Purpose_in_Life_and_Its_Relationship_to_All_Cause.2.aspx

42   https://www.kendallcottonbronk.com/

43   Martinez, Mario. *Mindbody Code: How to Change the Beliefs That Limit Your Health, Longevity, and Success.* Sounds True, 2016.

44   Brown, Brené, *Daring Greatly: How the Courage to Be Vulnerable Transforms the Way We Live, Love, Parent, and Lead*

45   https://brenebrown.com/articles/2020/08/31/pressing-on-with-purpose/

46   Pukui, Mary Kawena, and Samuel H. Elbert, editors. *Hawaiian Dictionary: Hawaiian-English, English-Hawaiian.* University of Hawai'i Press, 1986.pp 340-341.

PART III ~ STORIES OF RESILIENCE

47   Brown, Brené. *Atlas of the Heart: Mapping Meaningful Connection and the Language of Human Experience.* Random House, 2021, pp 91-95.

48   https://www.breatheforchange.com/

49   Maté, Gabor. *The Myth of Normal: Trauma, Illness, and Healing in a Toxic Culture.* Penguin Young Readers, 2022.

50   Kovacevich, W.D., *Planet 90s,* 2022.

51   Beattie, Melody. *Codependent No More: How to Stop Controlling Others and Start Caring for Yourself.* Spiegel, 2022.

52   https://spsp.org/news/character-and-context-blog/krauss-orth-low-self-esteem-eating-disorders

53   Pillemer, Karl. *Fault Lines: Fractured Families and How to Mend Them.* Penguin Young Readers, 2022.

54   Coleman, Joshua. *Rules of Estrangement: Why Adult Children Cut Ties and How to Heal the Conflict.* Sheldon Press, 2021.

55   https://www.youtube.com/watch?v=oARMo6YT0fs

56   https://adamgrant.substack.com/p/the-most-toxic-relationships-arent

57   https://www.nytimes.com/2023/05/28/opinion/frenemies-relationships-health.html

58   https://www.researchgate.net/publication/228079134_Social_Undermining_in_the_Workplace

59   https://www.youtube.com/watch?v=AEpD2o6MZOk

60   https://english.hi.is/news/association_of_stress_related_disorders_with_subsequent_autoimmune_disease

61   Brown, Brené. *Atlas of the Heart: Mapping Meaningful Connection and the Language of Human Experience.* Random House, 2021.

62   Colligan, Victoria, and Beth Schoenfeldt. *Ladies Who Launch: An Innovative Program That Will Help You Get Your Dreams off the Ground.* Saint Martin's Griffin, 2008.

63   Zuckerberg, Randi. *Pick Three: You Can Have It All (Just Not Every Day)*. Dey Street Books, 2019.

64   Ressler, Robert K., and Tom Shachtman. *Whoever Fights Monsters*. St Martin's Press, 1992.

65   Gaines, Chad. *Who Am i (The Chad Gaines Story)*. IngramSpark, 2023.

66   https://psychcentral.com/ptsd/complex-posttraumatic-stress-disorder-symptoms

67   https://www.youtube.com/watch?v=ydpd0-AqehE

68   https://www.tyla.com/celebrity/sally-field-76-praised-embracing-ageing-naturally-610724-20230420

69   https://www.youtube.com/watch?v=AEpD2o6MZOk

70   https://www.betterhealth.vic.gov.au/health/healthyliving/empty-nest-syndrome

71   https://www.healthline.com/health/mental-health/empty-nest-syndrome

72   https://psychcentral.com/health/empty-nest-syndrome#empty-nest-defined

73   https://www.webmd.com/parenting/how-to-manage-empty-nest-syndrome

74   https://cdhf.ca/en/mental-health-ibs-and-removing-the-stigma/

75   https://www.spinalcord.com/blog/2023-united-states-spinal-cord-injury-statistics

76   Peterson, Laura. *Whispers in the Wind: Communications from an Ascended Master*, 1999.

77   https://www.ncbi.nlm.nih.gov/pmc/articles/PMC5093909/

78   Brown, Brené. *Atlas of the Heart: Mapping Meaningful Connection and the Language of Human Experience*. Random House, 2021.

79   https://www.headspace.com/

PART IV ~ RESOURCES

80   https://www.calm.com/

81   https://www.psychologytoday.com/us

82   https://anlp.org/knowledge-base/definition-of-nlp

83   If you are in need of support, please do not hesitate to reach out to someone. If you aren't sure who to talk to, contact https://www.crisistextline.org/ - they can help. These suggestions come from their website.

Acknowledgements

I extend my heartfelt gratitude to those who generously shared their stories, my clients and their experiences, my own gut-wrenching life challenges, and each of my five children who served as my invaluable teachers throughout the creation of this book. Every conversation served as a poignant reminder that, in the realm of grief, there's a vast expanse of knowledge yet to be explored.

A special thank you to Heather Felty, my outstanding publishing coach. Your unwavering support, countless hours of dedicated work, and exceptional patience in guiding me through the tumultuous journey of writing and publishing. Your expertise and attention to detail have been nothing short of extraordinary. Your patience with the seemingly endless edits and meticulous rereads of my drafts have not only improved the quality of this book but have also honed my skills as a writer. In dedicating yourself to this project, you have not only been a publishing coach but also a trusted friend and mentor. I am profoundly grateful for your unwavering support and pivotal role in bringing this book to life.

I'd also like to thank key members of my team. To my dear friend and colleague, Cosette Remund, thank you for patiently listening to my Voxer messages as I processed thoughts and ideas for this book. To Kathleen Babcock, thank you for keeping me on track with this project, and to Veronica Martinez-Goodman, thank you for your help with marketing. This was truly a team effort.

In dedication: Michelle G., I gladly carry your torch to help more people know the profound impact of this work on the world. Health encompasses more than just diagnoses and treatments. The crucial focus is to prevent it before it takes hold in the body. We will eradicate pancreatic cancer! Kimberly M., you were an unstoppable force, leaving an indelible mark on this world that will forever be remembered. Your influence and the positive changes you brought about are a testament to your strength and character. Michelle and Kimberly, the legacies you've left behind continue to thrive within your children, your families, and the countless individuals, myself included, who were touched by your infectious smiles, laughter, warm hugs, and kind-hearted spirits.

Mother, I have strongly felt your spiritual presence and intuitive guidance in the thoughts, feelings, and nudges. You have whispered to me in the odd hours of the night and impressed upon me to write during the day. It may be my name on the front of this book yet I know these words were heavily influenced by more than me. Yes, Mother, I know there are more books for us to write!

Tyler, my dear son, you have been an endless source of inspiration and learning throughout your life. Your fingerprints are all over this book, from the private stories you allowed me to share, your technical expertise, and your unwavering support, even if it meant bringing me ice cream late at night. I love you immensely, and you mean the world to me.

Though I could spend another decade hidden behind stacks of books, immersed in research, scientific studies, client interactions, and the wealth of shared stories, it would be a disservice to you, dear reader, to withhold this book when you need it most. I sense that our journey together extends into future volumes, and I eagerly anticipate our continued exploration.

My guiding motto in life is simple: work with, learn from, and share with others. As you embark on your own path through grief, I invite you to do the same with me. Please share your stories, reflections on this book, or your personal journey through grief via email at HealthyGrief@DrKarenKramer.com. Your journey and insights are a wellspring of inspiration.

My dearest hope is that you will use your gifts to assist others in their pursuit of understanding and healing. Together, let us break down the barriers surrounding the conversations about grief.

Always remember, whether you or a loved one are navigating the complexities of a healthy grief journey, you are not alone.

With love and gratitude,
Dr. Karen

Photo Credits

Page 13: Dr. Karen Kramer
Page 104-105: Shutterstock
Page 107: Laura Peterson
Page 117: Donna Matthews
Page 128: Janaia Bruce
Page 135: Unknown
Page 140-141: Shutterstock
Page 143: William K. Kovacevich
Page 150: Rachel Best
Page 154: Artiphoria
Page 160: Suzanne Peterson
Page 167: Unknown
Page 176-177: Shutterstock
Page 179: Unknown
Page 190: Artiphoria
Page 196: Shutterstock
Page 204-205: Shutterstock
Page 209: Jon Taff
Page 219: Sabrina Cousineau
Page 226: Jan Ghilain
Page 231: Chad Gaines
Page 239: David Martin
Page 245: Michelle Petitpas
Page 252-253: Shutterstock
Page 255: Shutterstock
Page 262: Nicole Harvick
Page 268: Dr. Karen Kramer
Page 274-275: Shutterstock
Page 277: Unknown
Page 284: Cheryl Nelson
Page 291: Unknown
Page 302-303: Shutterstock
Page 306: Shutterstock
Page 317: Malia MacGilfrey
Page 323: Casian Photography
Page 339: Stephanie MacGilfrey
Page 351: Jamie Scott Lytle
Page 363: Jennie Edwards-Stock, Guided by Imagination Photography

About the Author

Dr. Karen Kramer (aka "Dr. Karen") is a guiding light who has transformed the lives of hundreds-of-thousands of individuals around the globe since the early 1990s.

With a profound understanding of the human mind and as a grief recovery expert, Dr. Karen's true passion as a mindset coach, speaker, and author lies in helping navigate heart-wrenching experiences such as divorce, loss of loved ones, and traumatic events. Through her meticulously tailored techniques, she skillfully liberates her clients from the chains of limiting beliefs and negative emotions, restoring their ability to seize control of their lives in 90 days or less!

Armed with an impressive academic background, Dr. Karen holds a Bachelor's in Business, a Master's in Leadership, another Master's in Organizational Development, and a Ph.D. in Human and Organizational Development. Her innovative dissertation sheds light on the intricate interplay between emotional intelligence and leadership.

Corporations and nonprofits including the CIA, United Way, American Express, Nike, Boeing, and Google have sought Dr. Karen's invaluable counsel. Her transformative expertise also embraces entrepreneurs, beauty pageant titleholders, actresses, counselors and therapists, stay-at-home moms, teenagers, and retirees.

In addition to her private practice, Dr. Karen has an illustrious travel record. As a faculty member, program manager, and executive coach at the esteemed Center for Creative Leadership, Dr. Karen guided leaders from new managers to C-suite executives. She also served as a co-facilitator and program director for Teen Wisdom Inc., certifying teenage girl life coaches. Moreover, Dr. Karen served as the Head Coach for Recalibrate360, with a pivotal role in certifying individuals in the life-altering realms of Neuro-Linguistics Programming (NLP), Time Line Therapy®, and Hypnotherapy.

In 2022, Dr. Karen unveiled the awe-inspiring VillaVision Wellness and Retreat Center – a sanctuary of tranquility, nestled in sun-drenched Southern California. Here, women overcome grief while rediscovering happiness, health, and inner wholeness through one-on-one Breakthrough Immersion coaching, women's retreats, and day events.

Dr. Karen draws her inspiration for *Healthy Grief* from personal experiences, including the loss of loved ones, two divorces, and various life challenges, as well as her son's remarkable recovery and powerful client results. With a wealth of international coaching experience, a profound understanding of techniques that unlock the subconscious mind, and her intuitive abilities, "Healthy Grief" becomes her gift to help create a better world for everyone.

Hailing from the vibrant city of San Diego, Dr. Karen cherishes her life in the embrace of sunny Southern California. As a woman-preneur and a mother who successfully raised five children in a blended family, she intimately understands the art of juggling life's priorities while maintaining a semblance of sanity... most of the time.

To contact Dr. Karen:

Email:
HealthyGrief@DrKarenKramer.com
Website:
www.DrKarenKramer.com

To seek support for one-on-one coaching or speaking opportunities, book a call at **bit.ly/BookWithDrK**.